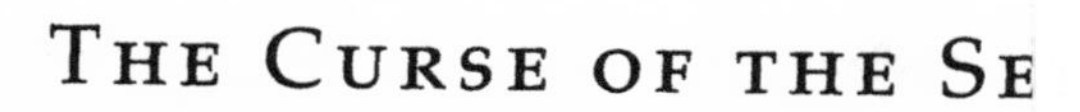

The Curse of the Se

The Curse of the Self

Self-Awareness, Egotism, and the Quality of Human Life

Mark R. Leary

OXFORD
UNIVERSITY PRESS

OXFORD
UNIVERSITY PRESS

Oxford University Press, Inc., publishes works that further
Oxford University's objective of excellence
in research, scholarship, and education.

Oxford New York
Auckland Cape Town Dar es Salaam Hong Kong Karachi
Kuala Lumpur Madrid Melbourne Mexico City Nairobi
New Delhi Shanghai Taipei Toronto

With offices in
Argentina Austria Brazil Chile Czech Republic France Greece
Guatemala Hungary Italy Japan Poland Portugal Singapore
South Korea Switzerland Thailand Turkey Ukraine Vietnam

Copyright © 2004 Mark R. Leary

First issued as an Oxford University Press paperback, 2007

Published by Oxford University Press, Inc.
198 Madison Avenue, New York, New York 10016

www.oup.com

Oxford is a registered trademark of Oxford University Press

All rights reserved. No part of this publication may be reproduced,
stored in a retrieval system, or transmitted, in any form or by any means,
electronic, mechanical, photocopying, recording, or otherwise,
without the prior permission of Oxford University Press.

Library of Congress Cataloging-in-Publication Data
Leary, Mark R.
The curse of the self : self-awareness, egotism, and the quality of human life /
Mark R. Leary.
p. cm.
ISBN 978-0-19-517242-3 ; 978-0-19-532544-7 (pbk.)

1. Self. 2. Egoism. 3. Conduct of life. I. Title.
BF697.L33 2004
155.2—dc22 2003059249

PREFACE

As a university professor, I regularly attend my university's graduation exercises each spring. As I've sat through my share of both excellent and dreadful commencement speeches, I have sometimes mused over what *I* would say to the graduating students and assembled guests if I were ever invited to give a graduation address. What important lesson could I impart in 15 minutes or less that, if heeded, might change the graduates' lives as they made their way out into the world?

A few years ago, as I listened to a speaker talk about the challenges that the graduates would face, I decided that my commencement speech would tell students that their greatest challenges in life would be ones that they inadvertently created for themselves. "You will face various disappointments, problems, and even tragedies in life," I would say, "many of which you will have little or no power to control. But the primary cause of your unhappiness will be you."

This claim is not new, of course. Others have suggested that people are often their own worst enemies. But others who have examined this topic rarely consider the possibility that people create so much unhappiness for themselves because of how the human mind is designed. As a social psychologist with interests in self and identity, I have come to the conclusion that the natural human tendencies to be egocentric, egotistical, and otherwise egoistic play a central role in our problems at both the personal and societal levels.

Although a few other animals can think consciously about themselves in rather basic ways, no other species possesses the powers of self-reflection that human beings have. The ability to self-reflect offers many benefits by allowing us to plan ahead, reminisce about the past, consider options, innovate, and evaluate ourselves. However, self-awareness also sets us up for a host of problems that are unlike the difficulties faced by any other species. Among other things, the capacity for self-reflection distorts people's perceptions of the world, leading them to draw inaccurate conclusions about themselves and other people, and prompting them to make bad decisions based on faulty information. Self-awareness conjures up a great deal of personal suffering in the form of depression, anxiety, anger, and other negative emotions by allowing people to ruminate about the past or imagine what might befall them in the future. The inherently egocentric and egotistical manner in which the self processes information can blind people to their own shortcomings and undermine their relationships with others. The self also underlies a great deal of social conflict, leading people to dislike those who are different from them and to fight with members of other social groups. It also leads people to endanger their own well-being by putting egoistic goals over personal safety. For those inclined toward religion and spirituality, visionaries have proclaimed that the self stymies the quest for spiritual fulfillment and leads to immoral behavior. And, ironically, using self-reflection to help us deliberately control our own behavior can often backfire and create more problems than it solves.

The Curse of the Self is about the personal and social problems that result from self-reflection, egocentrism, and egotism. I wrote it for readers who want to understand why they—like all other people—have such difficulty finding the peaceful, happy, and satisfying life they desire. I suspect that many of them already have a vague sense that at least part of the reason lies in an excessively self-focused and egoistic approach to life. This book will explain how and why our natural tendency to talk to ourselves, see the world egocentrically, defend our egos, seek self-validation, and engage in other acts of selfhood often works against our best interests.

I also wrote the book to counteract what I view as the glorification of egoism in Western culture and pop psychology. People are often urged to solve their problems and improve their lives by focusing on themselves, setting more egoistic goals, enhancing their self-esteem, and otherwise strengthening their sense of self. Although these strategies are sometimes useful, those who promote an egoistic approach to solving life's problems fail to recognize that an excessive emphasis on self and ego is often part of the problem.

Although I wrote this book primarily for nonprofessionals, I believe that behavioral scientists, mental health professionals, and students in psychology and related disciplines will find the material useful and provocative. For them, I have included references to the scholarly literature on which my claims are based.

I would like to thank my students and colleagues, many of whom have contributed to my thinking about the self. I particularly appreciate the feedback that Geoff MacDonald and Robin Kowalski provided on early drafts of certain chapters. I also thank Connie Kuhlman, Roger Charles, Carolyn Crump, John Bloss, and Alexa Moderno for many provocative discussions regarding ways in which the self is a curse. Finally, I wish to acknowledge assistance from an R. J. Reynolds Research Leave from Wake Forest University, which allowed me to write portions of the book.

Contents

The Curse of the Self ∷

1 ∷

The Self-Aware Animal

Self-awareness . . . is an evolutionary novelty; the biological species from which mankind has descended had only rudiments of self-awareness, or perhaps lacked it altogether.
—T. DOBZHANSKY

When 24-year-old John Scopes decided to challenge Tennessee's new law prohibiting the teaching of evolution in public schools, he could not have anticipated that he would be cast into the national spotlight during the hot, dry summer of 1925. On the surface, the matter seemed one of only local interest. Scopes, a high school science teacher, was accused of violating the Butler Act, which made it unlawful to teach "any theory that denies the story of the divine creation of man as taught in the Bible, and to teach instead that man descended from a lower order of animals." Yet the nation quickly became entranced with the dramatic courtroom performances of noted attorneys William Jennings Bryan and Clarence Darrow as they challenged one another and the court on issues that ran much deeper than a schoolteacher's run-in with the law—the conflict between science and religion, the separation of church and state, the infallibility of the Bible, and a teacher's right to academic freedom.

One issue at the center of the court proceedings was the question of how human beings differ from other animals. The prosecution strenuously objected to Darwin's view that human beings are a species of animal that evolved according to the same biological processes as all other animals. Pointing to the offending textbook that Scopes used in his course, William Jennings Bryan bellowed, "There is the book they were teaching your children that man was a mammal, and so indistinguishable among the mammals that they leave him there with 3,499 other mammals!"[1]

Bryan was not alone in his refusal to believe that human beings are animals. Human beings differ from other animals in so many striking ways that, even today, many people have difficulty thinking of us as having been cut from the same cloth. Yet those who try to distinguish human beings from animals disagree regarding precisely what it is that makes us so different. Like Bryan, many theologians and philosophers have asserted that only human beings have a soul or were specially created "in God's image," as the Bible asserts. The philosopher René Descartes promoted this view, arguing that whereas human beings possess a soul, animals are merely machines. However, many people disagree that possession of a soul distinguishes humans from other animals, either because they are unwilling to concede that other animals do not have a soul or that human beings do.

For many years, some scientists maintained that human beings are unique in their ability to make and use tools. However, this distinction collapsed when close inspection revealed that other species as diverse as beavers, chimpanzees, sea otters, and elephants also use tools. Human tools may be superior to theirs in some sense, but we cannot claim that tool use itself distinguishes human beings from other animals.

Others have suggested that we differ from other creatures in our ability to communicate through language. Certainly, human beings are facile with spoken and written language in ways that other species are not. Yet other animals do communicate quite effectively with each other through chirps, grunts, growls, and nonverbal behaviors. We may have a more sophisticated and flexible ability to communicate than do other animals, but it's largely a matter of degree.

Another possible difference is that people are simply more intelligent than other animals. *Civic Biology*, the textbook that landed John Scopes in court, took this view, noting that "we know that man is separated mentally by a wide gap from all other mammals."[2] But again, this is a matter of degree. People do solve novel problems and reason more effectively than most other animals, but we also must admit that every animal has domains of "intelligence" that people don't possess. And, despite our seemingly superior intellect, human beings do an untold number of very unintelligent things that pose serious threats to themselves and to the world at large, things that seem far more stupid than we observe in any other animal.

Without disputing that people differ from at least some other animals in all of these ways, I believe that the defining difference between human beings and other animals involves the nature of the human self. As we will see, evidence strongly suggests that most other animals do not have a self at all and that those species that do possess a self have only a very rudimentary one compared with human beings.[3]

People use the word *self* in several distinct ways, so let me make my use clear. As I am using the term, *self* refers to the mental apparatus that allows people (and a few other species of animals) to think consciously about themselves.[4] Of course, all animals can "think" in the sense that they process information about themselves and their environments, but few are able to think consciously about themselves or about what they are doing. Only animals with a self—those with the cognitive ability to focus their attention on and think consciously about themselves—can think deliberately about themselves, form images of what they are like (a self-concept), evaluate themselves (and react emotionally to their self-evaluations), talk to themselves in their own minds, and purposefully control their own behavior with some conscious goal in mind. Clearly, other species of animals get by just fine without having a self. Yet having this capacity for self-reflection opens up an entirely new world of experiences, opportunities, and challenges for animals that have one, including human beings.

What Difference Does a Self Make?

You are so accustomed to thinking about yourself that you may have never considered what an unusual ability this is or what life would be like if you couldn't do it. How would you be different if you were unable to focus on or think about yourself? Being able to think about oneself has five important consequences that not only account for most important behavioral differences between human beings and other animals but also create a wide array of personal and social problems that are the focus of this book. The ability to self-reflect is an essential feature of the human psyche, yet it is also a curse.

Planning

Perhaps the most important consequence of having a self is the ability to plan. All planning requires the ability to think about oneself so that one can play out various future events and imagine the consequences of one's actions. Having a self allows people to create what Julian Jaynes called the *analogue-I*.[5] The analogue-I is a mental representation or imaginary stand-in for the person—a thought or image of oneself that people can think about, manipulate, or move around in their mind. Sometimes people imagine seeing themselves in a particular situation, as if they were watching a hazy movie of what might happen. More commonly, the analogue-I is a person's imagined perspective on a scene as viewed from his or her own viewpoint. Using your analogue-I, you can imagine yourself in other situations, intentionally plan to do something in the future, consider your options, mentally rehearse future actions, retrospectively imagine how events might have turned out differently, and even contemplate your own death.

All planning requires the individual to imagine him- or herself at some time in the future. By manipulating a thought or image of oneself mentally, a person can think about what needs to be done now to achieve a particular goal in the future. Animals without a self cannot do this sort of mental time-travel. As a result, most other animals do not plan at all but, rather, respond to the environment on a moment-by-moment basis. Of course, some animals do things that appear to be in preparation for some future event. For example, squirrels hoard nuts as winter approaches, and pregnant animals often build nests for their unborn young. But it seems unlikely that these kinds of behaviors involve the same sort of deliberate planning that is involved when people buy food for the upcoming picnic or when expectant parents buy a crib before the baby is born. Animals are programmed to carry out particular patterns of behavior in response to certain environmental and internal stimuli (such as hormones), but without a self, they cannot really plan more than a few seconds ahead. Their responses reflect patterns of behavior that are elicited by internal or external stimuli rather than deliberate decisions based on conscious self-focused thought.

Decision Making and Self-Control

A self also allows people to make deliberate decisions to control their own behavior. With the ability to imagine what may happen in the future, people can make decisions to avoid problems or take advantage of opportunities, often well in advance of the time when those decisions can actually be implemented. Self-less animals do not have that option; they cannot "decide" to behave differently than they naturally do. The fact that our decisions are sometimes conscious and deliberate does not necessarily mean that they are better than those made automatically, but the process is different.

In every conscious decision, the individual tries to imagine the likely consequences of different possible lines of action. Think about trying to decide which of two job offers to accept. The cognitive task involves imagining the consequences of each decision—projecting oneself not only into the future but also into places and circumstances in which one has not been before. Being able to imagine themselves in the future allows people to play out the possible consequences of various actions, creating mental simulations of possible future outcomes.

Not all behavior is based on deliberate decisions. Often, people react automatically without consciously thinking about what they are doing. People possess two distinct mental systems by which they process information and make decisions: one is conscious and controlled, and involves deliberately thinking about what we are doing, while the other is nonconscious and automatic, and does not involve conscious thought. We move back and forth between these modes frequently, rapidly, and usually without effort.[6]

The nonconscious, automatic system, which is shared by all mammals (and perhaps all animals), starts on its own, operates very quickly, and runs automatically, without any intentional effort on the part of the individual. Automatic processes require little, if any conscious attention, and the processes themselves operate outside of the person's awareness.[7] In contrast, the conscious, controlled system appears to be unique to human beings after the age of about two years and perhaps a few species of nonhuman primates. The conscious system is involved in mental acts of which we are aware, that we intend, and that we can control with effort. Controlled processes begin intentionally and operate rather slowly as the individual thinks through options and makes deliberate decisions. Furthermore, the process itself is open to awareness so that the person is cognizant of the steps involved in consciously analyzing a problem, formulating a solution, or making a decision.

John Bargh, a leading researcher of nonconscious processes, maintains that most human behavior is controlled by automatic processes.[8] Right now, you are not consciously aware of reading the letters in each of these words (until I mention them, that is), nor of how it is that you are reading them or extracting their meaning. You are not conscious of the position of your body (again, until I mention it), despite the fact that you automatically reposition parts of it from time to time. You are not aware that you are occasionally blinking your eyes, or conscious of the fact that you are breathing. Assuming that you are reasonably engrossed in reading this paragraph, you are aware only of its meaning, which you are automatically decoding, and everything else lies outside your awareness. And, if you are not engrossed in this paragraph, you are not even aware of what you just read even though your eyes have nonetheless scanned the sentence!

From Bargh's perspective, it is fortunate that most of our behavior occurs automatically because people simply do not have enough cognitive resources to think consciously about everything that they do. Just as automatic devices such as answering machines and thermostats free people from having to respond actively to answer an incoming call or turn on the heat, automatic mental processes free us from having to think about tasks for which conscious thought is not needed. It would be impossible for us to deal with all of life's decisions in a conscious, self-aware, controlled fashion because we have only a limited amount of attentional capacity. Fortunately, most of our daily decisions, emotional reactions, and behaviors are the product of automatic processes rather than conscious choice.

One important difference between automatic and controlled processes involves the fact that controlled processes require a self, whereas automatic processes do not (although, as we will see, automatic processes sometimes involve self-reflection). To make deliberate decisions or control their natural reactions, people must be able to think consciously about themselves and the implications of their behavior. In fact, it is possible that the self's main function is to provide a way for people to override their automatic inclinations. Instead of responding nonconsciously and automatically as other animals typically do, people have the option, at least in principle, of restraining their automatic reactions or substituting behaviors of their choosing for those that occur naturally. So, no matter how much you might like to eat three pieces of cake or to hit someone who has infuriated you, the self allows the possibility of consciously exercising control over these urges.

Of course, self-control is by no means perfect, and sometimes our automatic reactions are too strong to be controlled by volition.[9] So, we all experience instances in which we have trouble making ourselves behave as we would like. Despite our best intentions, we gobble up the three pieces of cake or strike out at the other person. An intriguing question is why the self is not always powerful enough to override our urges, and what happens psychologically to make us "lose self-control." We'll address this question in chapter 8. For now, the important point is that possession of a self and the capacity for self-reflection allows at least the possibility of deciding to control one's actions.

Self-Conceptualization and Evaluation

An animal with a self can create a mental representation of itself, allowing it to think about its own characteristics and behaviors. This representation may be visual (I can "see" myself in my mind) or verbal (I can label, define, or characterize myself).

Behavioral researchers have been interested in how people conceptualize themselves because, once formed, people's self-concepts provide an important source of input to their decisions.[10] Our behavior is often affected by our beliefs about the kind of person we are—what characteristics and abilities we possess, for example. We sometimes do certain things because we see ourselves as the kind of person who does that sort of thing, and we resist doing other things because we're "not that kind of person." We undertake certain tasks because we believe that we have the ability to do them well, and we avoid other tasks because we think ourselves incompetent. Because an animal without a self does not have a self-concept, its behavior is not influenced by its beliefs about its personal characteristics.

Having a self also allows people to evaluate themselves. Although all animals can assess whether their ongoing behavior is accomplishing immediate goals, only animals with a self can step back and evaluate themselves and their behavior according to abstract standards, then react to those self-evaluations. For example, you are able to think abstractly about whether you are a "good" employee, student, friend, lover, athlete, musician, or person-in-general in ways that other animals cannot. When these self-evaluations are favorable, you experience positive feelings; when they are negative, you feel badly. Again, these self-evaluative reactions are possible only because you can think consciously about yourself.

Combining the ability to think about the future with the ability to self-evaluate gives human beings the potential to change themselves. Most people devote a good deal of effort to controlling and changing their behavior as they try to lose weight, stop smoking, control their temper, procrastinate less, or control other bad habits or vices. Deliberate self-change necessarily requires a self.[11] An animal that can think about itself and imagine the likely future consequences of its behavior is no longer a slave to environmental factors and automatic mental processes. Of course, simply having the ability to think about the future and to self-evaluate does not guarantee that people can always control their actions. If it did, we would always be able to make ourselves behave exactly as we desired. But even though our ability to control ourselves is imperfect, self-control would be impossible without the ability to reflect upon and evaluate ourselves.

An animal without a self cannot simply decide to behave contrary to its natural inclinations. A goose could not decide in a conscious and deliberate fashion to fly north rather than south for the winter, and a stallion could not decide to pass up the opportunity to mate with a sexually receptive mare. You, on the other hand, can truly decide whether to go north or south on vacation and whether or not to respond to another person's sexual advances. This is not to say that animals that lack a self never do things that are atypical for their species; they do. But such behaviors are the result of idiosyncratic patterns of physiology, experience, and environment, and not a self-directed decision.

Introspection

Although an animal without a self thinks, feels, and behaves, it cannot think about thinking, feeling, and behaving. In contrast, human beings can contemplate their own thoughts, feelings, and behavior. Not only are we alive, but we also know we are alive. We are not only having a good time, but we can also think about what a good time we are having. We are not only in pain, but we can also wish the pain would go away. We not only see the tree, but we can also think about how pretty the tree is. We are not only sexually aroused, but we can also think consciously about the object of our arousal and our reactions to him or her. We not only think but we can also think about our thoughts.

Possessing a self adds a layer of interpretation to the direct perception of the world and our experiences in it. Rather than simply perceiving the world and reacting to it, we can introspect about what we perceive and experience. As we will explore in chapter 2, introspection changes the nature of our experiences from what they would have been had we not thought consciously about them. For example, when we think carefully about things in life—such as products we buy, gifts we receive, courses we take, and even romantic partners with whom we are involved—the process of conscious thinking can change how we feel about these things. Paradoxically, thinking too much about life can interfere with our ability to process information about it accurately, and retrospectively examining decisions we have made may lower our satisfaction with them.[12] Contrary to what most people assume, it is sometimes better to think too little rather than too much.

Perspective-Taking

Nicholas Humphrey proposed that, once the emergence of self-awareness during evolutionary history provided human beings with the ability to think about their own behavior and inner mental lives, they could begin to infer things about the behavior and mental lives of others.[13] Essentially, they could imagine in their own minds what it might be like to be somebody else, based on their understanding of themselves. Thus, the ability to think about oneself goes hand-in-hand with the ability to imagine the world from other people's perspectives, including the ability to imagine how one is perceived and evaluated by others.

Evidence for this conclusion comes from two sources. First, animals without a self show little or no evidence that they can take other organisms' perspectives. For example, they do not realize that another organism has a different visual perspective on a scene than they do, and they do not seem to ponder how they are being viewed by another. However, the few animals that show evidence of having at least a rudimentary capacity for self-awareness also seem to be capable of taking others' perspectives.[14] In his book *Chimpanzee Politics*, primatologist Frans de Waal showed that chimpanzees, one of the few other species known to have the ability to self-reflect, are able to deceive one another deliberately, an action that requires imagining the perspective of another individual.[15] Likewise, Jane Goodall and others have reported instances in which chimpanzees appeared intentionally to suppress their normal reactions (such as studiously ignoring a piece of food that only they could see when another chimp was watching) in order to mislead another chimp.[16]

On the surface, many animals act as if they can infer the inner thoughts or emotions of other animals. For example, a low-ranking wolf may display submissive, appeasement behaviors in response to the angry stare of a high-ranking one. But such reactions are automatic responses to the other wolf's expressions and postures rather than the result of inferring that the high-ranking wolf is angry or has malevolent intentions. Only human beings and a few other primates appear to be able to put themselves in the minds of others.

A second piece of evidence about the link between self-awareness and perspective-taking comes from research in developmental psychology. Children develop the ability to take other people's perspectives at about the same time as they develop the ability to think about themselves. Prior to 18 to 24 months of age (the age differs across infants), babies lack the capacity for self-awareness. Not only can they not think consciously about themselves, but also they are unable to infer the mental states of others. After they begin to display evidence of self-awareness, babies also begin to demonstrate empathy, altruistic behavior, self-consciousness, and other reactions that require the ability to adopt the perspectives of other people.[17]

It is easy to see that these features of the self offer human beings many benefits. Being able to plan, self-evaluate, control one's own responses, introspect, and adopt other people's perspectives not only help people navigate life more successfully but also are responsible for most of the cultural innovations that we think of as human "progress." Science, philosophy, government, education, and health care would all be impossible if people could not consciously self-reflect. Perhaps you now understand why I think that having a self is the most important difference between human beings and most other animals.

The Search for the Self

If you are like most people, you may have the vague sense that there is, inside your head, a small, experiencing "thing" that registers your experiences, thinks your thoughts, and feels your feelings—some sort of conscious entity "in there" that is the center of your awareness, thought, and conscious experience. Many people report that this mental presence is at the core of whom they really or most essentially are, and some people have the sense that their body is just a vehicle for carrying around this important mental entity. For some people, the constant presence of this sense of self is what convinces them that they are the same person today as they were many years ago. Despite all of the changes that they have experienced, this inner self has remained constant. Some say that they could lose virtually everything else—their possessions, their family, their identity, even most of their body—and they would still be essentially the same person; only if they lost this mental presence would they be truly and completely gone. In fact, when many people think about dying, it is this mental consciousness that they imagine being extinguished at the time of death.[18]

When asked where their sense of self is located, most people reply that it is in their head. When researchers ask people to indicate where "you" are located by adjusting a pointing device, people usually locate their "egocenter" at a position between but slightly behind their eyes, somewhere along the median plane of the head from front to back.[19] Of course, there is not really any sort of identifiable structure such as this inside our skulls. We each have a brain, and the human brain has the ability to think about the person who carries the brain around. However, most people do not localize their egocenter as being the size and location of their physical brain but, rather, as something smaller.

The sensation one gets from close introspection is that there is a small inner space behind the eyes in which our conscious thoughts occur. If you close your eyes and introspect—for example, think about standing at the checkout in your local supermarket—you will likely get the sense that the scene, as hazy as it might be, is being played out in this inner space. You can even look in different directions—at your groceries, at the clerk, at the tabloids beside the counter. If you wish, you can even move through this space—for example by leaving the checkout line to retrieve a forgotten item from the shelves.

We are all accustomed to engaging in this sort of self-thought, but we rarely stop to think about what it means to "look" at a scene such as this. Where is the "space" in which this image is occurring, and who or what is looking at it? Most people are stymied by this question and feel vaguely uneasy even trying to understand what it is that they are experiencing when they imagine themselves in their own minds.

We all know, of course, that there is no empty space—neither a true egocenter nor a theater of the mind—inside our heads where the self does its work. Instead, our heads are filled with brain tissue of various sorts—mostly neurons and supporting tissue, permeated by a circulatory system. But if our craniums are full of biological matter, where does this perception of inner space come from? Given that it is not really there, we clearly must invent this space in our minds and then use it to think about and visualize ourselves, all the time knowing that it doesn't really exist anatomically.[20] How this happens is not understood, but it lies at the heart of people's sense that they have a self.

People not only think about themselves by imagining the analogue-I, but they also "talk" to themselves in their minds. Inner speech plays an important role in human behavior because it allows us to evaluate, direct, and control our own actions. People internally compliment and criticize themselves ("Boy, I'm getting fat"), offer themselves advice ("Whoa, slow down; the road's slick"), reassure themselves ("Just relax; it'll be just fine"), comment on their experiences and feelings ("Geez, I'm tired"), and talk to themselves in myriad other ways. Inner speech can be quite beneficial but, as we will see, it can also create a great deal of unhappiness, conflict, and other personal havoc.

We know relatively little about the specific brain structures that are associated with self-awareness, but neuroscientists are beginning to investigate where and how the brain creates self-awareness and our sense of self. Given that the self appears to be a relatively recent evolutionary adaptation, we might expect that the neurological processes that underlie it occur in the parts of the brain that have developed most recently, such as the prefrontal cortex. The prefrontal area is the foremost portion of the frontal lobes of the brain, lying immediately behind the forehead. (It's interesting, then, that most people do not feel that self-reflection occurs in the area behind their forehead.) Recent research evidence suggests that the prefrontal area of the brain is particularly active when people engage in self-relevant thinking, but experimental research on the neuroanatomy of the self is in its infancy.[21]

Most of our knowledge about the functions of the frontal lobes comes from studies of individuals whose brains have been damaged by injury or modified by surgery. Case studies and experiments over the past 150 years have shown that damage to the frontal lobes produces disturbances of self and awareness. For example, people with damage to their frontal lobes are typically completely unconcerned about their injuries. Despite the fact that they understand fully that their injury is quite serious, they simply do not seem interested in it—much as if the problem were someone else's rather than their own! As one researcher observed, frontal lobe patients "seem to be entirely uninterested in themselves as persons."[22] Clearly, something about their sense of self has gone awry.

People with frontal lobe injuries also have trouble evaluating themselves accurately. For example, they do not have insight into deficits in their behavior that are obvious to everyone else, and they seem oblivious to how others view them. They also tend to lose their ability to be self-absorbed and to introspect, and thus no longer daydream or brood over their problems. Some such patients appear unable to initiate purposeful behaviors, suggesting that the executive functions of the self that control intentional behavior have also been affected. The frontal lobes seem to be involved in the executive control by which people initiate, monitor, and control their own behavior, as well as in consciousness itself.[23]

Frontal lobe patients also often display disturbances in their experience of time. They may react normally to concrete situations in the present yet be unable to think clearly about the past or future. Without the ability to imagine themselves in other time frames, it is as if a person with compromised frontal lobes lives constantly in the present. Studies of cerebral blood flow have confirmed that the recollection of past events about oneself is associated with activity in the frontal lobes.[24] Frontal lobe patients also have problems planning, formulating goals, and exerting self-control, all of which require a functional self. Although not all patients with frontal lobe disturbances show all of these symptoms, the patterns are consistent enough to suggest that activity in the frontal lobes of the brain underlies our ability to think about ourselves as separate individuals whose identity extends from the past to the future, and possibly our ability to initiate and control volitional behavior, as well.

Self-Awareness in Other Animals

Evidence suggests that most other animals are not able to think about themselves consciously in the ways that human beings can. Of course, all organisms have some very primitive sense that allows them to distinguish themselves from their environment—what Ulrich Neisser has called "ecological self knowledge."[25] If they didn't have some sense that their body was theirs, they would just as easily attack or eat themselves as they would a plant or another animal. But the sense of bodily self possessed by most sentient organisms is very rudimentary, based on physical sensations rather than conscious thought. A snake, gopher, or cow distinguishes itself physically from the rest of the world but cannot think about itself in the ways that a human being does.

If we were going to find evidence of a self among other members of the animal kingdom, we might expect to find it among our closest relatives—other primates such as chimpanzees, bonobos, gorillas, and orangutans—with whom we share the most genetic similarities and in whom the frontal lobes are most highly developed. Comparative psychologist Gordon Gallup, Jr., was among the first to demonstrate that chimpanzees do indeed possess a rudimentary form of self-awareness.[26] Gallup had observed that, although chimpanzees that were shown their reflection in a mirror initially reacted as if the image were another chimp, they quickly seemed to realize that the image was, in fact, them. They would then use the mirror to explore parts of their bodies that they could not see directly, pick their teeth, and groom—much as human beings do.

To convince skeptics that the chimpanzees actually recognized themselves in the mirror, Gallup anesthetized his chimps, then painted an odorless, nonirritating red dye on the brow ridges above their eyes and on the tips of their ears—parts of their bodies that they could not see directly. After the anesthetic had worn off, the chimps were placed in a cage with a mirror. Gallup's question was this: Would the chimp respond to the red marking by touching its own body (as you and I presumably would if we saw red paint on our faces in the mirror) or by touching the mirror (as an animal would if it didn't know that the red reflection in the mirror was itself)? As it turned out, Gallup's chimps touched their own ears and brows, suggesting that they knew that the face in the mirror was theirs.[27] The same phenomenon has been demonstrated in both orangutans and gorillas.[28] Very recently, researchers have found preliminary evidence that dolphins may also possess self-awareness, but more research must be done before we are certain.

Importantly, no other species, including any species of monkey, has demonstrated any ability to recognize itself in a mirror. Even when they are given months (or in some cases, years) of exposure to mirrors in their cages, monkeys continue either to ignore their reflections or react to them as if they were other animals. They may threaten the image, or they may run away and hide. But they do not seem to have any recognition that the image in the mirror is their own.

Two points should be made about these mirror tests. First, it is conceivable that a self-aware organism might fail the mirror test, leading us to erroneously conclude that it did not have a self. Some researchers have suggested that in order to recognize its own reflection in a mirror, an animal must not only possess self-awareness but also realize that mirrors provide accurate images of objects that are placed in front of them. An animal with a self that nonetheless did not understand the contingent nature of mirror reflections might not react to its own reflected image. However, animals that fail the mirror test for self-awareness do not show any other evidence of having a self, either.[29]

Second, simply because chimpanzees and orangutans recognize themselves in a mirror does not indicate that their selves are identical to ours. Mirror recognition involves a rather rudimentary form of self-awareness, and chimps and orangutans do not appear capable of some of the more advanced mental activities that use a self. For example, Daniel Povinelli's research has suggested that, although chimpanzees recognize themselves in mirrors, they do not seem to appreciate that they are a unique individual with a past and a future.[30] As a result, they cannot engage in human acts of selfhood such as long-term planning.

The Evolution of Self-Reflection

If we accept the premise that "lower" animals (going all the way back to one-celled organisms) do not have a self but that human beings do, then we need to account for how and why the human self developed. Unfortunately, we may never have a definitive answer to this question. Brains, much less brain functions, are not preserved in the fossil record, so archeologists and paleontologists cannot trace the evolution of the self in the same way as they trace the evolution of the horse's hoof or the human spine. In the absence of concrete evidence, we should not be surprised that experts disagree considerably about when the self first emerged.

If it is true that chimpanzees and orangutans have a rudimentary ability to self-reflect, the basic foundations for the human self were probably laid down long ago, possibly in a common ancestor of human beings and chimpanzees before their family trees diverged over 5 million years ago. Furthermore, we might surmise that, for the first couple of million years of hominid evolution, our human ancestors possessed a level of self-awareness that was roughly comparable to that of a modern chimpanzee.[31] This would have certainly been an improvement over having no self at all for, by virtue of having a rudimentary self, chimpanzees can engage in sophisticated social behaviors and inferences that most other animals cannot. The more interesting question, though, is when the human self in its present form—with its sophisticated ability for abstract self-reflection, introspection, and planning—first appeared.

Some psychologists have made the argument that the human self emerged around 1.7 million years ago with the appearance of *Homo erectus* in the late Pleistocene era.[32] They base this conclusion on the assumption that hominids could not have successfully moved from being forest foragers to grassland hunter-gatherers at that time without the special abilities that self-awareness confers. Although hominids undoubtedly experienced increases in their cognitive abilities about this time, the evidence for the appearance of the self is much weaker, and I place the emergence of the modern human self later in the course of human evolution.

I said earlier that we cannot find evidence of a self in the archeological record, but that is not entirely true. Although we do not find fossilized selves or even brains, we do find the products of selves and brains—human artifacts that may provide hints about the evolution of self-reflection. Prior to around 40,000 to 60,000 years ago, the archeological record contains little evidence to suggest that human beings or their hominid ancestors had a self such as people have today. Crude stone tools appear in the fossil record with the remains of *Homo hablis* around 2 million years ago, but these are little more than rocks with a few flakes chipped off. Tools improved only slightly over the ensuing 2 million years, becoming barely more sophisticated than those used by chimpanzees today. Not until after the arrival of *Homo sapiens* do we find any evidence of the kinds of thought processes that involve a self —no evidence of innovation, culture, personal identity, art, or advanced technology.[33]

Then, between 40,000 and 60,000 years ago, we see a pronounced change in human artifacts. Not only do tools become more sophisticated and specialized, with different tools designed for different tasks, but we also begin to see the first evidence of culture. The first body adornments—beads and bracelets—appear, suggesting that, for the first time, people could think about how they were being perceived by others. Representational art first appeared about this time as well. As archeologist Richard Klein observed, "There was a kind of behavioral revolution 50,000 years ago. Nobody made art before 50,000 years ago; everybody did afterward."[34]

We also see the first evidence of boat-making—a task that requires mentally imagining one's analogue-I using a boat at some later time—as well as the first burials that contain grave goods. Earlier people, including the Neanderthals, sometimes buried their dead in shallow graves, but only after about 40,000 years ago did people appear to attach much importance to death or entertain the idea of an afterlife.[35] Some experts even date the appearance of human language to about this same period. Given that much of self-focused thought involves "talking to oneself" in one's mind, there may be a direct link between language and the self.[36]

These changes in human lifestyle have led archeologists to label the period around 40,000 years ago, which is technically known as the Middle-Upper Paleolithic transition, the "cultural big bang." Just as physicists trace the beginnings of the universe to the cosmic Big Bang—the point at which everything in the universe seemed to appear from nowhere—archeologists trace the beginnings of human culture to the cultural big bang—the point at which sophisticated cultural practices also seemed to appear from nowhere. After millions of years with little change in the lifestyle of hominids, we begin to see extensive evidence of innovation and culture.[37]

Experts disagree regarding many aspects of the Middle-Upper Paleolithic transition, including whether it was a sudden "revolution" or a gradual "evolution." They also disagree whether this period was the result of a biological change in the brain or the development of cultural innovations by people who had been capable of culture for tens of thousands of years but who, for some reason, had not shown it. Yet most agree that something happened about this time that radically changed human behavior.

My speculation is that the cultural big bang was a direct consequence of the emergence of the modern human self. If we could travel back in time over 60,000 years ago to the time before this important transition, I think we would regard the humans we met as essentially intelligent apes. Although they would look roughly human and possess certain human characteristics, we would see little evidence of the attributes that we expect human beings to possess. They would not exhibit foresight or planning, be able to consider options, or communicate purposefully about what they were thinking or feeling. From our present standpoint, it is virtually impossible for us to imagine what human behavior and life were like before humans had the capacity for self-awareness. Prior to the transition, early human beings (such as *Homo erectus, Homo neanderthalensis,* and *Homo heidelbergensis*) were not people "like us" who just happened to live more primitively, with less complex tools, social systems, knowledge, and culture. Rather, these species were probably so different from us psychologically that it is as impossible for us to imagine what their lives and experiences were like as it is to imagine what it is like to be a cat or a gorilla. As White observed, "life in the Lower Paleolithic may have been so different from the modern human condition that it is barely recognizable to us."[38] After the transition of the cultural big bang, however, we would find ourselves able to identify with the people we met. They would plan ahead, worry about the future, be concerned with what others thought of them, and perhaps even ponder existential questions.

Some people have difficulty imagining that early human beings could have survived and functioned without a self because they assume that our ability to self-reflect, plan, and reminisce are essential to human survival. But, in fact, people could have gotten by quite well without a self, particularly in the environment in which they lived at the time. After all, most other animals function quite well without a self, and it's hard to imagine what an otter, dog, or salmon would do with a self if it had one! As products of natural selection, early hominids evolved with the necessary physical and mental attributes to survive and reproduce at least well enough that the species did not die out.

Another piece of evidence that early human beings could have functioned reasonably well without self-reflection is that each of us does it every day. Most people assume that they think consciously about most of what they are doing, but more often than not, they don't. As I noted earlier, people can function in either an automatic (nonconscious) or controlled (conscious) mode, and most of our behavior even today occurs automatically without conscious self-thought. People can engage in highly complex behaviors without any self-awareness or self-related thought whatsoever.[39] One familiar example involves "highway hypnosis," in which people drive a car for miles with no conscious thought. The individual is obviously processing incoming information and responding effectively by turning the steering wheel, using the turn signals to change lanes, and reacting to the movement of other cars, but the person is not self-aware. Similarly, we can carry on lengthy conversations with no conscious, self-related thought. Our words often seem to come from nowhere without any forethought, mediated entirely by automatic processes that operate below the level of our awareness. Of course, there are instances in which we are very self-focused during conversations as we choose our words carefully, wonder about what other people are thinking about us, ruminate over stupid things that we said, or worry that the conversation will turn out badly. But we can converse quite well on automatic pilot and without self-focused thought.

We spend much of each day in an automatic mode with our selves quiescent. We cannot only drive and talk without a self, but we can eat, read, watch TV, listen to music, play sports, make love, and do myriad other things as well. The self is sometimes engaged as we do these things, but it's not necessary. (In fact, as we will later see, self-thought is sometimes impedes these actions.) Seeing how well modern human beings function on automatic pilot makes it easier to imagine prehistoric people managing quite well without the ability to self-reflect.

Why the self emerged at this time during evolutionary history is difficult to say. One possibility is that the human brain had changed in ways that for the first time permitted self-awareness. Perhaps it is no coincidence that the first human skeletons that are indistinguishable from modern humans date approximately to this same period. The self may have been a by-product of anatomical changes in the brain and other parts of the body.

Having a self was presumably beneficial (or at least not generally detrimental) to our prehistoric ancestors or else it would have not evolved through natural selection. If animals that were able to think about themselves fared more poorly in the struggle to survive and reproduce than those without a self, *Homo sapiens* would most likely not have the ability to self-reflect. In fact, though, people who had selves had a distinct advantage over both other animals and people without selves (there must have been a transition period during prehistory in which some people had a self and other people didn't). Despite the remarkable things that animals can do without a self, the capacity to think consciously, plan, consider, and debate gave human beings the upper hand.

The Dark Side of the Self

Thus far, the self sounds like a rather beneficial evolutionary adaptation. It allows us to think about who we are and what we are doing, anticipate future contingencies, plan ahead, control our own behavior, and cognitively adopt the perspectives of other people. Yet despite the many ways in which having a self enhances human functioning, the self is not an unmitigated blessing. It is single-handedly responsible for many, if not most of the problems that human beings face as individuals and as a species.

As we will explore in subsequent chapters, the capacity to self-reflect distorts our perceptions of the world, leads us to draw inaccurate conclusions about ourselves and other people, and thus prompts us to make bad decisions based on faulty information. The self conjures up a great deal of personal suffering in the form of depression, anxiety, anger, jealousy, and other negative emotions by allowing us to ruminate about the past or imagine what might befall us in the future. The inherently egocentric and egotistical manner in which the self processes information can blind us to our own shortcomings and undermine our relationships with other people. The self also underlies a great deal of social conflict, leading people to dislike those who are different from them, fight with members of other social groups, and perpetrate horrible acts of cruelty. Ironically, the self also leads people to endanger their own well-being by putting egoistic goals over personal safety. And, for those inclined toward religion and spirituality, visionaries throughout history have proclaimed that the self stymies the quest for spiritual fulfillment.

It seems a paradox that the mental capacity that is responsible for many of the best aspects of being human also underlies our most serious deficiencies and problems. The paradox may be explained, at least in part, by the fact that the self evolved under conditions much different from those under which most people live today. Whatever date we place on the appearance of the self, the capacity for self-awareness emerged among beings who lived as hunters and gatherers (and possibly scavengers) on the plains of prehistoric Africa—the so-called ancestral environment. Self-reflection presumably had adaptive value in the ancestral environment because being able to think and plan more than a few seconds ahead gave humans an advantage over other animals and the natural environment. Further, the capacity to imagine what other people (and other animals) might be thinking likewise enhanced the probability of survival and reproduction. In such an environment, self-awareness would have likely had many benefits and relatively few liabilities.

To see that this is so, let's put ourselves, as best we can, in the world in which these early people lived. (Incidentally, we are able to engage in this imaginary time-travel only because we have a self!). As nomadic hunter-gatherers, we would have lived day to day—hunting, gathering, and scavenging what we needed to survive. Because we had no way to preserve or transport large amounts of food, we would have collected only as much as our clan could eat in a day or two. Furthermore, because we lived in an environment in which our basic needs were clearly met or unmet on a daily basis, we would have had little reason to look more than a few days into the future. Even when things were not going well for us—when food was scarce, for example—we could do nothing other than keep looking. We would not have spent a great deal of time considering ways to improve our lot in life because we didn't have many options.

As prehistoric hominids, we would have had no long-term aspirations to succeed, achieve, or accumulate possessions. We might have owned a few things that could be easily carried, but we certainly had no reason to acquire extra belongings. We would have met few other people in our nomadic wanderings, but they would have been living just like us, so we wouldn't have gotten new ideas about what else we might need to be happy. With no desire to accumulate wealth or possessions, we would not have been oriented toward long-term achievement and success as people are today. Nor would we have struggled with the issues of identity that plague many modern people. People today think a great deal about who they are, the lives they live, and what they hope and fear becoming in the future. But as prehistoric people, we could not fathom other options. Because we knew only one life since birth, we couldn't imagine alternative futures for ourselves. What else could we imagine being other than what we already were?

Given our circumstances as prehistoric hunter-gatherers on the African savanna, we would have had little reason to imagine ourselves in the future or to pursue long-range goals. We would have thought about our lives mostly from a short time perspective—hours or, at most, a few days into the future—and having a self would have been very useful in that regard. But we would probably not have spent much time wondering and worrying about the distant future or about greater existential questions.

The lives of modern people are markedly different from those of our ancestors at the time of the cultural big bang. Because we live in sedentary communities, we are able to accumulate not only vital commodities such as food but also personal possessions. Because we see a universe of possibilities for ourselves reflected in the people whom we know, read about, and see on television, most of us desire many things that we don't have and, thus, live with a mild degree of discontent. We aspire to do new things, own more possessions, live different lifestyles, and pursue new identities. Because they can see a great number of possibilities laid out before them, many people today feel not only that they are missing out on important aspects of life but also that they are faced with an endless array of choices that prehistoric people could not have imagined. Each person faces decisions about what job to pursue, how much education to attain, where to live, what political and religious beliefs to adopt, who to live with, and so on. Even our decisions about friendships and romantic partnerships are complex in contrast to our prehistoric ancestors, whose options for friends and mates were limited to the other members of a small clan.

Compared to the short-term goals of our prehistoric ancestors, many of the outcomes for which we strive today lie far in the future. Whereas prehistoric peoples looked only a few days ahead, we spend a great deal of time thinking about and waiting for paychecks, educational degrees, promotions, retirement, and other distant goals to be realized. And, because we do not always know whether what we are doing today will result in attainment of these rewards in the future, we live with a great deal of uncertainty that was not common among prehistoric people.[40]

In short, we are living today with a mental apparatus for self-reflection that evolved because it had adaptive value for intelligent, bipedal animals living in Africa tens of thousands of years ago. Because the conditions under which people live today are so far removed from those under which the self evolved, the benefits it provides are now accompanied by numerous liabilities. The self is not in any way inherently flawed; indeed, it is a remarkable biological adaptation. Rather, self-reflection has become a double-edged sword because the inclinations that served us well in the ancestral environment are often detrimental in the modern world. In this respect, the self is much like the bodily systems that control human eating. The natural penchant for sugar and fats that facilitated the survival of prehistoric people has become a detriment to people's health in a society in which they can easily obtain large quantities of sweets and fats at a nearby store or fast food restaurant.

This book is about the downside—the curse—of having a self in modern life. I will repeatedly stress that the self has decided value as well. Without a self, we could no longer reminisce about the past or plan for the future. We couldn't purposefully control our own behavior or make deliberate decisions. We would also lose much of our ability to put ourselves in the minds of other people, and we couldn't think about what they might be thinking. I doubt that many people would choose to trade places with an animal that does not have a self or, if it were possible, to have a "selfectomy" that excised their self and everything that it entails. In many ways, the emergence of self-awareness was what turned prehistoric hominids from intelligent apes into human beings as we know them today, and without it, we would have none of the social or cultural affordances that are the hallmark of human existence. Self-reflection is much more a mixed blessing than an unmitigated curse, but our focus will be primarily on the downside of having a self.

The point of this book is not that the self is "bad" or that it ought to be eradicated, but rather that the same ability to self-reflect that makes us wonderfully human and underlies the best features of civilization also creates havoc with people's lives, leading to suffering, selfishness, troubled relationships, disastrous decisions, and behavior that is dangerous to ourselves and to others. The self is at once our greatest ally and our fiercest enemy, and many of the biggest struggles each of us faces in life are either directly or indirectly the doing of the self. Understanding how the self creates many of our problems can provide important insights into the nature of the human condition and offer solutions for how we can counteract many of the detrimental effects of selfhood.

2

Living in Two Worlds

The person who thinks all the time has nothing to think about except thoughts, and so he loses touch with reality.
—ALAN WATTS

During two weeks in June and July of 2001, three young children died in separate incidents after being left for too long inside hot cars. Such cases are tragically common; nationwide, several children die in hot vehicles each summer. The twist that made these three events noteworthy was that, in each case, the child died because his or her parent forgot that the child was in the car! In June, an Iowa woman forgot to drop her 7-month-old baby girl at a babysitter when she went to work. Then, in July, a father in Minneapolis forgot to take his infant son to the day-care center, leaving him in the sun-baked car until the baby's body was discovered six hours later. The same week, a North Carolina father forgot to take his 6-month-old son to the babysitter's house before going to work.

Many people found these events incomprehensible. People accidentally leave their checkbooks in the car or perhaps their cell phones or sunglasses, but their children? It might be possible to dismiss these cases as the actions of uncaring, neglectful, or stupid people except for the fact that they were, by all accounts, good parents and respected professionals. (The woman was chief executive officer for a hospital, and the two men were a mortgage lender and a veterinarian.) So, how does a caring parent forget something as important as a child, particularly a child who is in the car at the time?

Although we don't know what was going on in these parents' minds on the mornings that they overlooked their children in the backseat, it's probably safe to assume that they were preoccupied. Rather than focusing on the requirements of the present moment, their minds were somewhere else. Perhaps they were thinking about the upcoming workday, or about problems they had to face at the office. Maybe they were replaying an argument they had at home over breakfast, or thinking about how stressful it is being the parent of a small child. Maybe they were mulling over the news on the radio, worrying about their financial situation, or planning an upcoming vacation. Whatever they were thinking, it's my guess that their attention was engaged by the self.

Each of us lives in two worlds. One is the world outside of our bodies—the so-called real world of objects, people, and events. The other is the world inside our heads—the subjective world of our own thoughts, experiences, plans, feelings, and fantasies. Each of us lives in both of these worlds every day, moving back and forth between them easily and often.

We live in the external world as we crane our necks to look at the accident along the highway, watch the climactic ending of an engrossing movie, listen to strange sounds in the night, read a fascinating book, or watch the rain falling in the back yard. We live in the internal world when our attention switches from these objective things to our plans for tonight, a nagging worry about an upcoming presentation at work, a bodily ache, or the memory of a long-lost love.

The transitions from one world to the other typically go unnoticed, and our experience of life is an ongoing, interwoven meld of our outer and inner worlds. As you are reading this page, you will focus for a time on my words (external), but then you may be distracted by a thought about something you must do later today (internal). Your attention shifts to the clock to check the time (external), then to the thought of what you will eat later (internal). You wonder whether this book is going to be interesting (internal), then look around the room (external), suddenly realizing that your attention is shifting around in just the way I'm describing (internal). And so it goes; all day, every day, our attention seldom rests on one thing for very long but rather is a stream of consciousness that includes both the external objective world of people, things, and events, and the internal psychological world of thoughts, images, and feelings.[1]

Much of what happens in our inner world involves the activity of the self. Our thoughts are often about ourselves—memories of our past, plans for the future, ruminations about our personal abilities and characteristics, analyses of sensations and feelings, and fantasies about our desires. These thoughts may be concrete (pondering a specific memory of what you did yesterday, for example) or quite abstract (such as wondering about one's purpose in life). But all of them involve self-relevant thinking, and thus, the self.

The inner worlds of other animals do not include these sorts of self-related thoughts. Their attention is focused on the external world, as well as on physical sensations (such as pain, cold, and hunger) and their emotions. But they do not spin introspective webs of self-related thought. It seems unlikely that cats or cows or butterflies think consciously about themselves and their experiences as they sit quietly, graze, or flit from flower to flower. "I wonder why my owner feeds me this dry cat food." "Am I better than the other cows in my herd?" "Which flower garden should I flit to next?" In contrast, human beings live with an ongoing chatter of thoughts in their heads. Unlike other animals, we might, in fact, ask ourselves why someone treated us in a certain way, whether we are better or worse than other people (in general or on some specific dimension), or where we should go to eat. This sort of ongoing introspection and rumination adds an additional layer to our experiences. We live not only in the external world as all animals do but also in an internal world of self-generated thought.

Who Is Talking to Whom?

Much of the thinking that people do about themselves is experienced as internal "talking" in which an inner "voice" makes observations ("It looks cold outside this morning"), asks questions ("Should I wear my coat today?"), and provides answers ("Nah, it'll warm up by this afternoon"). We have all had the experience of talking to ourselves, "hearing" (in an odd sort of way) ourselves think. In fact, we talk to ourselves so often that these inner voices rarely attract our attention unless the questions are difficult or the answers distressing. But why do we talk to ourselves, and why does thinking about oneself seem like a conversation? Who is talking to whom inside our heads?

Philosophers, psychologists, and neuroscientists have attempted to understand the nature of self-talk for centuries.[2] Most have tended to regard talking to oneself as a monologue rather than as the dialogue that it sometimes seems. Even when internal talking appears to be a conversation—as when I consciously wonder whether to wear a coat, then answer myself—most writers have assumed that a single mental apparatus is involved that simply alternates roles. Plato held this view, for example, observing that "when the mind is thinking, it is simply talking to itself, asking questions and answering them."[3]

Sometimes, however, the talking in our heads seems like a real conversation between two or more distinct entities. Consider, for example, the conversation-like quality of self-talk when a person is trying to consider multiple perspectives in order to make a decision. I have the thought that I would like to go on a cruise for my vacation, but a "voice" immediately reminds me that I may not be able to afford it. As the conversation plays out, various "speakers" chime in with their analyses of the pros and cons, sometimes in the first person ("I don't have enough money saved up") but sometimes in the second person as well ("Yes, but you always wanted to go on a cruise"). This inner dialogue feels rather like a true conversation among two or more distinct parties that have competing interests and concerns.

Self-talk also appears to be a dialogue when a person suggests something to him- or herself, only to reject the idea immediately. For example, I might think to myself, "I think I'll fix some coffee," only to immediately counter, "No, I'll have tea instead." If I knew I wanted tea (which I presumably did), why did I first suggest coffee to myself? This kind of internal exchange gives one the sense that there are two separate inclinations inside of me having a conversation about whether to drink coffee or tea, much as when a friend suggests that we see one movie and I counter with a different suggestion.

James Blachowicz, a philosopher, has suggested that our self-talk often feels like a conversation because it sometimes involves an exchange between two distinct mental systems.[4] One of these systems is particularly adept at articulating questions, and the other is particularly good at finding answers and meaning, but it offers its answers in the form of brief, guttural, often visceral responses that are then interpreted by the first system. I ask myself a clearly articulated question ("Should I take the job in Seattle or Miami?"), but rather than getting a clear and thorough verbal response, I often receive bits and pieces of answers, both verbal ones ("Seattle's rainy . . . Miami's hot") and nonverbal, visceral "gut" feelings. I might feel excited when I read information about Seattle but dread when I read about Miami, or vice versa. The first system then organizes, amplifies, and articulates the piecemeal responses that the second system provides, explicitly exploring their meaning and implications and possibly posing more questions ("Which do I like least—rain or heat?"). Blachowicz compares this type of self-talk to a game of charades in which the receiver asks questions and interprets the sender's behaviors as the sender responds in a piecemeal, nonverbal fashion until the receiver arrives at an answer.

Although it sometimes seems that several mental speakers are competing for our attention, we each know that the "voices" in our heads—the various questioners and answerers who participate in our inner conversations—are actually all part of us. Despite the sense that there are different voices in your head, you know that the decision that you ultimately make whether to go on a cruise or to have tea or to take the job in Seattle is *your* decision. You don't have the sense that one of the voices in your head has somehow won the day and that the others have unhappily sulked away in silence. Your ability to self-reflect allows you to realize that you are, in fact, the source of all of these disparate thoughts.

But what if you didn't know that the voices you heard in your head were yours? Julian Jaynes, a Princeton psychologist, offered the provocative and highly controversial hypothesis that human beings were, in fact, precisely in this position until relatively recently in their history. Pulling upon a variety of literary, archeological, and historical evidence, Jaynes proposed that people did not realize that the voices in their heads were actually them until sometime after 1000 B.C.E., less than a mere 3,000 years ago! Among other things, he based his conclusion on analysis of the use of mentalistic terms in ancient writings. Jaynes claimed that mentalistic terms conveying that people intentionally decided to do something (verbs such as *decide, intend, want,* or *initiate*) or consciously reflected on themselves (*wonder, understand, anticipate,* or *regret*) were absent from the earliest known writings. Rather, ancient writers described people as simply behaving in a particular way (with no intentions, motives, or decisions imputed) or being ordered to do things by the gods. After around 800–1000 B.C.E., however, mentalistic concepts began to appear in ancient writings, being used much as they are today to indicate that people made conscious decisions, thought about the future, introspected, and looked back on their actions with pride or regret.[5]

According to Jaynes, people prior to 1000 B.C.E. were, in fact, "talking to themselves" in their minds just as they do today; they simply didn't know it. Not having the capacity to realize that they were the source of the voices they heard in their heads, they came to the not unreasonable conclusion that the instructions, ideas, and warnings they received came from external sources. Jaynes believes that his analysis explains why people of ancient Greece, Egypt, and Mesopotamia regularly heard and responded to the voices of the gods. These ancient gods were not much like the monotheistic God of many modern religions but, rather, were a group of entities that regularly instructed people regarding what they should do, warned them of dangers, criticized them, and gave them ideas—precisely the kinds of things that self-talk does.

Jaynes suggested that, around the time that people were first able to recognize that the talk in their own heads was self-created, the voices of the gods largely disappeared. So, for example, the Greek gods became increasingly weak and uninvolved in human affairs at about this time, and in the Middle East, the Hebrews set out to discover why Yahweh had withdrawn from them. In fact, Jaynes suggested that the first five books of the Bible tell the story of a people trying to come to terms with the fact that the voice of Yahweh was not being heard as clearly and frequently as before. It was also at this time that divination, prophecy, and angels become popular, possibly as replacements for the previous certainty of having a god tell one what to do directly.[6]

Jaynes's hypothesis is quite controversial and has been criticized on many fronts. Yet it raises the provocative question of how people would respond if they didn't know that they talked to themselves. Much like a child who cannot distinguish nighttime dreams from waking life, the person who could not distinguish self-talk from external voices would live in a world in which disembodied voices instructed, warned, and criticized them. Jaynes suggested that many modern cases of schizophrenia (in which people "hear" voices) and possession (in which people seem to be controlled by unknown entities) may be related to a permanent or temporary inability to distinguish self-talk from real voices.[7]

Whatever the merits of Jaynes's analysis, he is correct that something seems to have happened to human consciousness toward the middle of the first millennium B.C.E. The philosopher Karl Jaspers used the term *axial age* to refer to the period of a few hundred years on each side of 500 B.C.E. because he saw this period as the "axis" of world history.[8] From the beginnings of civilization until after 1000 B.C.E., human culture progressed relatively slowly, but in a short few hundred years, culture exploded to develop fundamental ideas in philosophy, religion, science, and government that still guide civilized human life today. Cultural innovations in Greece, Israel, Iran, India, and China dramatically changed human civilization as figures such as Plato, Pythagoras, Zoroaster, Isaiah, Confucius, Gautama Buddha, and the unnamed sages who wrote the *Upanishads* and *Tao te Ching* offered radically new ways of thinking and living. Clearly, people of this era began to think consciously about themselves and their worlds more than ever before.

Self-Preoccupation

There is no doubt that the voices in our heads are often useful. Because the self allows us to think deliberately and consciously about people, objects, and events that are not immediately present, we can retrospectively analyze things that have happened to us, anticipate what may occur in the future, make decisions about what to do, and plan for expected contingencies. We can conjure up our memory of this morning's argument with our boss to think about why it happened and whose fault it was. We can imagine what might happen when we meet with the boss tomorrow to complain about how he or she treated us unfairly. And we can think through various options about where to look for a new job should the boss not respond favorably to our complaint. In each case, our ability to think consciously about ourselves allows us to examine past and future events deliberately and carefully.

Yet, although self-talk is sometimes useful, a great deal of this internal chatter seems unnecessary. The self is often engaged whether we need it or not. People live in their inner worlds when there's no pressing reason to do so and even when it pulls them away from attending to life in the external world. Self-generated rumination is not always helpful for making decisions, figuring things out, planning for the future, or coping with what happens. Even when a certain amount of self-reflection might be beneficial, most people tend to overdo it, ruminating far more than necessary to solve the problem at hand. More problematically, too much inner dialogue is not only unnecessary, but, as we will see, it can actually be detrimental, and in this sense, it contributes to the curse of the self.

People have only a limited capacity for attention. Devoting attention to one thing necessarily precludes paying complete attention to anything else, and it is difficult to focus one's attention on more than one thing at a time.[9] Thus, to the extent that we are self-focused and living in the inner world inside our own heads, we are not able to live fully in the world outside. As a result, thinking about oneself can distract people from the events that occur around them. Most of us have had the experience of walking or driving from one place to another so absorbed in self-thought that we arrive with no memory whatsoever of the sights along the way. Because we were planning, worrying, reminiscing, or engaged in some other sort of self-reflection, our attention was commandeered by the self rather than focused on the environment in which we were moving. The fact that we navigated successfully from one place to another while lost in self-thought is a testament to our ability to function on automatic pilot. Even so, we substituted self-generated internal thoughts for the sights and sounds of the real world.

Distracted From Real Life

This fact is demonstrated by research showing that self-preoccupation interferes with memory. When being held captive by their own thoughts, people often miss part (or all) of what happens around them. Imagine that you are attending the first day of a new class or the first meeting of a new group. To begin, the teacher or group leader asks each person to introduce and say a few things about him- or herself. As members of the group start introducing themselves, your thoughts turn to what you will say when your turn arrives. Your self shifts into high gear as you consider various possibilities, imagine how the other people might react to each disclosure, finally settle on what you will say, then rehearse in your mind how you will say it. Although you have now prepared for your introduction (which is undoubtedly beneficial), your self has distracted you from what the other people in the group have been saying. As a result, you have no idea who these people are or what they just said about themselves. This phenomenon is called the next-in-line effect because people are least likely to remember what the person who immediately preceded them said because that was when they were most self-absorbed.[10]

Self-preoccupation also interferes with people's ability to remember things that they already know. When people devote too much attention to themselves, they leave little cognitive room for other kinds of mental processes, including those associated with remembering. We can see this effect quite clearly in the case of test anxiety. I talk regularly to students for whom taking tests is an exceptionally anxiety-provoking ordeal. In general, their chief complaint is not that they feel anxious and upset while taking tests (although that is true) but, rather, that test anxiety interferes with their ability to do well on the test. Burdened by excessive anxiety, these students find it difficult to remember things that they have learned. The problem arises because, rather than focusing single-mindedly on the test questions, students' minds are filled with a cacophony of irrelevant, self-generated thoughts that edge out their ability to think about the test itself.[11] "Why didn't I study more for this test? Boy, am I stupid! I should know this stuff. I'm going to be so embarrassed when I get my grade back. Mom and Dad are gonna kill me if I fail this course." And so their self goes, on and on. After this sort of experience, students often say that their "mind went blank" as they tried to answer the test questions. In reality, however, their mind was not blank at all but, rather, filled up with the self's competing chatter. Once they leave the testing situation, the answers often come immediately to them because their ruminations are no longer monopolizing the attentional and cognitive resources needed to remember the answers.

I suspect that the parents who forgot to take their children to day care before going to work were sidetracked by this sort of self-created distraction. We have all had the experience of forgetting what we were doing because our minds were abuzz with self-chatter.

Choking Under Pressure

In other instances, the problem is not that people's self-thoughts interfere with cognitive processes (such as memory) but, rather, that they pay conscious attention to tasks that are best performed automatically and nonconsciously. Once a behavior becomes well-learned, self-preoccupation can interfere with its execution. In such cases, the self not only fails to help performance but dramatically hinders it.[12]

Many complex behaviors initially require a great deal of effort and attention to learn successfully, but once mastered, they can be executed skillfully without self-attention. After people have learned to play the piano, shoot a free throw in basketball, or recite the Gettysburg Address, for example, they do not need a self to execute the behavior. They may need the self to decide to initiate the action, but once the behavioral sequence begins, the behavior seems to flow out of them without much conscious thought. However, if we purposefully lead people who have mastered a complex skill to think consciously about what they are doing—to monitor carefully the placement of their fingers on the piano keys, the movements involved in shooting a basketball, or the pronunciation of each word in the Gettysburg Address—the quality of their performance will typically deteriorate. Directing conscious attention to the execution of a well-learned, complex action short-circuits the automatic process and undermines the quality of the behavior.

This process is responsible for what we commonly call choking under pressure. Most people have had the experience of performing dramatically below their capacity because they were excessively self-focused. Athletes choke in games, public speakers and actors choke when they stand in front of an audience, and job applicants choke during job interviews. In each case, the individual knows that he or she is capable of behaving skillfully but cannot pull it off at the critical time. When people begin to monitor, think about, and try to control behaviors rather simply behaving automatically as they know how, the quality of well-learned complex behaviors is compromised. By devoting conscious attention to the process of the action and deliberately trying to execute certain behaviors correctly, the self interferes with automatic, habitual, well-learned responses.[13]

After all, people don't really "know"—at a conscious level, at least—precisely how they perform complex behaviors. A pianist could not describe the infinite number of neuronal processes that allow her to execute an elaborate arpeggio, nor could a basketball player tell us precisely how he judges the arc and distance of a shot. Once learned, such behaviors happen automatically without deliberate, self-directed control. Because the conscious self is not privy to precisely how these actions occur, it cannot help us perform them and, in fact, will interfere with the execution of the responses that we have worked so hard to master.

People who choke—in a game, on stage, in social interactions, or wherever else—are bewildered when, as soon as the key moment is over, they are able to execute the shot, remember their line, or converse fluently. As soon as the pressure is gone—after the missed free throw, the scene is over, or the stilted conversation has ended—the person will often be able to execute the desired responses smoothly because the self is no longer trying to control the action. It is obvious to the person that he or she had the ability to do well all along but was unable to do so when it counted, which can make such failures all the more upsetting.

Researchers have studied choking by having research participants perform skilled behaviors under conditions that increase their self-awareness. Leading people to focus on the process of performing a behavior—such as focusing on the movement of their hands during a task that requires fine motor control—causes their performance to deteriorate, much like the centipede in the children's nursery rhyme:

> The centipede was happy, quite, until a toad in fun
> Said, "Pray, which leg goes after which?"
> This worked his mind to such a pitch,
> He lay distracted in a ditch, considering how to run.

Ironically, research shows that as the importance of performing well goes up, people are increasingly likely to choke.[14] Thus, people may perform worse the more important it is for them to perform well! One factor that raises the importance of performing well is being observed by other people. Thus, people often perform worse when others are watching than they do when by themselves. Simply being observed can raise the stakes and create excessive self-awareness that interferes with behavior.

In one study, researchers approached people playing video games in a video arcade and asked them to try to obtain as high a score as possible on a game they had just played. Because the researchers had surreptitiously watched each participant beforehand, they knew how well the person could potentially play the game. On average, participants showed a 25% drop in performance when being observed by the researcher, indicating that trying to obtain a high score while the researcher watched undermined their performance.[15] I'm reminded of seeing children who are able to execute a complex behavior (doing cartwheels, executing a trick on a bicycle, or playing a musical piece) suddenly fall flat on their faces when they invite their parents to watch. Even behaviors as automatic and natural as walking become awkward and uncoordinated when people "try" to walk naturally while others observe them.

Offering incentives for good performance also increases the probability of choking. Think of something you do consistently well—singing, playing a musical instrument, serving a tennis ball, or hitting a particular golf shot, for example. Imagine now being offered $1 million to execute this behavior flawlessly. Studies suggest that the incentive to perform well will likely make you perform the behavior more poorly than if you were doing it just for fun![16] With so much riding on your behavior, you will pay more attention to what you are doing than necessary, thinking that paying careful attention will help. Instead, it interferes with the processes that allow you normally to perform the behavior so well. Choking occurs in this instance because the offer of a sizable reward causes you to pay conscious attention to behaviors that should be automatic and mindless. Experienced musicians and athletes need not think consciously about the execution of routine movements, but being offered a reward leads the self to sit up and take notice.

The fact that choking increases as the importance of performing well increases may be responsible for a "home-field disadvantage" in sports. Normally, athletic teams have an advantage when they play at home.[17] Because players know the idiosyncrasies of their home field or court, are desensitized to stimuli in the setting that may distract visiting players, and do not have to travel when they play at home, the home team has a slight edge over the visitors in most sports. However, when the stakes of a game are particularly high, playing at home may actually promote choking and lead to a home-field disadvantage. In decisive games, such as championships, both teams are likely to be more self-conscious than in regular season games and, thus, choking may increase. But the home team has the added pressure caused by the possibility of losing "the big one" in front of friends, family, and fans. Presumably, it is worse to lose a championship at home than away, particularly if one's personal performance is implicated in the loss. Ironically, being on the verge of victory may also induce choking as the athlete starts thinking about being the champion and worries about not blowing the game in the waning minutes. So, teams may be particularly likely to choke in critical games that are played at home because they start thinking consciously about what they are doing.

An analysis of data from baseball's World Series and basketball's National Basketball Association (NBA) playoffs supported this prediction. Social psychologists Roy Baumeister and Andrew Steinhilber found that, for both baseball and basketball, home teams tended to win the early games in the championship competition but tended to lose the later, decisive games. Between 1924 and 1982, home teams won 60% of the first and second games of the World Series but only 41% of the last game. Similarly, between 1967 and 1982, NBA home teams won 70% of the first four games they played in the championship semi-finals and finals, but only 46% of the last game. Importantly, these effects appeared to be due to the home team's executing less successfully in decisive games rather than to the visiting team suddenly performing better. For example, compared to visiting teams, home baseball teams had more fielding errors, and home basketball teams missed more free throws in decisive games.[18] Another study showed a similar effect among golfers: golfers playing on their home courses played better than visiting players early in a tournament but the advantage went to visitors later in the tournament.[19]

Choking is most likely to occur on tasks that require careful muscular control and is less likely for behaviors involving strength or stamina. This is because self-attention does not interfere as markedly with the execution of major muscular movements as with fine motor control. Thus, athletes whose performance depends on raw strength are less likely to choke than those whose performance requires finesse.

Intuition and Insight

We have already seen that human beings process information in two distinct ways—one involving processes that are automatic and nonconscious, and the other involving processes that are deliberate and conscious. For most of life's routine actions, automatic processing serves us quite well. In fact, we would not have the cognitive capacity to think deliberately about every decision, action, or movement we made even if we wanted to. Most of the time we react automatically with little conscious thought and, thus, with little involvement of the self.

Ideally, people would switch from the automatic, nonconscious mode of responding to the deliberative, self-reflective mode only when self-controlled thinking was needed to produce a better decision or more optimal behavior than the automatic mode allows. Normally, we do not need conscious self-attention in order to walk down the street, but we might like the self to kick in when we must choose our steps carefully to avoid slipping on a patch of ice. Unfortunately, because people's selves are active even when they are not needed, self-related thought can override automatic reactions that might actually be more effective.

One example involves what many people call intuition. Intuition is sometimes viewed as some kind of magical or spiritual experience in which people receive ideas, information, or insights by some nonphysical route—something like mental telepathy or extrasensory perception. In fact, intuition is no such thing. Rather, intuition occurs when people experience a feeling or thought that results from the automatic information-processing system.[20] Because automatic processes are not open to inspection, when the end results of an automatic process appear in consciousness, people have no awareness of the process that produced them. They are oblivious not only of the mental processes that produced the thought or feeling but often of the external stimuli to which they are responding as well. As a result, some thoughts and feelings seem to spring unbidden from nowhere, leading some people to assume that they must have been "received" from outside. (In this respect, we are in much the same position as the ancient people whom Jaynes suggested did not realize were talking to themselves in their minds.)

Automatic, nonconscious processes often serve us quite well. However, because people needlessly process information consciously even when automaticity would be better, self-directed thought can obscure, confuse, or supplant their automatic, intuitive reactions. The self can interfere with intuition in two ways.

First, people may purposefully disregard their intuitive, gut-level reactions altogether. Western thinkers have typically advocated that people use rational approaches to make deliberate decisions rather than intuitive ones. Reason and conscious choice have been assumed to be superior to emotion and intuition, and philosophers from antiquity have advocated thinking carefully about one's life. (As Socrates said, an "unexamined life is not worth living.") Many of us have been so socialized to emphasize rational deliberation over intuition that we disregard intuitive signals that might provide us with important information. So, we ignore subtle indications that a friend is having difficulties, our relationship is in jeopardy, or our work is no longer fulfilling. All of the signals are there, but if they can't be explicitly articulated through self-reflection, we may ignore, downplay, or dismiss them.[21]

Second, even when the signals are received clearly, we may deliberately override them through self-reflection. Even though many everyday judgments and decisions are automatic, some people think it is better to make decisions rationally by systematically analyzing the pros and cons. Thus, they purposefully use their head instead of their "heart" (which is, in actuality, in their head as well) even when the heart may know best. For example, some people analyze their romantic relationships logically, tallying the pros and cons of being involved with another person while disregarding how they feel about him or her. Although thinking rationally about one's relationships is certainly beneficial (and a purely intuitive approach to love can create problems of its own), it is hazardous to ignore one's feelings simply because they are not "logical," as if one were *Star Trek*'s Mr. Spock.

Research by Timothy Wilson and his colleagues has shown that deliberately thinking about one's preferences, decisions, and actions can actually make them worse than if we had not examined them so closely. Consciously thinking about things that ought to be judged intuitively can be a hindrance. In one study, research participants tasted and rated five brands of strawberry jam that had been rated previously by a panel of trained experts for *Consumer Reports*. Participants in one experimental condition were told explicitly to analyze why they felt as they did about each jam, whereas participants in the other condition were not given any specific instructions to guide their ratings. The question of interest was which group of participants would rate the jams most like the experts. Results showed that, left to their own devices, participants' ratings of the jams corresponded closely with the ratings made by the experts. Presumably, participants who were given no explicit instructions about how to rate the jams went with their immediate gut reactions: they either liked the jam or they didn't. However, the ratings of participants who were explicitly told to analyze their reasons for liking or disliking the jams did not jibe with how the experts had rated them. To say it differently, when participants consciously analyzed their preferences, their ratings did not correspond as closely to how good the jams actually were! Given that participants were assigned to the two experimental groups at random, differences in their ratings must have been due to the fact that one group analyzed the reasons for their ratings and the other group didn't. In thinking carefully about rational reasons for liking or not liking the jams, participants allowed conscious (but less accurate) judgments to override their automatic, intuitive inclinations.[22]

In another study, university students read descriptions of actual courses and rated the likelihood they would take each one. One group of students was instructed to stop and think carefully about each piece of information about each course. Another group of students was simply told to read the descriptions carefully before making their ratings. Again, students who thought carefully about their choices made less optimal judgments. Not only did they base their course selections on criteria that are objectively less important to the quality of a course, but they also were less likely to register for and remain in courses that had received high evaluations by former students.[23] In brief, introspection about the reasons for their reactions actually changed students' responses in a less optimal direction.

Perhaps not much damage is done if we make less than optimal decisions about relatively trivial matters such as the taste of jam or which university course to take. But here's the unsettling part: Consciously thinking about your personal relationships can change how you feel about your loved ones. Research has shown that interviewing newlyweds annually about their relationships changed the couple's attitudes toward their relationships compared with newlyweds who were not interviewed. Similarly, when university students were asked to think about their romantic relationships, doing so changed how they felt about their partners and relationships. Importantly, the effects of introspection about one's relationship were not consistently positive or negative. Some students' attitudes became more positive, and other students' attitudes became more negative. But there was no doubt that thinking consciously about their relationships affected how they felt about them.[24]

These effects of introspection on people's judgments—whether of jams, courses, or relationships—appear to occur because the rational criteria that people consciously use to evaluate their lives are sometimes at odds with their subjective preferences and feelings that arise spontaneously. People often do not know precisely why they like one taste more than another, why they are drawn to particular college courses, or why they love their romantic partners—they just do. These kinds of reactions largely emerge from the automatic, nonconscious system, and their causes are often not obvious to the individual. Thus, when people consciously analyze their reactions, asking themselves why they feel as they do, they do not necessarily identify the "real" reasons that underlie their feelings. Rather, they focus on reasons that seem plausible, come easily to mind, or are easy to articulate.[25] Some of these may be the real reasons for their feelings, but many of them may not be, and some contributing factors may be ignored entirely. Our conscious self simply does not know all of the factors that affect our reactions and, when it tries to analyze our preferences and decisions consciously, it may get them wrong.

In the case of pondering their relationships, for example, people may think about features of their partner and relationship that are, in reality, unrelated to how they feel. They may think about their partner's sense of humor (or lack of it) or their kindness (or lack of it) simply because these factors are commonly viewed as contributing to relationship satisfaction and dissatisfaction. In their particular case, however, how they feel about their relationship may have nothing to do with the partner's sense of humor or kindness. Even so, once they start thinking about these once-irrelevant factors, these considerations begin to influence their feelings, creating reactions that would not have occurred had they not tried to figure things out consciously. If people think about positive aspects of their relationship, their attitude may become more positive, but if they focus on negative features, their satisfaction with the relationship may decline. In either case, the simple fact that they thought consciously about their nonconscious reactions changed their feelings and, possibly, the course of the relationship.

Many people have difficulty believing that they often don't know why they feel the way they do. It seems obvious to them that they have privileged insight into the causes of their emotions and behaviors, and know precisely what causes them to respond as they do to the people and events in their lives. Of course, in many instances, people undoubtedly know what caused their reactions, but in many others, they truly have no idea (even though they may steadfastly insist that they do). Not only are people incapable of being consciously aware of everything that influences their feelings and behavior, but many reactions occur automatically outside of awareness and with no conscious thought. When people try to analyze these automatic reactions consciously, they may misidentify the causes.[26]

These studies do not, in any way, suggest that people should never think carefully about what they are doing and why. Clearly, making informed choices often requires studious attention to the pros and cons of various options, and analyzing trouble spots in one's life is the first step to taking constructive action. Furthermore, automatic gut-level reactions can mislead us as well when they are based on irrelevant nonconscious associations. Our intuitive, knee-jerk reactions can be as misguided and maladaptive as our conscious, deliberate decisions.

Rather, what these studies do suggest is that we should not assume that self-directed, conscious thought is necessarily better than intuition. Our automatic, natural inclinations may be based on nonconscious information-processing schemes that are quite effective in leading us to satisfying personal choices, despite the fact that we have not reasoned through our options consciously. To put it differently, sometimes intuition is the rational way to make decisions.

Problems of Preoccupation: Sleep and Sex

Two of the most natural and ordinary behaviors, not only for human beings but for the rest of the animal kingdom as well, are sleeping and mating. Given the importance of both sleep and sex to human well-being, we might expect that they would be impervious to being disrupted unnecessarily. However, both are surprisingly sensitive to interference by the self.

Insomnia

Everyone has trouble sleeping from time to time, and many people consistently have difficulty falling and remaining asleep. Insomnia can occur for many reasons: caffeine, spicy foods, medications, shift work, jet lag, and certain medical problems may make it difficult for people to sleep. But of all causes, the self may be the greatest thief of a restful night's sleep. When asked how her self affects the quality of her life, one female university student pointed immediately to its effects on her sleep: "I often lay awake at night worrying about what will happen after

I graduate this May. Will I in fact graduate? What if I don't pay a parking ticket that I have forgotten about and they withhold my diploma? What if my boyfriend never asks me to marry him, or what if he doesn't like the names I have picked out for our children? I could 'what if' myself all night long."

Research confirms that people who are worrying, planning, or making decisions do not fall asleep easily.[27] In addition, because many of the things that we ruminate about are emotionally charged, our bedtime thoughts create a state of anxious arousal that prevents us from calming down enough to sleep. It is no surprise, then, that people find it particularly difficult to sleep when under stress. Not only are they thinking intensely about the troubling situation, but they are also too physiologically aroused to sleep.

Even when a person's sleeplessness is not initially caused by too much self-thinking, the self can nonetheless exacerbate the problem. Imagine, for example, that you are having trouble falling asleep for a perfectly good reason—for example, you took a long nap late in the afternoon, you uncharacteristically drank a caffeinated beverage an hour before bedtime, or you have heartburn from eating a late, spicy dinner. As you lie there staring at the ceiling, you are likely to start thinking, planning, or worrying. In such instances, these thoughts are initially the result rather than the cause of the fact that you couldn't sleep, but once they begin, they may delay the onset of sleep even more.

Furthermore, when many people have insomnia, they begin to obsess about the fact they can't sleep. They begin to castigate themselves for their sleeplessness ("I knew better than to drink coffee before bedtime") and worry about the consequences of insufficient sleep for the next day ("I'm going to be exhausted at work tomorrow"). These intrusive thoughts about their insomnia can further fuel the problem by cluttering their mind with chatter and by inducing arousing emotions such as frustration, anger, and worry.[28]

The age-old remedy for sleeplessness is to "count sheep." The benefits of sheep-counting have not, to my knowledge, been empirically investigated, but the rationale behind such practices is sound. Occupying one's mind with meaningless tasks prevents the person from worrying, planning, and thinking about self-relevant topics. Counting sheep (or one's breath or whatever) uses mental resources that are then not available for ruminating about troubling aspects of life. The problem, of course, is that imaginary sheep do not hold one's attention as strongly as the drama of one's life, so people typically lose count after a few sheep and fall back to thinking about themselves. Counting is so easy that it can be done rather automatically, leaving plenty of consciousness free for the self to operate.

Sexual Dysfunction

Like other animals, human beings do not need a self in order to have sex. Sexual arousal can occur quite automatically and nonconsciously in response to certain visual, tactile, and olfactory cues. Having a self does, however, allow human beings the option of having more varied and creative sexual experiences than other animals. Whereas all members of other species tend to mate in approximately the same manner, people can consciously decide to engage in a great variety of sexual behaviors in a variety of situations.

That being said, it's also true that the self is perhaps the greatest enemy of sexual satisfaction. Many experts believe that the single greatest cause of problems involving sexual arousal and orgasm stem from people being overly self-focused during sex. *Spectatoring* refers to the process of monitoring one's own engagement in a sexual event rather than being unself-consciously immersed in it. Most people spectator from time to time during sex, but focusing excessively on what one is doing, whether one is performing well sexually, and how one's appearance and performance are being judged by one's partner is an impediment to satisfying sex.[29]

Two processes may underlie the effects of spectatoring on sexual pleasure. First, to the extent that people are thinking about themselves and their performance during sex, they will be distracted from attending to the visual and sensory stimuli that foster arousal. (In fact, people who desire to slow down the progression of their mounting arousal often intentionally distract themselves from the erotic stimuli.) In addition, because spectators may critically judge the adequacy of their appearance and performance, they may become nervous, and thus allow anxiety to interfere with sexual arousal at a physiological level.

Flow and Spontaneity

Psychologists have often been criticized for emphasizing the dysfunctional, dark side of human life. Both psychological researchers and mental health professionals have tended to focus on the myriad ways that people fail to function optimally. Doing so has shed much more light on why things go wrong for human beings than on how things can go right.

This state of affairs led to a movement during the 1990s that has become known as positive psychology. Positive psychology involves the study of the sunny side of human experience, such as the capacity for love, courage, compassion, resilience, creativity, integrity, self-control, and wisdom.[30] One of the leaders of the positive psychology movement has been Mihaly Csikszentmihalyi, who has studied the optimal states of human experience for more than two decades. Among Csikszentmihalyi's contributions is his analysis of the flow experience.[31] Flow involves a state of focused concentration in which an individual becomes completely absorbed in an activity. When they are in a state of flow, people feel alive, strong, and vibrant, as if they are being carried along by a current on which their actions flow smoothly and effortlessly. Problems and time both disappear as people become "lost" in the activity.

According to Csikszentmihalyi, the most satisfying experiences in life occur when people are in flow. Skilled athletes, musicians, performers, and speakers often talk about times in which their behaviors were relaxed and effortless, seeming to flow out of them rather than being drawn out by effort. More mundanely, people may experience flow in everyday life when they play with their children, work on an important and meaningful task, play sports, socialize with friends, or make love.

People often describe the flow experience by saying that they "lose themselves" in the activity. This characterization seems apt because they did indeed lose their self. Whether we say that shutting down the self helps to create flow or that flow quiets the self, people in a state of flow are not self-aware. Instead, they are focused singularly on the experience at hand, lost in concentration, and responding largely automatically. If self-thinking does arise during flow, it involves exceptionally concrete thoughts. A rock climber in flow may think, for example, about where on the rock face he should place his next step, but the thought is focused on immediate action and does not involve deeper, abstract thoughts—those that would include an element of self-evaluation or cause him to feel self-conscious.

Closely related to flow is spontaneity. People behave most spontaneously when their selves are disengaged. When people act spontaneously, they are responding automatically, with little forethought or conscious attention to their actions. The opposite of spontaneity occurs when people are so self-conscious that they are nearly unable to act. A cacophony of internal chatter impedes their natural ability to respond. "What should I do? What are these other people thinking about me? This is awful!"

The common element in flow and spontaneity involves a selfless immersion in whatever is happening in the present moment. When people are living in the moment rather than in their own minds, they experience flow and react spontaneously. This state not only decreases the likelihood that self-preoccupation will interfere with one's thoughts or actions (as in test anxiety or choking under pressure) but also is quite pleasant. Phil Jackson, who coached the Chicago Bulls to six NBA championships, recognized the importance of this fact and made efforts to teach his players to enter this state more easily. As Jackson wrote in his book, *Sacred Hoops*, "In basketball—as in life—true joy comes from being fully present in each and every moment, not just when things are going your way. Of course, it's no accident that things are more likely to go your way when you stop worrying about whether you're going to win or lose and focus your full attention on what's happening right this moment."[32]

The problem is that the self continually drags us out of the present moment. Instead of focusing on what is happening here and now, we spend much of our time distracted by self-generated thoughts about what has already happened in the past and about what may (or may not) happen in the future. Although thinking about the past and future is sometimes beneficial, much of the time it is not. Eckhart Tolle, author of *The Power of Now*, puts it this way: "Make the Now the primary focus of your life. Whereas before you dwelt in time [in your mind] and paid brief visits to the Now, have your dwelling place in the Now and pay brief visits to past and future when required to deal with the practical aspects of your life situation."[33]

Unfortunately, most people are virtually powerless to slow down, much less halt, the self's ongoing chatter about the past and future. To see what I mean, take just a moment to quiet your thoughts. Close your eyes, take a deep breath, and tell your self to be quiet. For the next three minutes, do not think any self-focused thoughts. Focus only on things that are happening around you at this moment and do not think about yourself. Don't think about anything that has happened in the past, don't think about anything that might happen in the future, and don't even think anything about yourself right now. Attend only to what is going on around you right here, right now, in the present moment. (Stop for three minutes and try this exercise.)

I suspect that most readers will have given up on trying to silence their self long before three minutes have expired. Within a matter of seconds, a self-related thought will pop into consciousness, and then another, and another. And though you warned your self to be quiet, it couldn't resist, after just a short time, to pipe up again. So you chastised your self for being intrusive (which was, itself, another self-thought) and tried again. But there came the stream of thoughts, the inner voice that won't go away. You've probably tried this same sort of exercise many times before (for example, trying to go to sleep at night while your self obsessed about the next day's problems) and the outcome is usually the same. Despite our best efforts, the self chatters on. Most of us can identify with the person who once told me, "When I start tormenting myself over every conceivable thing that might happen, I desperately wish that the voice inside of my head came with a mute button!"

Quieting the Self

Had the human self been installed with a mute button or off switch, the self would not be the curse to happiness that it often is. Of course, with the self switched off, people would have no volitional ability to turn it back on again, and such an individual would be incapable of functioning in modern life. We all must occasionally remember, contemplate, and plan, and the self is thus essential. The goal is not to eliminate the self but rather to use it only when necessary. Sometimes, we absolutely need to plan, to think ahead, to consider, to reflect on ourselves. On those occasions, the self is needed to perform these essential cognitive activities. But when self-talk is unnecessary, or worse detrimental, we want the self to be quiescent, much like a computer in standby mode, inactive but able to be powered up in a flash by a single keystroke.

Rowland Miller has offered the useful analogy of the self to a thermostat. We want the thermostat in our apartment or house to regulate the temperature only when the temperature really needs to change. We don't want it to be on all of the time (or else the furnace would run continuously) but neither do we want it not to come on at all. Many of us have lived in apartments and houses with inexact thermostats that triggered the furnace either too much or too little. In the same way, an ideal self would be one that "turns on" only when conscious self-thought is needed for optimal functioning.

Unlike malfunctioning thermostats, which are probably just as likely to be underactive as they are to be overactive, the human self clearly leans in the direction of turning on when it really isn't needed as opposed to not turning on when self-reflection is required. I have never heard someone complain, "I wish I thought about myself more" or "I tried to dwell on myself, but I couldn't." What most people need is a way to reduce the amount of time that the self is engaged. By minimizing the time that we spend in self-thought, we lower opportunities for the self to harm our well-being.

Perhaps the most tried-and-true method of quieting the self and reducing its effects on behavior is meditation. Although meditation sprang up in the context of various spiritual practices, it has taken on a secular life of its own as people have come to see meditation as a remedy for many of the self's curses. The rationale for meditation is straightforward: if the self is too chatty, too intrusive, too catastrophizing, perhaps one should simply turn it down a bit.

Mediation is often misunderstood in the West, regarded either as a peculiar Eastern practice tied to esoteric religions or as a New Age fad on a par with astral projection and channeling. In fact, it is neither one, but rather a set of mental approaches for quieting down the self's chatter. As we will see, many people report that meditation results in clearer thinking, more even emotions, and a more magnanimous approach to life.[34] By reducing the activity of the self, many of the problems that it creates diminish. Importantly, there is nothing remotely magical or esoteric about the effects of meditation. Of course, many people combine meditation with spiritual practices of various kinds, but at heart meditation is simply a way to quiet the mind.

The Practice of Meditation

My intention here is not to try to teach you to meditate. Readers who are interested in learning to meditate may wish to seek one of the many available books, tapes, and classes on the topic.[35] Rather, I want to describe briefly how people meditate so that we can examine its effects on the self.

People meditate in many different ways, but they all aim to induce a state of consciousness that involves a minimum of self-chatter going on inside the skull. Contrary to what many people think, meditation typically does not involve thinking deeply about something (that sort of practice is more accurately characterized as contemplation) but, rather, at least in its purest form, an effort to still one's thoughts.

Meditation requires four conditions: a reasonably quiet place to meditate, a comfortable yet alert posture, a stimulus on which to focus one's attention, and a mental state of poised awareness. To begin, the meditator assumes a position that, although comfortable, is not conducive to sleep. Many meditators sit on a cushion on the floor with their spine straight and legs crossed (and some even use the classic, but nearly impossible lotus position), but there is no one correct posture for meditation. Sitting cross-legged on the floor has the advantage of providing a balanced position (the rear end and the knees create a tripod) and promoting alertness, but so does sitting in a straight-backed chair with both feet on the floor. Meditating in an easy chair or on a soft sofa too often leads to sleep, as does meditating lying down. (Some people use meditation in order to get to sleep, in which case lying down is obviously okay.)

Once seated, the person relaxes and begins to focus on some stimulus, most often one's own breath. No attempt is made to change how one is breathing but only to track the breath's movement in and out. Some people count their inhalations (up to 10, then repeat), whereas others simply observe carefully the sounds and sensations of breathing. There is nothing magical about the breath except that it provides something for the person to focus attention on that is always present and free of self-related content. Unlike many other stimuli that a person could focus on, the breath does not lend itself easily to self-related thinking. Some people use visual stimuli, such as a candle flame, or auditory stimuli, such as the bubbling sound of a desktop fountain. Many people like to meditate outdoors where they can focus on the gentle blend of wind, birdsong, and rustling sounds. Devotees of some meditation practices, including Transcendental Meditation, focus their attention on a mantra—a tranquil word or syllable. Whether one focuses on the breath, objects, sounds, or mantras, the purpose is to give the mind something else to keep it busy rather than whatever thoughts the self conjures up.

Some people meditate with their eyes closed; others prefer to keep them open or partly opened, focused on a point somewhere a few feet in front of them. Many meditation teachers suggest that beginning meditators should start with their eyes closed, but again, there's no one correct way to meditate. It really depends on whether one is more distracted by self-thoughts with one's eyes open or closed.

The meditator's goal is simply to maintain a mental state that is characterized by alert, poised awareness. The aim is to be totally present, alert to the breath or aspects of one's surroundings, but forgoing all thoughts about the past or about the future. The person doing this pure form of meditation is not looking for insights (although certain contemplative practices do have this goal) or trying to achieve a particular experience. Rather, he or she is simply present without judging.

Inevitably, within a surprisingly short amount of time, a self-related thought will come up. "Shoot, I forgot to return that phone call." "My legs are starting to cramp in this position." "Am I doing this right?" "I wish that dog would stop barking." Most people, when they first try to meditate, are surprised, if not shocked, by how intrusive and uncontrollable their thoughts are. Most have never realized how noisy it is inside their own heads. Often, people wonder if there is something wrong with them—whether their self is unusually verbose or whether they are psychologically disturbed. Probably not. The self's "job" is to talk to us in our heads; that's just what it does. Most of us have simply not sat quietly for long enough while monitoring our internal state to realize how incessantly our self jabbers.

An important part of meditation is learning not to react to whatever thoughts come up. Rather, the person just lets each thought arise and dissipate without either following it or berating oneself for having the thought. In the untrained mind, one self-generated thought typically leads to another, which leads to another, and another, and another in a relatively unbroken stream. Meditators try to break the cycle by simply not getting caught up in whatever thoughts arise. Whatever the thought is, they just let it slide through their mind without judgment. Certainly, one shouldn't talk to oneself about not talking to oneself!

Once people start watching their thoughts in this way, they realize that thoughts typically have a short life span. If we don't latch on and follow them to yet more thoughts, thoughts rise up, float through consciousness, and disappear in a matter of seconds. Some meditation teachers instruct their students to imagine that their thoughts are sticks or leaves floating by in a river. Each stick or leaf appears upstream, floats by, then disappears downstream. The meditator's goal is not to follow them with one's attention. Although you notice the stick appear, then float by, you stay focused on the river and let the stick glide on through.

Another useful analogy involves looking through an aquarium filled with colorful fish. As interesting as the fish may be, you are interested for the moment not in the fish but on whatever is on the other side of the aquarium. The fish are your self-thoughts, which, if you aren't careful, will distract you from what you really want to see—the world on the other side of the tank. Looking through the tank, it is easy to be distracted by the fish. But, with practice, the meditator is able to let the fish swim by without losing focus on the image of the world beyond the tank. Nor will the mediator fuss about the fish swimming around or about being distracted by them. After all, swimming is what fish do. In the same way, thinking is what the self does.

Beginning meditators should probably start with relatively brief sessions (10–15 minutes), but with time, the session can be extended to 30 minutes, or even longer. The first few efforts at meditation are typically exasperating because the person is flooded with unwanted thoughts (or, more precisely, the person becomes aware of the cacophony of thoughts that have always been there). Over time, however, unwanted self-chatter slowly diminishes as thoughts decrease in both number and intensity. The person will still be pulled into self-conscious thought from time to time, but the thoughts become easier to escape and the periods of inner stillness longer and longer.

Effects of Meditation

The most immediate effect that most people experience when they start meditating is a sense of relaxation and peacefulness. In part, this may result from simply sitting still and breathing deeply, but much of the effect comes from the diminishment of self-talk. A great deal of unhappiness and distress arises, not because the person's immediate situation is problematic, but because he or she is thinking about upsetting things in the past or future. Quieting the self through meditation allows a respite from these self-generated emotions, at least for most of the meditation session.

Scientific research has documented the effects of meditation on the nervous system. Meditation produces signs of deep relaxation, such as decreased heart rate, blood pressure, and respiration, decreased plasma cortisol (a hormone associated with stress), and brain waves that are associated with relaxation. Muscles relax, as indicated by a fall in skin resistance, as do blood vessels.[36] Recent research has suggested that many of the effects of meditation are more pronounced than those that occur from mere relaxation.[37] In fact, merely telling people to try to relax sometimes increases arousal because they are trying to relax by force of will.

Because it helps them to relax, some people use meditation as a sedative. As we have seen, one reason that people have trouble sleeping is that their self-talk keeps them upset and aroused. Replaying the hassles of the day, worrying about the problems of tomorrow, pondering important decisions, and judging the quality of one's life can make sleep elusive.

But meditating before going to bed can quiet the chatter and promote sleep. The effect is similar to the practice of counting sheep. Whether one is watching one's breath or counting sheep, the self cannot spin the web of thoughts that trap us in wakefulness.

Initially, the relaxing effects of meditation are relatively short-lived. At the end of meditation, the person feels more relaxed and refreshed than beforehand. However, as the person reenters active life, self-thoughts arise with all of their emotional baggage, and stress returns. However, after a relatively small number of meditation sessions, its effects begin to carry over into normal life. People not only begin to feel more relaxed and less stressed out, but they react to normal problems with increased composure and equanimity. They feel more relaxed more of the time, and their responses to daily hassles are less extreme.

Over time, meditation affects the self's normal mode of operation—not just during meditation itself but also during the rest of one's day. With less unnecessary self-chatter, the person is not always planning, thinking about problems, or worrying about what needs to be done. As a result, the person's normal emotional state is less aroused and more calm, and thus less likely to be pushed over the edge by frustrations and hassles. I've had several people tell me that one of the first signs that meditation was "working" for them in everyday life was that they got angry at other drivers on the highway less often.

Most meditators also report increased clarity in their perceptions and thoughts. The world is experienced as more vivid, and they begin to notice things they never noticed before. As we saw, self-preoccupation distracts people from the world. With meditation practice, people are less preoccupied by inner thoughts about themselves, thereby freeing up attentional resources that can be directed outward. People have told me that, after meditating, their daily commute to work became on ongoing surprise as they began to notice things along the way that they hadn't "seen" in years of driving the same route in a self-preoccupied fog.

Many people also report that their thinking is clearer and they can focus their attention more single-mindedly. For this reason, some meditators meditate just briefly before tackling tasks that require thought—such as writing, solving problems, or complex planning. They find that even a brief period of meditation allows them to focus their attention more fully on the task at hand and that they are not as distracted by extraneous thoughts.

The effects of meditation dissipate over time, and even experienced meditators must continue to meditate regularly (though not necessarily every day) to maintain the desired effects. In this way, meditation is a bit like physical exercise: one loses what one has gained if it is not repeated on a regular basis. The biggest problem with meditation is making oneself do it. Like exercise, it takes a commitment of time and often requires relinquishing some other enjoyable activity. And, paradoxically, the times when a person most "needs" to meditate are usually those in which there is little time to do so. When one is exceptionally busy, living on insufficient sleep, preoccupied with problems, and generally stressed out, meditation often takes a backseat.

Meditation is not a panacea for one's problems or a way to escape the real world. Rather, it is simply a demonstrated method for reducing the degree to which one's attention and thoughts are commandeered by one's self. Most of one's problems are still there, although some of the self-generated ones may disappear. But meditators report that spending time each day quieting their jabbering self allows them to approach problems in a more balanced, less self-centered way as they live less in their inner, self-generated world and more in the world outside.

3 ∷
Through the Eyes of the Ego

We don't see the world as it is. We see it as we are.
—ANAÏS NIN

According to Greek myth, Narcissus was a handsome young man whose high opinion of himself led him to dismiss the advances of the nymphs who sought his attention. One day, a maiden whom Narcissus had spurned prayed that he, too, might feel what it was like to love someone and receive no affection in return. Nemesis, the goddess of righteous anger, granted the maiden's prayer by causing Narcissus to fall in love with his own reflection. When Narcissus glimpsed his reflection in a clear pool, he became so enamored that he could not tear himself away from his image, losing all interest in food or sleep until he pined away and died. Even as he was being ferried to Hades across the River Styx, Narcissus could not resist leaning over the edge of the boat to catch one last glimpse of himself in the water.

The English language has borrowed Narcissus's name to refer to people who have a particularly inflated view of their appearance, cleverness, importance, or worth. At the upper extremes of narcissism lies the *narcissistic personality disorder*, a psychiatric classification applied to people who not only have a grandiose self-image of being special and unique, but who also insist on excessive admiration and special treatment and feel entitled, by virtue of their superiority, to use and exploit other people.

The narcissistic personality disorder is a fascinating phenomenon in its own right, but we are not interested here in the exceedingly annoying behavior of the pathological narcissist. Rather, our focus is on the everyday variety of narcissism that characterizes virtually everyone. Because we view ourselves and our worlds through the eyes of our own egos, our perceptions are often biased in ways that flatter ourselves. We are all occasional narcissists who believe that we are a tad more wonderful than we really are.

Most people go through life assuming that they perceive themselves and the world accurately. We are all aware, of course, that our senses can be fooled by optical illusions, and from time to time, each of us realizes that we have misinterpreted a situation, misjudged a person, or drawn some other mistaken conclusion. But most of the time, we regard these mistakes as atypical errors in judgment against a broad backdrop of general accuracy. Most of us fail to realize, much less come to terms with, the fact that our perceptions of the world are often distorted in ways that are impossible for us to discern.

Contrary to our strong sense that we usually know what's going on around us, people don't perceive the world as it actually is. Never mind that our senses are designed to register only certain kinds of stimuli—certain wavelengths of light or frequencies of sound, for example—and that everything that lies outside our sense modalities goes undetected. Even in the realm of the knowable, our experience of the events that unfold around us is accompanied by an ongoing internal commentary about them that modifies the nature of our experience. In everyday language, we "talk to ourselves" about what we experience. Furthermore, what we say to ourselves about what's happening is often not correct.

This stream of internal chatter about our ongoing experiences is far more pervasive than most people realize. We are quite aware of those times in which we consciously deliberate about something, carrying on an explicit conversation in our heads about its pros and cons. But we are usually not aware that our ordinary daily activities are accompanied by an ongoing inner interpretation about what we are experiencing, what it means, whether it is good or bad, what we ought to do about it, and often whether we'd rather be somewhere else doing something different. Right now, you may be thinking to yourself "I see what he means" or "that doesn't make sense" or "so what?" Whatever your reaction, you are not having the pure experience of simply reading this book. Rather, you are adding new layers of meaning and interpretation on top of the original, real event. When you watch TV, talk to other people, go to work, or eat dinner, your experience is also a blend of the actual event and your analysis of it. "My neighbor doesn't seem to like me much." "My job is so boring." "This show is an insult to my intelligence." "This food is delicious." The way that you talk to yourself about what happens to you becomes an inseparable part of the experience itself, just as when we watch a sporting event on television, our experience is a combination of the actual competition plus the ongoing patter and analysis of the sports announcer. Only in this case, the announcer is us.

In many ways, this running commentary creates the world we experience. I don't mean that the world itself does not really exist but, rather, that our ultimate experience is of our perceptions, ideas, and opinions about what happens rather than of the world itself. As the Yacqui shaman Don Juan explained to his apprentice, Carlos Castaneda, "the internal dialogue is what grounds us. The world is such and such or so and so only because we talk to ourselves about its being such and such or so and so."[1] We are almost always at least one step removed from the real world, separated from it by our ongoing thoughts, interpretations, opinions, and judgments. Only rarely do we experience events with no conscious interpretation or self-related comments about them.

If the self's commentary on our experiences was consistently fair, objective, and accurate (as it sometimes is), there would be no problem. In fact, it might be useful to have an objective analysis of our lives as we go along—something like a sports announcer's play-by-play coverage of a fast-paced event. Difficulties arise, however, because our self-talk puts a decidedly one-sided spin on our experiences. The play-by-play announcer in our mind is unabashedly biased in favor of the home team. As a result, the self sometimes leads us to perceive a world that differs in important respects from the one that really exists "out there." This biased announcer provides us with a one-sided, somewhat distorted picture of ourselves, other people, and the world.

Perceiving Ourselves

Ever since the Oracle at Delphi admonished the ancient Greeks to "know thyself," people have regarded having an accurate understanding of oneself as a hallmark of maturity and personal adjustment. People cannot function optimally if they do not know themselves well or are deluded about who they are.

Most people assume that they understand themselves reasonably well. Each of us can easily see that other people's self-views are often distorted, if not deluded, but most of us believe that we have a relatively dispassionate view of who and what we are. We admit that we may sometimes be misled and even occasionally biased, but in general, most of us think that we see ourselves plainly, warts and all.

In reality, each of us holds illusions about ourselves that distort the truth in a variety of ways. I am not talking here about the fact that we simply don't know certain facts about ourselves because we lack sufficient information or have never thought carefully about certain things. Rather, I'm referring to the fact that we are systematically biased in how we think about ourselves. Instead of having a clear and unencumbered view of who we are, our self-perceptions are occluded and distorted in a number of ways. And, perhaps most troubling, we are nearly blind to the illusions we have about ourselves.

Perhaps the biggest bias in people's perceptions of themselves involves their penchant for overestimating their own positive qualities. People have a pervasive tendency to interpret events in ways that maintain an image of themselves as being competent, capable, and good.[2] This is not to say that people never admit their failures, shortcomings, and ethical lapses; they do, of course. But even so, they display a broad tendency to see themselves as better than they really are. Rather than holding a balanced view of their personal strengths and weaknesses, people dramatically overperceive their positive qualities and underperceive their negative ones. Thus, even when they think they are seeing their faults accurately, their self-perceptions of their deficiencies are still often distorted in a positive direction!

In an influential article on what he called the "totalitarian ego," social psychologist Tony Greenwald compared the self to a totalitarian political regime.[3] Totalitarian regimes are well known for their ongoing programs of propaganda that promote an image of the dictator as a capable and benevolent leader. To maintain a desired image of the dictator, the government's office of public misinformation rewrites the country's history in ways that reflect well on the government, hides ugly truths about the leader's failures and misdeeds, and embellishes, if not fabricates, the dictator's accomplishments. Greenwald suggested that the human ego operates much like a totalitarian office of misinformation, fabricating and revising our personal histories to cast us in an unrealistically positive light.

Everyone Is Better Than Average

Author Garrison Keillor describes fictitious Lake Wobegon as a place "where all the women are strong, all the men are good looking, and all the children are above average." In fact, we all live in a private Lake Wobegon of our own making. Most people think not only that they are better than the average person, but that their friends, lovers, and children are above average as well.

People tend to judge themselves as better than the average person on virtually every dimension that one can imagine. In one study of the "better-than-average effect," university students rated themselves and the "average college student" of their own sex on 20 positive traits (such as dependable, intelligent, mature, and friendly) and 20 negative traits (such as insecure, humorless, mean, and unpleasant). Results showed that the average participant rated him- or herself more positively than average on 38 of the 40 traits![4] Similarly, most people rate themselves as safer than the average driver, more sexually adroit than the average lover, and more ethical than the average person.[5] A study from Australia revealed that 86% of employees rate their job performance as "above average," whereas only 1% say that they perform below average at work. Most people also tend to see themselves as less prejudiced than other people they know.[6] Other research has shown that most people also say that their chances of encountering life misfortunes such as divorce, a serious accident, or personal bankruptcy are lower than the average person's. On only a select few dimensions, such as computer programming ability, do most people rate themselves as average or worse.[7]

People also think that they are more likely to go to heaven when they die than other people are. A *U. S. News and World Report* survey asked 1,000 Americans to rate whether they and various celebrities were likely to go to heaven. Of the celebrities, Mother Teresa ranked highest on the list; 79% of the respondents thought Mother Teresa was likely to go to heaven. Oprah Winfrey (66%), Michael Jordan (65%), and Princess Diana (60%) were not far behind. In contrast, only 19% thought that O. J. Simpson was heaven-bound. The most interesting finding, though, was that when asked about themselves, 87% of the respondents indicated that they were destined to go to heaven.[8] Put simply, respondents thought that they were personally more likely to go to heaven than anybody else on the list, including Mother Teresa!

A moment's thought will show the logical absurdity of the better-than-average effect. Virtually every human characteristic—intelligence, physical attractiveness, social skill, kindness, athletic ability, morality, driving ability, sexual skill, and so on—falls into a normal, bell-shaped distribution. Thus, on every characteristic that is normally distributed, the same number of people fall below average on the characteristic as above average. Whether we are talking about kindness, laziness, driving ability, or skill in bed, 50% of all individuals will, by definition, fall at or below average and 50% will fall at or above average. If every person knew where he or she fell along the distribution of a particular characteristic (for example, if each of us knew precisely how we compared to everyone else in "creativity"), half of us would acknowledge that we are above average and half of us would acknowledge that we are below average on that dimension. Yet only a few people indicate that they are below average on any given attribute, and even then, they probably underestimate how far below average they really are! This, of course, is a statistical impossibility. A great number of people who think they are above average on any given dimension are fooling themselves.

When people do encounter someone who is clearly better than they are on some important dimension, they naturally conclude that the other person is a uniquely superior individual! By viewing people who unambiguously outperform them as exceptional, people can preserve a positive view of themselves. It's not that they themselves are personally deficient on the dimension in question, but rather that the "superstar" is so unquestionably good.

In a demonstration of this effect, researchers provided participants with feedback indicating that they had performed somewhat worse than another person (who was actually an accomplice of the researcher) on a bogus test of "perceptual intelligence." After seeing the scores, both the participant and an uninvolved observer rated the perceptual intelligence of both the participant and the accomplice. Given that the accomplice had outscored the participant, it is not surprising that both the participant and the observer rated the accomplice as having greater perceptual intelligence than the participant. The interesting finding, though, was that although the participant and the observer rated the participant's perceptual intelligence about the same, the participant (who had been outperformed by the accomplice) rated the accomplice's intelligence significantly higher than the observer did. By concluding that the person who outperformed them was a genius, participants could reassure themselves that the disparity between their and the accomplice's performance was due more to the accomplice's obvious superiority than to their own incompetence. The observers, whose egos were not involved in this judgment, did not show this self-serving effect.[9]

In addition to seeing themselves as better than average, people also tend to view themselves more favorably than they are viewed by others. When researchers compare people's ratings of themselves to other people's ratings of them, they invariably find that most people rate themselves more positively than other people rate them.[10] This is a sobering fact because it means that other people rarely perceive us as positively as we perceive ourselves! Even if we don't like some aspect of ourselves very much, chances are that other people like it even less. The bias toward egotistical self-perceptions is strong and pervasive and, as we will see, it can undermine the quality of people's lives.

Self-Serving Attributions

Psychologists use the term *attributions* for people's explanations of the events in their lives. For example, people may make attributions as to why their lovers left them, why their children are not doing well in school, why they are having a problem at work, or why they won or lost an important game. Psychologists are interested in attributions because the attributions that people make for an event influence their reactions to it. Attributing the breakup of a relationship to a lover's problem with alcohol results in different reactions than attributing the breakup to one's own shortcomings as a lover. Even though the event (the breakup of one's relationship) is the same, the attribution a person makes can evoke quite different reactions to it.

Hundreds of studies have shown that the attributions that people make tend to be biased in ways that portray them in a positive light. In many of these studies, people take what they believe is a test of intelligence, interpersonal sensitivity, or problem-solving ability, then receive feedback indicating that they performed relatively well or relatively poorly on the test irrespective of how well they actually performed. (In fact, the participants' tests are never actually scored.) Then participants answer questions about why they performed well or poorly on the test.

Virtually without exception, these studies show that people make attributions that are biased in a self-serving direction.[11] When they perform well, research participants indicate that they did well because they're smart or skilled. When they perform poorly, however, they tend to say that their performance was due to an unfair or excessively difficult test, distracting testing conditions, or bad luck. In essence, people claim more personal responsibility when they think they performed well than when they think they performed poorly—even though they all took exactly the same test! We all see these kinds of self-serving reactions almost every day, each time somebody makes a lame excuse for doing poorly or claims too much credit for doing well.

Receiving low scores also leads participants to question the validity of the test. Even though all participants took exactly the same test, those who think they did poorly rate its validity and accuracy lower than those who think they did well.[12] All schoolteachers have observed this pattern of self-serving attributions. When students receive grades on a test, students who get good grades feel smugly satisfied about their performance and think the test was fair, whereas those with lower grades tend to see the test (and by extension, the teacher) as unfair. I've even seen students in class argue among themselves about the fairness of a test, with students who received good grades defending the test to the disgruntled students who did poorly.

People also make self-serving attributions when they behave badly by pointing out that they had little or no choice but to do what they did.[13] Denying responsibility for or control over one's actions helps to deflect the negative implications of bad behavior. For example, people who get caught cheating often claim that they were led to cheat by the nature of the situation (such as an unfair teacher or the fact that "everybody else does it"), but those who don't cheat boast of their own moral scruples. We don't find many cheaters who say they cheated because they are immoral people, or many noncheaters who say they didn't cheat because the situation pressured them to be honest. Anytime people's behavior leads to negative consequences, they are inclined to assert that they had little or no choice but to do what they did. One is reminded here of the guards in Nazi concentration camps who repeatedly insisted that they were just following orders.

Similar self-serving attributions may be seen when people work together in groups, such as on committees or teams. When the group does well—wins the game, reaches a good decision, makes a profit, successfully completes a task—each group member tends to feel that he or she was more responsible for the group's success than most of the other members were. When the group performs poorly, however, each member feels less responsible for the outcome than the average member.[14] As an old saying goes, "Success has many parents, but failure is an orphan." Everybody wants to claim some of the responsibility for success; no one wants to accept responsibility for failure.

The ironic consequence of this pervasive bias is that both success and failure can lead to conflicts within the group. Understandably, the members of failing groups usually are unhappy, and each tends to think that the failure was mostly other members' fault. If they then learn of one another's attributions, each person will feel that he or she is being unfairly blamed by other group members and that the others are not accepting their rightful responsibility for the fiasco. However, conflicts may also arise after a group success because each member feels that the others are claiming more responsibility than they deserve while not giving him or her the credit that is due.[15] People sometimes leave successful music groups, athletic teams, and corporations when they believe they are not receiving adequate recognition for their contributions. Yet the self-serving attributional bias virtually assures that most of the members in any group will feel that they are not receiving adequate recognition. It may also help to explain why virtually everyone feels that he or she is underpaid at work. Although we might imagine that a great number of employees are, in fact, not worth what they are paid, nearly everybody thinks that he or she is not receiving his or her due.

Why Peter Piper Picked a Peck of Pickled Peppers

Our tendency to judge ourselves positively extends to objects, symbols, and events that are associated with us. We tend to view things that are somehow connected to us in a more favorable light than things that are not connected to us.

One example of this phenomenon is the mere ownership effect. People evaluate things that they own—their houses, cars, clothes, books, and other possessions—more favorably than things that they don't own. On one level, it is not surprising that people own things they like. However, experimental research suggests that this effect is due to more than just the fact that people own things that they like; people also come to like things that they own.

Researchers in one study asked research participants to rate how much they liked a number of objects such as a candy bar, stapler, comb, and drink insulator. However, before making their ratings, each participant was given one of the objects to keep; some participants randomly received the candy, some got the stapler, and so on. When they then rated all of the objects, the participants tended to evaluate the object that they now owned more positively than the objects that they didn't receive.[16] Those who received staplers rated staplers more highly than those who did not receive staplers, new comb owners rated combs particularly highly, and so on. Interestingly, this effect was even stronger after participants thought that they had failed a test than when they thought they had performed well, supporting the idea that the participants' judgments of the objects were affected by their desire to feel good about themselves.

Of all of the things that we "own," few are more intimately tied to our sense of who we are than our names. This observation suggests that people may come to like their names, and even the letters in their names, better than other names and letters that are not in their names. As outlandish as this possibility may seem at first, research clearly shows that it is true. People do, in fact, like the letters of the alphabet that appear in their own names much more than they like letters that are not in their names, and the effect is particularly strong for people's first and last initials. This preference for the letters in one's own name has been documented in at least 14 countries.[17]

Brett Pelham, a social psychologist, reasoned that, if people feel particularly positively about the letters in their names, this preference might manifest itself in the choices they make in life. Pelham proposed the bold hypothesis that people may prefer occupations and cities that begin with the letter of their name over those that do not! Of course, people's choices of jobs and locations to live are affected by many factors, and we should not be surprised if Mark is a university professor in North Carolina rather than a Mercedes mechanic in Minnesota. Yet Pelham and his colleagues believed that people would gravitate toward occupations and cities that shared the letters of their names at a higher rate than would be expected based on chance.

A series of 11 studies showed that this was the case.[18] The researchers found, for example, that people are overrepresented in states that start with the same letter as their names. Among women, Louises are overrepresented in Louisiana, Marys in Maryland, Michelles in Michigan, and Virginias in (you guessed it) Virginia. Among men, California had more Carys than we would expect on the basis of chance, Delaware had too many Dales, Georgia was overrepresented by Georges, Texas by Teds, and Kentucky by Kenneths.

To examine the possibility that this effect occurs because parents give their children names that resemble the state in which they are born, the researchers also examined the relationship between the first letters of people's last names (which aren't typically chosen) and their state of residence. The letter-preference effect was obtained for last names as well. Furthermore, people whose names matched one of the 35 U.S. cities that begins with "Saint," such as St. Louis and St. Helen, were disproportionately likely to live in a namesake city. So, there are more Louises than one would expect in St. Louis and more Helens than one would expect in St. Helen. To be precise, compared to what one would expect given the frequency of various names in the United States, 44% more women and 14% more men live in cities named for saints who share their names than would be expected on the basis of chance.

Bolstered by their success, Pelham and his colleagues then tested the even bolder hypothesis that people select occupations that resemble their names—that dentists are more likely to be named Denny or Denise, and lawyers are more likely to be named Lawrence or Lauren. Not only was this prediction supported, but a subsequent study showed that roofers are more likely to have first names that start with the letter *R* than people who own hardware stores, whereas hardware store owners are more likely to have names that start with *H*.[19] Now we understand why Peter Piper picked a peck of pickled peppers!

Given Pelham's findings, we can only assume that many other life decisions are affected, albeit subtly, by the name-letter preference effect. Are we unconsciously influenced to choose colleges, products, and romantic partners because they share the letters in our own name? If so, we have a case of an extraneous feature of self-processes—the tendency to overvalue things with which we are associated—entering subtly into important decisions in which it ought to be irrelevant. If we like the letters in our own names better than the other poor letters of the alphabet, is it any wonder that we tend to think that others things that are linked to us—our children, occupation, local sports team, country, and religion, for example, are also particularly special?

Beating Ourselves Up

Although people typically keep their egos well inflated, occasionally the balloon pops, sending self-image into an uncontrolled dive. Even minor failures, setbacks, rejections, and disappointments can prompt harsh self-criticism. "How could I have been so stupid?" "I'll never amount to anything!" "No one likes me!" People self-flagellate for many reasons—for example, to deter criticism from other people ("If I castigate myself severely enough, maybe no one else will"), to elicit compliments and support, to show that the person has insight into his or her deficiencies and weaknesses, or to give one the license to criticize other people.

However, a great deal of unnecessary self-criticism arises from precisely the same source as excessive self-congratulation: the general tendency to perceive ourselves too positively. As we have seen, people like to think of themselves as better than most other people, so when failure or disgrace arrives, their self-image sustains a serious blow. They keep their egos defended as long as possible through various self-serving tactics, but when the walls are finally breached, the ego's defenses temporarily collapse. The fact that people react so strongly to these ego-threatening events shows that they usually feel pretty good about themselves. If they didn't, they could accept failures and other setbacks in stride. ("Yeah, I got kicked out of college, but so what? I've always known than I'm a loser.") The same egoistic desire to be special that leads to self-inflation also sets people up to be greatly deflated from time to time.

Judging Other People

The same natural tendency to self-enhance that biases our perceptions of ourselves and the things that are associated with us also affects our perceptions of other people. We usually think that we are perceiving and evaluating other people accurately and that our feelings about other people are a reaction to who they are and what they are like, but in fact, the self has again intruded into our view of reality.

For example, merely sharing the same birthday with another person can influence our evaluations of him or her. In one study, participants read one of two essays about Rasputin, the "mad monk of Russia."[20] Rasputin exercised considerable influence over the royal family of Russia in the early part of the 20th century despite the fact that he was widely despised. He was filthy and violent, drank heavily, and sexually assaulted women; moreover, as it turns out, he wasn't even a monk but was married and had three children. Rasputin certainly isn't the sort of person who attracts a great deal of admiration. The two essays that participants read about Rasputin were identical in all respects except that one of the essays listed his birthday as the same as the participant's, whereas the other essay listed a birthday that was different from the participant's. This one, trivial personal connection affected participants' evaluations of Rasputin. Participants who thought that they and Rasputin were born on the same day of the year rated him significantly more favorably than participants who did not think he shared their birthday. Given that our evaluations can be influenced by such a minor, egocentric matter as whether another person shares our birthdate, it should not surprise us to learn that factors even more intimately related to our views of ourselves also influence our judgments of other people.

People's perceptions of other people are affected by their views of themselves in several ways. For example, people overestimate how common their own behaviors, reactions, and attitudes are in the general population. This false consensus effect leads people to believe that they are in the majority even when they are not.[21] We each assume that other objective and fair-minded people (like ourselves) will reach the same conclusions as we do. In some ways, using oneself to make assumptions about other people is not unreasonable because one's own response may be a useful indicator of how other people might respond. However, research shows that people over-rely on their own reactions when guessing how most other people will act. Even when presented with information that many of their peers would unanimously react in a way that was different from how the participant would react, participants in one study still concluded that most other people would react as they personally would.[22]

More interesting is the fact that the false consensus effect occurs more frequently on characteristics that people view as undesirable than on characteristics that they view as desirable.[23] People tend to think that most other people share their personal weaknesses and shortcomings, and thus overestimate the prevalence of their own negative traits in other people. Along the same lines, people who make mistakes are more likely to assume that other people would make the same bad choices than people who make correct decisions. This bias allows people to feel better about their undesirable characteristics and bad decisions; if almost everybody else shares my bad traits and makes the same stupid decisions as I do, I need not feel too badly about them.

In contrast, people underestimate the prevalence of their positive characteristics in the population, concluding that their strengths and abilities are relatively unusual. This false uniqueness bias allows people to feel particularly good about their desirable characteristics. Thus, the motive to see oneself positively leads to false consensus on negative traits but false uniqueness on positive ones.[24]

These biases influence people's assumptions about what most other people are like and thereby their reactions to others. When meeting a stranger, for example, your expectations about this person's characteristics may be influenced by your perceptions of yourself, leading to errors in judgment. If you believe that you possess an undesirable attribute such as a hot temper, you will perceive that many other people, possibly including this stranger, also have hot tempers. This ego-driven assumption will undoubtedly affect how you respond to the stranger, leading you to behave differently than if you had not projected your hot temper onto him or her. On the other hand, if you believe that you are compassionate, you may be inclined to see others as less compassionate than you are because false uniqueness occurs on positive traits. But, again, your biased assumption will influence your behavior and increase your chances of reacting inappropriately.

Occasionally, people also project their own positive attributes on other people, but usually only on those whom they perceive favorably. When drawing conclusions about strangers, for example, people are more likely to assume that attractive, desirable individuals possess their positive characteristics than unattractive, undesirable ones.[25] Doing so allows people to maintain positive views of themselves. After all, it does not enhance one's ego to conclude that some incompetent or despicable person also possesses some of one's own best qualities.

People tend to perceive friends and romantic partners more positively than they regard other people. Just as most people see themselves as better than average, they also evaluate their friends and relatives more positively than they rate the "average person."[26] They make the same sorts of self-serving attributions for intimates that they do for themselves, giving them more credit for success and less blame for failure than they give to other people.[27] These kinds of effects can also be seen at the group level. People tend to see their own groups (schools, clubs, occupations, towns, nations, and so on) as better than average, and this effect occurs even in controlled studies where they are assigned to one of two groups at random.[28] All of these biases help people feel good about themselves. Our sense of self-worth is enhanced by believing that our friends, lovers, children, and groups are all better than average. However, this tendency creates problems when it leads us to devalue and discriminate against people who are not associated with us in some way.

To top things off, people tend to think that the characteristics that they personally possess are more important and desirable than the characteristics that they do not possess. For example, whether you think it is generally better to be extraverted or introverted depends a great deal on whether you see yourself as an extravert or introvert. Extraverts think that extraversion is better; introverts think that introversion is better. Similarly, the degree to which you value creativity depends on how creative you think you are, the importance you place on physical appearance depends on your own level of attractiveness, whether you think it is good to be ambitious depends on whether you see yourself as ambitious, and so on. Even when researchers tell people that they possess a fictitious trait based on nonsensical criteria, people conclude that possessing the trait is better than not possessing it. Of course, people who believe they don't possess the bogus trait think that it is better not to have it.[29]

Why do our views of ourselves influence our perceptions of other people? In part, it is because people's judgments of others have implications for how they evaluate themselves. David Dunning, a psychologist who has investigated how the self relates to our perceptions of other people, put it this way:

> When people judge others, they act as though they are also implicitly judging themselves, that the conclusions they reach about other people imply certain conclusions about themselves. As a consequence, they tailor those judgments to ensure that those judgments comment favorably on themselves, making sure that those judgments are symbols that reaffirm positive images of self. They ensure that their pronouncements of others keep faith with the notion that they are wonderful, capable, and lovable human beings. As a consequence, it is inevitable that what they think about themselves becomes entwined in what they believe about others.[30]

Meta-Biases

We have seen that people perceive themselves and others in self-serving ways. They think they are better than average, make self-serving attributions, judge their possessions (including the letters in their names) unusually favorably, evaluate people close to them unrealistically positively, and think that their personal characteristics are particularly good ones to have. To make matters worse, people are not only biased in all of these egotistical ways but also biased to believe that they are not biased!

I noted earlier that far more people believe that they are better than average than is statistically possible. Typically, research shows that between 70 and 80% of people think that they are better than average on any particular trait.[31] But do they have any idea that their self-perceptions might be biased in a positive direction? A study by Emily Pronin, Daniel Lin, and Lee Ross suggested that most people do not.[32] In their study, 87% of the participants rated themselves better than the average student at their own university, demonstrating the typical better-than-average effect. However, when the researchers carefully explained the better-than-average bias to the participants and asked whether they thought that their self-ratings might have been influenced by this tendency for people to see themselves too favorably, only one-fourth of the participants who had rated themselves higher than average conceded that their ratings might be biased. The vast majority of the participants did not recognize that their ratings were biased even though they had just fallen prey to the better-than-average effect.

People are relatively blind to their own biases, but they see other people's biases much more clearly. Research on this bias blind spot shows that people tend to think that they are less susceptible to biases of all kinds than other people are. Pronin and her colleagues asked research participants to indicate how much they personally showed eight specific biases in perception and judgment, including the self-serving attributional bias and better-than-average effect described earlier. In addition, participants indicated how much the "average American" shows each bias. Results showed that participants indicated that they were affected less by all eight biases than the average American. To be certain that this effect was not due to the participants assuming that, as university students, they were less biased than other uneducated people, a second study asked participants to rate the degree to which they and their university classmates showed these biases. Again, participants thought that they were less biased than their peers, although the magnitude of the difference was smaller than when they compared themselves to the average American. In a similar study using a noncollege sample, people waiting for flights at the San Francisco airport rated themselves as significantly less biased compared to how they rated other travelers who were passing through the airport at the time![33]

Perhaps the meta-bias to see oneself as unbiased shown in these studies is due to people's having a faulty memory for their own biases. If we asked participants about their biases immediately after they showed one, maybe they would see the bias clearly. To test this possibility, pairs of participants in another study took a difficult test, and each participant obtained feedback indicating that he or she had performed well or poorly on it. As found in other research, participants who did poorly rated the test as significantly less valid than those who did well, presumably to feel better about their performance. However, when asked whether their and the other person's ratings of the test's validity might have been affected by the scores they had obtained on it, participants indicated that the other person's rating of the test was more likely to have been influenced by the score they received than their own rating had been. Again, participants were more likely to see other people's self-serving biases than their own even right after they exhibited one.[34]

The implications of these findings are staggering. We each tend to think that our view of the world is the correct one and that other reasonable, fair-minded people will (or at least should) see things the same way we do. When other people disagree with us, we naturally assume that they are deluded, ignorant, or biased. As Ichheiser put it: "We tend to resolve our perplexity arising out of the experience that other people see the world differently than we see it ourselves by declaring that these others, in consequence of some basic intellectual or moral defect, are unable to see things 'as they really are' and to react to them 'in a normal way.' We thus imply, of course, that things are in fact as we see them, and that our ways are the normal ways."[35]

In fact, our biases lead us to conclude that our perceptions of ourselves and other people are more accurate than other people's perceptions of us and themselves. Somehow, we believe that we have special and objective insights into our own and other people's psyches that most other people do not have. People think that they understand other people better than other people understand them, and people assume that they understand themselves better than other people understand themselves. Furthermore, people expect others to be less objective and fair than they themselves are. Not only do these assumptions lead us to think that we have an inside track to accuracy and that other people's interpretations are wrong, but it leads us to underestimate what we might learn from other people and overestimate what they might learn from us. Perhaps this explains why most people offer advice much more freely than they accept it from others.

Research has also revealed a tendency to believe that we have a greater ability to respond rationally than most other people do. For example, people think that they are personally less affected by advertising, propaganda, and other calculated efforts to change their behavior than other people are. We often conclude that other people are reacting irrationally, but how often have you concluded that you were personally behaving irrationally?

Underestimating our own biases leads to a good deal of conflict with other people. Many disagreements center on people's interpretations of events—why things happened, who was responsible, whose perspective is correct.[36] To the extent that each person sees him- or herself as a relatively objective arbiter of the truth, any disagreement will be attributed to the biases of other people. Although we each see the world through ego-colored glasses, we think that our glasses have clear lenses (if we even stop to wonder whether we are wearing glasses at all), but that other people look through cloudy lenses that are warped by egoistic imperfections. When we then accuse others of being biased, we fuel disagreement and mistrust and exacerbate the conflict further.

Of course, no reasonable person would claim that he or she is never biased and, in fact, most people are willing to concede that they have their preferences and biases, some of which may be unfounded. Yet these admissions of personal bias are typically made in the abstract rather than with respect to a particular situation. I may agree that I do not always act rationally, but I am unlikely to agree that I am behaving irrationally right now.

None of us can step completely outside the blinders of our own self-interest. Perhaps the best we can do is to practice attributional charity by assuming that other people are generally just as accurate and honest as we are (though not necessarily more so) and that our perceptions are as likely to be distorted as theirs. In this way, we can live more easily with the fact that we may disagree with other people in our interpretations of events without necessarily assuming that we are right and they are wrong.

The Costs of Self-Generated Distortion

Psychologists and other behavioral researchers have debated for several years whether the kinds of self-serving distortions of reality described in this chapter are generally beneficial or detrimental to the individual's well-being. Some theorists have made the case that a certain amount of self-serving distortion is advantageous both for the individual and for his or her relationships with other people. Other theorists have argued that, although misperceiving reality can sometimes make people feel good, it is rarely helpful in the long run.

Shelley Taylor and Jonathon Brown championed the view that certain self-serving illusions contribute to mental health and general well-being.[37] Taylor and Brown pointed out that having positive illusions about one's characteristics, overestimating the amount of personal control one has over events in life, and holding unrealistically optimistic views of the future provide several benefits for people. Most obviously, these illusions reduce negative emotions. After all, acknowledging that one possesses negative personal characteristics, has minimal control over life events, and will encounter occasional disappointments, setbacks, and tragedies in the future is understandably sobering, if not downright depressing. Maintaining an unrealistic, rosy view of one's characteristics, control, and future reduces many concerns and promotes a positive mood. It is instructive that people who show the least evidence of self-serving illusions also tend to be the most depressed and that people who show the greatest biases in self-enhancement are most happy.

Furthermore, Taylor and Brown suggested that having a positive view of oneself may enhance motivation and persistence, increasing people's overall likelihood of success in life. Having positive views of oneself is associated with working harder and longer on difficult tasks, possibly because the individual feels more certain of eventual success.[38] Research also suggests that people who feel good about themselves are more benevolent and helpful in their relations with other people than people who are down on themselves. Thus, biases that enhance our own self-satisfaction may have positive effects on how we relate to other people.

Self-serving illusions can also help our closest relationships. Sandra Murray and John Holmes have studied how positive illusions influence romantic relationships. Their studies suggest that people who view their romantic partners in overly positive ways and who overestimate how much their partners care about them are more satisfied with their relationships than people who perceive their partners and their commitment more accurately.[39] Believing that one's partner is a wonderful, devoted person enhances relationship satisfaction even if the belief is partly illusory.

Altogether, it would seem that holding excessively positive views of oneself and the important people in one's life is a blessing rather than a curse. However, this tells only part of the story. There seems little doubt that positive self-illusions have precisely the effects that have been described: they make us feel better, and they may lead to both greater motivation and a more sociable and caring style of relating to others. Furthermore, holding illusions about our intimate partners appears to make us more satisfied with our relationships. Even so, I question whether it is beneficial in the long run to feel good about oneself and one's life if these positive feelings come at the expense of perceiving oneself and other people inaccurately. Perhaps seeing the unpleasant reality about ourselves and our lives is actually more beneficial in the long run because, despite occasional pangs of unhappiness and uncertainty, we will make better decisions based on accurate information that is untainted by self-serving illusions.

My inclination is to assume that all organisms fare better in the long run when they have an accurate perception of reality. Only through an accurate understanding of both their personal characteristics and the challenges they face can any animal, human beings included, deal effectively with the opportunities and threats they confront in life. Consistently overestimating oneself and one's capabilities may have short-term benefits but will come to little good in the long haul. Without denying that self-serving illusions can provide temporary benefits, let's take a look at some of the problems that they create.[40]

Holding an overly flattering view of one's personality, abilities, and other attributes is often a recipe for personal disaster. Success in life comes largely from matching one's abilities, interests, and inclinations to appropriate situations, jobs, and relationships. To the extent that they misperceive who or what they are really like, people are more likely to make bad decisions. How many people are in jobs, relationships, and lives for which they are unsuited simply because they perceived themselves inaccurately?

Furthermore, when self-serving illusions blind people to their shortcomings and weaknesses, they are unlikely to try to improve. The person who blames an uncontrollable temper on everyone else, poor school performance on unfair teachers, or a long string of romantic failures on other people's inability to handle intimacy will not do what is needed for positive change. The most important step in improving oneself and one's life is to discern where the problems lie. Similarly, people who convince themselves that their partners are wonderful and their relationships were made in heaven may fool themselves into staying in relationships that are not actually serving them as well as they might.

Although seeing oneself through ego-colored glasses may help to ward off negative emotions such as anxiety, frustration, and shame, biased self-perceptions may create unpleasant feelings of their own. Carl Rogers, one of the founders of humanistic psychology, discussed what happens when people distort reality to make it congruent with their views of themselves. He suggested that holding a view of reality that is at variance with the truth creates anxiety and unhappiness. The person may not be able to grasp what is wrong yet has a vague sense of tension and discontent.[41] On the surface, things may appear to be going well, but on another level, something is clearly amiss. A round peg trying to fit in a square hole does not fit even if the peg believes it is square.

This is why virtually every theory of mental health assumes that having an accurate view of reality is a hallmark of psychological adjustment. Denying or distorting reality to ward off anxiety and other unpleasant emotions is uniformly regarded as a sign of instability or disorder. According to most views, adjusted individuals are able to nondefensively accept their weaknesses alongside their strengths. Abraham Maslow, who spent much of his career studying people who functioned unusually well in life, observed that such individuals "can take the frailties and sins, weaknesses and evils of human nature in the same unquestioning spirit that one takes or accepts the characteristics of nature."[42]

Some researchers have suggested that the self-serving biases described in this chapter are culture-bound and not universal to all people. They note, for example, that people in certain other cultures, such as Japan, do not self-aggrandize or show the same egotistical tendencies as Americans. In fact, the Japanese not only seem to bend over backwards to be modest, but they also do not seek positive feedback to the same degree.[43] However, it is possible that either self-effacement or self-aggrandizement can make a person feel good about him- or herself depending on what the person's culture values. In most Western societies, characteristics such as confidence, individualism, autonomy, and superiority are valued, so people want to see themselves in these ways. In other societies, greater value may be placed on modesty, collectivism, and interdependency so that people prefer to possess these kinds of characteristics. The Japanese individual who downplays his or her positive traits may, in fact, be just as self-serving (and feel as good about him- or herself) as the American who exaggerates them. In both cases, the individual's perceptions and actions are biased in ways that protect his or her ego and foster positive feelings.

Why Do Self-Serving Biases Exist?

Given the many ways in which egotistical biases can be problematic, why do people distort the truth about themselves as they do? It seems unlikely that a general tendency toward self-serving distortion is a product of evolution. Biological and psychological systems seem generally designed to provide accurate information regarding the state of the organism and the state of the world. Animals need to know when opportunities and threats are present, and it is difficult to imagine how a system that diminished the perceived seriousness of threats could have ever evolved. As noted psychologist Leon Festinger observed, "inaccurate appraisals of one's abilities can be punishing or even fatal in many situations."[44] If anything, evolution seems to have favored animals that were threat-sensitive because underestimating threats is more likely to be disastrous than overestimating them. A species that chronically overestimated its ability and degree of control over its environment would make potentially fatal miscalculations at every turn. Yet this is precisely what the ego appears to do.

In fact, it is often advantageous to experience negative emotions, such as anxiety and sadness, because they signal to us that all is not well with our world. As unpleasant as they may feel, negative emotions are inherently functional in warning us of problems and motivating us to take action to remove the bad feeling.[45] Feeling afraid, for example, focuses our attention on a potential threat to our well-being and motivates us to protect ourselves by avoiding or confronting the threat. Similarly, the negative feelings associated with low self-esteem serve to alert us to problems with how we are being perceived and evaluated by other people.[46] We will see later that the self can create and prolong unpleasant emotions artificially, leading to other problems, but negative emotions are fundamentally adaptive. So, I cannot imagine that the self evolved in such a way to lead us to see ourselves and the world in an artificially rosy fashion simply to assuage our fears. Then why do self-serving tendencies exist that artificially make us feel better? The answer to this question is by no means clear, but let me suggest one possibility.

Human beings, like all other animals, possess various systems that monitor the state of their inner and outer worlds. Many of these systems monitor internal biological processes, such as blood sugar level or heart rate, and others monitor aspects of the external world, including both the physical and social environment. These systems evolved to maintain internal and external environments within certain optimal limits in which the animal can survive, function, and ultimately reproduce. Detecting conditions that constitute a possible threat to the animal elicit either physiological reactions to restore homeostasis (such as increasing heart rate when muscles need more oxygen) or behavioral reactions to promote the animal's well-being (as when hunger prompts the animal to seek food or fear elicits running).

Most of the internal states that signal a threat to an animal are experientially unpleasant. Hunger is certainly aversive, as are fear and disappointment. Indeed, the aversiveness of emotions is part of their value because the unpleasant feelings shift the animal's attention to the threat and provide an incentive to do something to eliminate it.[47]

Moreover, most of the systems that monitor the animal's well-being are designed to ensure that they do not overlook potential threats. As a result, most of these monitoring systems are more likely to detect false positives—events that are initially treated as threats but in fact are not dangerous—than false negatives, or true threats that are registered as benign.[48] For example, both human and nonhuman animals are more likely to react fearfully to stimuli that later turn out not to be dangerous than to be calm in the face of stimuli that pose a true threat. A deer is more likely to bolt at a small and harmless sound than to remain calm in the face of loud noises or clear danger. This bias in the detection of problems and threats is a very reasonable evolutionary adaptation. Animals that occasionally overreacted to false alarms were more likely to survive and reproduce than those that disregarded real threats. Evolution seems to have strongly endorsed the motto "It's better to be safe than sorry."

So, where does the self come in? When prehistoric human beings developed the ability to think consciously about themselves, they acquired the capacity to override many of their natural reactions to events. In most ways, this new ability was very beneficial. Being able to think carefully about potential opportunities and threats, rather than always reacting automatically to them, was clearly advantageous. By virtue of their ability to talk to themselves, people could decide, within limits, how to respond instead of always reacting automatically.

Yet one by-product of selfhood was that human beings could change how they felt about events by deliberately changing how they thought about them. Although this, too, was sometimes useful, it allowed people to reduce negative emotions through thought rather than through action. The rabbit that hunkers down under a bush at the sight of a wolf can reduce its fear only by finding safety. In contrast, the human being who confronts a possible threat can reduce his or her fear by either seeking safety or by cognitively reinterpreting the situation in a less threatening way. This is essentially what people are doing when they think about themselves, other people, and the world in biased, self-serving ways.

The tendency for people to perceive themselves and the world in self-serving ways reflects a method of reducing anxiety, uncertainty, and other unpleasant feelings by a back door route. In the short run, doing so undoubtedly makes us feel better about ourselves and our plight, and, as we have seen, it may have other beneficial consequences as well. But, in the long run, these illusions may compromise our ability to deal effectively with the challenges of life.

The Case for Ego-Skepticism

As we have seen, each of us is equipped with a mental apparatus that, despite our best intentions, biases our perceptions of ourselves and our worlds in self-serving ways. Knowing that our views are sometimes distorted in this way should lead us to develop an attitude of ego-skepticism. Anytime our beliefs about ourselves or other people are consequential, we should caution ourselves that those beliefs just might be biased in our favor. Rarely do they actually seem biased, of course, and deep down we probably think that our perceptions of reality are more or less on target. Yet just knowing that we are prone to think that we are more competent, correct, and in control than we really are ought to caution us to be more tentative in our conclusions. Recognizing that we are probably overestimating our responsibility for good things and underestimating our culpability for bad ones should temper our confidence in our attributions. Realizing that we overvalue those things and people who are associated with us should make us strive to be more objective.

Of everything that I learned in college, the lesson with the greatest impact was not to trust my perceptions of reality. This lesson was driven home to me on two fronts. First, my courses in psychology convinced me that people take great liberties in how they construe events. With no final arbiter of the "truth," people have great latitude to interpret (and misinterpret) events in ways that are to their liking. The fact that participants in countless psychological studies had been shown to interpret events in biased ways convinced me that my own judgments were more fallible than I had ever imagined. Knowing that I could not avoid making such errors nor know when my views were and were not accurate made me committed not to take my own perceptions of reality too seriously.

Second, while in college, I read Carlos Castaneda's books about his apprenticeship with a Yacqui shaman named Don Juan. (Castaneda's writings were later challenged as a hoax, but they nonetheless contained provocative insights.) I was particularly struck by one question that Don Juan asked Castaneda: "Why should the world be only as you think it is? Who gave you the authority to say so?"[49] Don Juan could have easily been addressing me. I realized that there was no reason whatsoever why the world should be only as I thought it was, and that I had no inside route to the truth. Clearly, the certainty with which I held my views of myself and the world was unwarranted.

A person who understands that his or her experiences are filtered through the lens of the ego can never look at the world in quite the same way again. Or, more precisely, the world may look the same, but the person doesn't trust his or her perceptions as much as before. Knowing that the possibility of misperceptions is always present, the person clings less strongly to his or her interpretation of reality. The person cannot give up all beliefs about him- or herself and the world because they are essential in order for the person to function in day-to-day life. Even so, it is worth striving to hold those beliefs more tentatively.

4 ∷
Making Ourselves Miserable

My life has been filled with many tragedies, most of which never occurred.
—MARK TWAIN

The Wizard of Oz, released in 1939, remains one of the most popular films of all time. In the movie, Dorothy and her three companions travel to Oz, seeking something that each of them believes will make them happy and complete. The scarecrow is troubled by his lack of a brain, the tin woodsman sadly claims that he doesn't have a heart, the cowardly lion is ashamed by his lack of courage, and the whole adventure begins when Dorothy and Toto run away from home in search of a place where there "isn't any trouble," far away from wicked Almira Gulch, who wants to take Toto away.

Dorothy, the scarecrow, the tin man, and the lion are each dissatisfied with some aspect of their lives, believing that they lack some essential ingredient for a full and happy life. Telling themselves that they are deficient in some way, they undertake a long and dangerous journey in search of the wizard whom they assume can fill their needs. When they finally find the great and powerful Oz, Dorothy and her companions learn not only that he is not really much of a wizard but also that they already possess what they had been seeking all along. After the wizard gives the scarecrow a diploma, the tin woodsman a large heart-shaped watch, and the lion a medal for valor, they are transformed by his gifts, but, in fact, nothing has changed except how they view themselves. Dorothy herself understands this important lesson at the end of the movie when she concludes, "If I ever go looking for my heart's desire again, I won't look any further than my own backyard. Because if it isn't there, I never really lost it to begin with!"

Like the characters in *The Wizard of Oz*, most people are dissatisfied with some aspect of their lives. Much like Dorothy and her friends, their lives are tainted by an undercurrent of dissatisfaction, unhappiness, anxiety, envy, or other unpleasant emotions that arise because they think that things are not as they should be. And, as in the movie, people go to great lengths to find someone or something that will help them fix their problems. However, most people have not learned the lesson that Dorothy learned—that the problems for which they seek solutions are often in their heads, fueled by troublesome beliefs about themselves and about how life should be.

Undoubtedly, some personal problems are real ones that truly need to be fixed. Negative emotions are sometimes direct and automatic responses to an undesirable state of the world. However, viewing emotions as natural reactions to real events overlooks the fact that people's emotions are often affected by how they talk to themselves, if not created entirely by the self. Part of the curse of having a self is that, like Dorothy and her companions in Oz, we create a great deal of misery in our own minds without realizing that we are reacting to our self-generated thoughts.

Emotions Without a Self

Animals clearly do not need a self in order to experience emotion. Although we cannot know for sure what other animals feel, their behavior suggests that they experience a wide array of emotions, including fear, sadness, joy, and rage.[1]

Animals experience natural, innate emotional reactions to certain stimuli. For example, most species react naturally with fear to certain cues, such as when the silhouette of a hawk in flight elicits fear in ducklings, or the threatening gesture of a dominant member of the group causes fear in apes. Human beings may also be innately prepared to experience fear in response to certain stimuli. For example, the rapid approach of looming objects automatically creates fear, as does a sudden loss of physical support (as when one begins to fall down the stairs or an elevator lurches suddenly). Stimuli such as snakes, bared fangs, and darkness appear to naturally create fear in many animals, including human beings. These reactions likely evolved because animals in an earlier era who experienced fear in the presence of these stimuli survived and reproduced at a higher rate than animals for whom these stimuli evoked no response or, worse, a pleasant feeling.

In addition, animals may be conditioned to experience emotions in response to previously neutral stimuli through the process of classical conditioning. In classical conditioning, animals learn to respond with a negative emotion to a previously neutral stimulus that has been paired with aversive events, or respond with positive emotions to a neutral stimulus that has been associated with rewarding events. An early example of classical conditioning of human emotions was provided by John Watson, the founder of behaviorism, who conditioned fear in a young boy known as "Little Albert."[2] After demonstrating that Little Albert was not initially afraid of certain animals and inanimate objects, Watson and his colleagues banged loudly on a steel bar behind Albert's back each time Albert tried to touch a white rat. After several pairings of the rat and the clanging of the steel bar, Albert began to react fearfully whenever the rat was present, and continued to be afraid of the rat even after Watson stopped banging on the bar. Albert also showed signs of being afraid of objects that resembled the rat, such as cotton and a rabbit, a process known as stimulus generalization. In the same way, each of us has come to dislike or fear certain people, objects, and events because they are associated with past aversive experiences.

Both of these emotional processes—one involving automatic reactions and the other involving classical conditioning—can occur without conscious self-awareness. We do not need to think anything at all to respond to a natural fear-evoking stimulus or a classically conditioned event. However, the capacity for self-relevant thought renders human beings' emotional lives far more extensive and complex than those of self-less animals. Specifically, having a self permits people to evoke emotions in themselves by imagining events that affect them, perceiving threats to their egos, thinking about other people who are significant to them, worrying about how they are perceived by other people, and contemplating the causes of their emotional experiences. This chapter will deal with these five ways in which self-talk contributes to human emotion.

∷ Self-Imaginings

Although we do not know for certain, it is plausible that nonhuman animals may experience emotions when they remember past events. Charles Darwin thought so, asking whether we can be sure "that an old dog with an excellent memory and some power of imagination . . . never reflects on his past pleasures in the chase."[3] However, although animals without a self might experience emotions when they remember actual experiences they have had, they would presumably not be able to think about what might happen to them in the future nor imagine having experiences that have no basis in reality whatsoever. Without the ability to create the analogue-I in their minds, they could not imagine themselves in situations they had not actually encountered.

In contrast, people often become quite emotional simply from imaging themselves in various situations and may even work themselves into an emotional frenzy by doing so. Many emotional experiences occur not because anything good or bad is happening but only because the person imagines it. People can experience strong emotions by reliving past experiences in their own minds, thinking about things that may happen in the future, and even imagining events that have neither happened in the past nor have much likelihood of occurring later. The past, anticipated, and fantasized experiences of the analogue-I often have emotional power similar to that of real events. Although most emotions can be triggered purely by self-thoughts, I will focus here on the one that is perhaps the most common.

Worry

Without a self that allows them to imagine what might or might not happen in the future, people would not worry. Nonhuman animals experience fear in the presence of real threats or stimuli that have become associated with aversive events, but one does not get the impression that they worry about what might happen to them tomorrow or next week. All worry about future events is the result of self-relevant thought and, thus, requires a self.

Anticipating future threats is sometimes adaptive because it allows people to take steps to avoid danger.[4] Anticipating the risks of driving on worn-out, treadless tires may prompt us to replace our tires before a long trip, and considering the possible negative consequences of risky behavior may lead people to stop smoking or to practice safe sex. Even when avoiding danger is not possible, thinking in advance about a potential problem or threat sometimes helps people prepare to confront or cope with it. A person can plan ahead about how to deal with a difficult situation at work or how to handle an unpleasant medical procedure. Without the ability to imagine themselves in the future, people could not deliberately behave in the present in ways that may promote their well-being in the future. This ability to anticipate the future is perhaps the greatest benefit of having a self.

If people worried only about things that had some reasonable probability of occurring, and if worrying always helped them deal more effectively with future events, the ability to worry would be a great gift. But the fact is that most worry is unnecessary. Many, perhaps most, of the things that people worry about never materialize and, even when they do occur, worrying about them in advance is rarely beneficial. In retrospect, people are far more likely to conclude that "there wasn't any reason for me to be so worried" than "I wish I had worried more!"

When it motivates precautionary behavior, worry is well worth the unpleasantness it brings, but worry serves no noticeable good when nothing can be done to thwart the danger. The airplane passenger who worries during a flight about an accident cannot reduce the likelihood of a plane crash by worrying. Parents worried about a new teenage driver who hasn't returned home on time with the family car don't increase their child's safety. The person who has a suspicious, potentially malignant mole removed for biopsy can't change his or her prospect of skin cancer by worrying while waiting for the results. Worrying about such events is, of course, absolutely natural, and almost everybody does it. My point is not that worrying about such things is abnormal or a sign of weakness, but rather that, from an objective point of view, a great deal of worry serves no good purpose and may even cause harm. Yet most people cannot stop the inner self-talk that keeps the worry-machine churning.

Some people believe that even when it doesn't help them to avoid danger, worrying prepares them to cope with misfortune once it arrives.[5] Anticipatory worry is viewed as a down payment on future trauma. Evidence does not support this positive view of worry, however. Not only does much of our worry not prevent a disaster (as in the case of the white-knuckled airplane passenger or the worried parent waiting for the teenager to come home), but worrying now about a potential tragedy does not seem to inoculate us against being upset if it actually takes place. It seems unlikely that worrying about one's child being killed in a car accident buffers one against the trauma of learning that an accident has, in fact, occurred. This is not to say that a realistic appraisal of possible outcomes, both good and bad, is not appropriate, but rather that anticipatory worry is not likely to steel the person against disaster once it arrives.

As Mark Twain's quip that opened this chapter suggests, our self fills our lives with many tragedies, most of which never really occur.

But, although imaginary, these tragedies take their toll. People who are in the grasp of worry are miserably anxious, preoccupied, and distracted. They often have trouble functioning efficiently, react distractedly and irritably to other people, and may have difficulty sleeping. People who worry a great deal tend to be more depressed, report more physical symptoms, and have higher blood pressure than people who worry less.

Why Do We Worry So Much?

If worry is so often useless or maladaptive, then why are people so prone to worry? Although we may concede that a certain amount of appropriate worry is beneficial, why are people plagued by anxiety when it is not useful or is even detrimental? Why does our self inflict so much unnecessary distress on us?

Social psychologist Leonard Martin has provided an intriguing answer to this question.[6] Martin speculates that self-generated worry about the future became prevalent and problematic only with the emergence of agriculture around 10,000 years ago. As we saw in chapter 1, people probably possessed a modern degree of self-awareness before this time (at least by 40,000–60,000 years ago), but the hunting-gathering lifestyle of human beings prior to the advent of agriculture did not evoke a great deal of rumination about the future. Life was lived mostly day to day, with no long-term goals to accumulate possessions, succeed, or improve one's lot in life, and, thus, few distal events to worry about. People's attention was focused primarily on what needed to be done today, and tomorrow was left largely to take care of itself.

With the emergence of agriculture, however, people moved from an immediate-return environment (in which they could see the results of their behavior on an ongoing basis) to a delayed-return environment in which important outcomes, both good and bad, often lay weeks or months in the future. People who rely on agriculture think about the future a great deal. Farmers must plan for planting, as well as for how their crops will be tended, harvested, and stored. Because so many things can ruin their yield, they fret a great deal about the weather, pests, and whether their crops will grow, and then about protecting whatever is produced from thieves, rodents, and rot. As the growing season progresses, feedback regarding progress toward their goal of producing sufficient food for the coming year is sporadic and uncertain. No matter how good one's prospects for a bountiful yield at the moment, a drought, infestation, storm, stampede, fire, or marauding horde could undo one's hard work in the blink of an eye, leaving one's family to starve. A farmer can never feel really secure about his or her future even when everything seems to be going well at the moment.

Along with agriculture came a change from nomadic clans to sedentary communities. With communities came houses and property ownership, and thus worries about protecting one's belongings. For the first time people had to be vigilant about protecting what they owned. Furthermore, agriculture brought a division of labor and social roles, so that people began to worry not only about their personal futures but also about the well-being of the other people on whom they depended. If I plan to trade some of my corn for one of your cows, I will worry not only about my own corn crop but about your herd and your health as well.

If Martin is correct, agriculture brought with it a new set of psychological stresses because it moved people from a hunting-gathering lifestyle that was characterized by day-to-day living and immediately available returns to a lifestyle in which people invested their efforts today for uncertain outcomes in the often distant future. And, because human beings and their ancestors had spent millions of years in an immediate-return environment, they were ill-prepared to deal with the anxiety of living for the future.

Modern society is a profoundly delayed-return environment. People spend much of their time thinking about, planning for, working toward, and worrying about future goals. Many such goals (such as one's paycheck or vacation) lie days or weeks ahead, whereas others (such as educational degrees, job promotions, new houses, and retirement) may be years in the future. Unlike prehistoric hunter-gatherers, people today rarely receive ongoing feedback about their progress toward these important goals. Our prehistoric ancestors knew day-to-day whether they were achieving the important outcomes that dominated their lives (particularly obtaining food and avoiding danger), whereas much of our lives focuses on distal, uncertain events. No matter how hard I work today, I have no assurance that my long-term goals will be met. Martin's analysis suggests that anxiety is much more pervasive in contemporary society than it was before the agricultural revolution because modern human beings spend far more of their time engaged in self-focused thought about the future.

To make matters worse, the psychological systems that monitor the world for potential threats are biased toward false positives.[7] All animals are far more likely to react to a benign stimulus as if it is a threat than to react to a threat as if it is benign. From an evolutionary standpoint, a bias toward false positives makes adaptive sense. Animals who overreact to false alarms are more likely to survive and reproduce than animals who fail to react (even once) to a real threat. Thus, all animals, including human beings, generally read more danger into events than is warranted.

For animals without a self, the emotional effects of a false alarm are short-lived. The deer, rabbit, or cat that startles and runs when it hears a sudden noise returns to normal soon afterwards. No real harm is done if many of the noises that scare the animal are, in reality, false alarms. But with their ability to dwell on future events in their minds, people can conjure up and dwell for long periods of time on bad things that might happen in the future. (I saw an advertisement recently suggesting that it was not too soon for parents of newborns to start worrying about their child's college education and their own retirement.) Many, perhaps most, of the things we worry about may turn out to be false alarms, but in the meantime, the self imposes a heavy price in the form of anxiety and preoccupation as it dwells incessantly on them.

The Ultimate Worry

For most people, death is the ultimate anxiety-evoking event. Some surveys show that people rate speaking in front of large groups as more anxiety-arousing than death, but this finding is probably due to the perceived remoteness of death for most people. I suspect that most of us would feel somewhat more anxious if we learned that we were going to die tomorrow than if we discovered that we had to give a speech.

Anticipatory anxiety about death seems to be a uniquely human characteristic, another by-product of our ability to self-reflect. Only because we are able to imagine ourselves in the future can we worry about death at all. Other animals may show fear when their lives are actually at stake, but they don't appear to worry about death in the absence of threatening situations or stimuli. And they certainly don't worry about what will happen to them after they die, whereas human beings find the afterlife both fascinating and frightening.

Many people expend a good deal of emotional energy worrying about death. The white-knuckled passenger on a turbulent plane flight, the person who has a suspicious symptom of a deadly disease, and the individual whose family must live in unsafe housing all think about the possibility of dying. These self-generated thoughts about death can be anxiety-arousing to the point of panic. When Shakespeare's Julius Caesar observed that "cowards die many times before their deaths; the valiant never taste of death but once," he was noting that the imagined deaths of the analogue-I in one's mind can be nearly as traumatic as the real thing.

As with worry about other dangers, a certain degree of anxiety about death serves an important function. If we weren't concerned about death, we might not protect ourselves and the people we care about. Because we can worry, we buckle our seat belts, discard tainted food, practice safe sex, and install smoke alarms. However, again, the active imagination of our self often causes us to worry about dying even when the worry doesn't serve any useful purpose and is probably misplaced to begin with.

The self is involved in our fears about death in yet another intriguing way. Most of the time when we think about ourselves in the future, we imagine not our self (in the sense of the psychological system that is the focus of this book) but rather about ourselves as living human beings. Thus, our worry about the future centers on what may happen to us as people and not as mental selves. A person who contemplates going to court next week for a traffic violation is thinking about him- or herself as a flesh-and-blood person and not about him- or herself as a psychological self. Any worry that arises from imagining the court appearance involves concerns about the person and not the self.

However, when people think about their death, their reactions appear to arise not only from the fact that they will no longer function as a living organism but also that they will cease to exist as a mental self.[8] As I noted in chapter 1, most people experience the self as an organic, conscious "thing" inside their head that registers their experiences and thinks their thoughts. When many people think about death, they think about the fact that this conscious thing—the self that seems most central to their existence—will no longer exist. After all, people do still exist as a physical body (for a while) after they die, and the atoms of which they are composed will presumably last indefinitely. What does not exist after death is the experiencing "self" that people imagine exists inside them. One of the most disturbing aspects of death for many people is the idea that this flame of consciousness will be snuffed out when they die.

The Undesired Present

We have seen that people often create negative emotions for themselves when their self becomes a time machine that allows them to travel to the past or the future. For this reason, it has often been suggested that people should make an effort to keep their attention anchored in the present as much as possible. This is excellent advice, but it comes with a caveat. People may be focused on the present moment yet still conjure up a good deal of unhappiness by wishing that, at this moment, they were somewhere else. I know of no research that has examined how often people wish they were somewhere else, doing something different from whatever they are currently doing, but I suspect that it's quite often. Many employees spend their working days wishing they were not at work, students spend a good deal of time wishing they were not in class, parents sometimes wish their children will fall asleep so that they can do something else, and virtually everyone has sat alone at home on a weekend night wishing he or she had somewhere else to be. Imagining a more ideal version of the present moment can create a good deal of unhappiness and frustration.

In fact, people may become unhappy even when current circumstances are pleasant if they think that being somewhere else would be even better. I may really be enjoying my steak at dinner yet feel vaguely dissatisfied because the shrimp on the menu might have been better. I like my job a great deal, but perhaps I could find one I like even more. I'm having a good time during my vacation in the mountains, but perhaps going to the beach would have been more fun. Because their selves can always imagine better circumstances than the one they're actually in, people often suspect that they're not getting the most out of life and thus live with simmering discontent.

The solution to this particular curse of the self is to fully accept whatever situation one is in at the moment. This does not mean that people should not try to change or leave an undesirable situation, if that is possible. However, if the situation cannot be changed or escaped (at least for now), one should recognize the absurdity of feeding one's own unhappiness by dwelling on the fact that one does not wish to be there or that being somewhere else would be better. This is, of course, easier said than done because self-reflection often involves comparing the present situation to alternatives. But just because our spontaneous self-chatter is often like a runaway train to unhappiness does not mean that we have to jump on board.

Threats to the Ego

The story is told of a Chinese prime minister during the Tang Dynasty who considered himself a devout and humble Buddhist. One day, during his visit to the temple, the prime minister asked the master to explain Buddhism's perspective on egotism. The master's expression turned grim and his eyes glared as he asked in a condescending and insulting tone, "What kind of a stupid question is that?" Understandably, the prime minister became angry and defensive. "How dare you speak to me that way!" he shouted. The master then sat back and smiled. "That, your excellency, is egotism."

When nonhuman animals become angry or enraged, they are typically responding to one of four kinds of threats. Most anger among other animals stems from either physical attacks upon themselves or other animals to which they are genetically or socially related (particularly their offspring), competition for food, competition over mates, or for animals that are territorial, encroachments by other animals upon their territory. Animals often respond quickly and violently to these kinds of situations, then calm down just as quickly once the threat has dissipated.

Human beings also become angry in response to these sorts of events. Physical attacks upon themselves or their loved ones, theft of property (including food), competition for mates, and territorial violations all cause people to become angry and, often, aggressive. However, the vast majority of things that make people angry do not involve these kinds of fundamental threats to their well-being. Of all of the situations that have ever made you angry, how many have involved your physical well-being, food, mating rights, or territory?

Human beings expend much of their anger on symbolic events that "threaten" something abstract that they hold dear, such as their ideas, opinions, and particularly their egos. Most people become upset when they fail, feel belittled, or are criticized; and suggestions that they are incompetent, unlikable, or undesirable can send them into the depths of despair or a surge of blind rage.[9] We react with anger, anxiety, or deflation to all kinds of events that, in one way or another, challenge our mental images of ourselves.

If we step back and look at this common reaction objectively, it begins to appear quite peculiar: we defend our mental ideas about ourselves with almost as much vigor as we defend ourselves against real physical attacks. As long as our cherished ideas about ourselves are confirmed by our own behavior and by other people's reactions to us, all is well. Events that stroke our egos generally produce positive feelings such as pride, happiness, and satisfaction. But when events threaten our egos, and particularly when other people call our competence or goodness into question, we experience negative emotions such as anxiety, despondency, frustration, shame, and anger. By virtue of having a self, we become invested in our thoughts about ourselves, forgetting that we are often reacting to ideas about ourselves rather than to consequential events. Failure, criticism, ridicule, and other threats to the ego can upset us even when nothing tangible is really at stake.

In addition to having beliefs regarding who they are and what they are like, people have goals for how they would and would not like to be in the future—what psychologists call future or possible selves.[10] A person may desire to be an attractive, successful, happily married businessperson (all desired future selves) but fear being overweight, unemployed, and alone (undesired future selves). These future selves serve as guides for people's decisions and behaviors. People's choices in life are often affected by their ideas about what they do and do not want to become.

People compare themselves to these imagined future selves and experience various emotions depending on whether they believe they are moving toward or away from them. Progress toward desired future selves evokes positive emotions, whereas lack of progress (and particularly movement toward undesired future selves) evokes negative emotions. People's emotions are not simply reactions to the current state of their lives, but rather the result of believing that their lives are or are not moving toward their desired future selves.[11] One woman wrote to me: "I am currently applying to graduate schools. I sometimes imagine getting into the school of my choice and feeling a great sense of happiness and excitement. But at other times, I imagine not getting into any school and feeling like a complete failure. When I think about not getting into graduate school, I begin to worry and feel depressed. I realize that it is just a thought that has not happened, but I still get real emotional. I don't want to think about the negative side, that I might not get into grad school, but I can't help myself." The self can curse people by conjuring up visions about what they might become in the future, thereby creating unhappiness even when everything is going well at present.

People also judge what happens to them in comparison to other outcomes that might have occurred.[12] The ability to think about one's analogue-I allows people to consider how things might have turned out differently. Thus, people may feel good or bad about their lot depending on whether they think the alternatives that could have happened are better or worse than what actually transpired. People's reactions to events are as much a function of the alternatives that they imagine as of whatever actually happened.

Would you be happier to win second or third place in a competition in which three winners would be recognized (the Olympics, for example)? Most people insist that they'd be happier coming in second than third, but research by Medvec, Madey, and Gilovich suggests that this is not the case. The reason lies in the alternatives that people imagine could have happened to them. In a study of the reactions of silver and bronze medal winners in the Olympics, these researchers found that bronze medal winners (i.e., third-place finishers) are actually happier about the outcome of the competition than silver medal winners (i.e., second-place finishers).[13] Presumably, this is because bronze medalists compare finishing third to the imagined alternative of not winning a medal at all, whereas silver medalists compare their second-place finish to the possibility that, with just a bit more effort or luck, they might have won the gold. Differences in how they construe alternative outcomes lead to different emotional reactions. In some ways, finishing second is more of a threat to one's ego (I'm not the best) than finishing third (Wow, I won a medal).

Imagining Significant Others

William James, the first psychologist to write extensively about the self, observed that a person's sense of identity involves not only the person him- or herself but also his or her house, romantic partner, children, friends, prized belongings, and accomplishments.[14] To see that this is so, we need only observe the strength of people's emotional reactions to the fortunes of their possessions, partners, reputations, families, friends, and bank accounts.

Animals without a self may react emotionally when events have direct and observable implications for their offspring or territory, but we see little evidence that they mentally conjure up thoughts of individuals or things that affect their extended, mental sense of self. It seems doubtful, for example, that other animals worry about the security of their nests or burrows while they are away from home, feel happy thinking about their "loved ones" when they are not physically present, or worry about their offspring once they strike out on their own. In contrast, human beings regularly experience various emotions when they think about these psychological appendages of themselves. Because people construe other individuals and inanimate objects as aspects of their identities, imagining events that involve individuals or belongings that are parts of one's identity can evoke emotions.

Jealousy

Jealousy is a particularly potent emotion that can be caused by imagining people in whom one is personally invested. It is certainly understandable that overt evidence that a relationship is threatened would make people feel jealous, but people may suffer painful bouts of jealousy simply from imagining that the loved one is interested in or spending time with someone else, whether or not that fantasy has any basis in reality.[15] A young woman wrote poignantly about how her self-talk creates jealousy about her boyfriend:

> When Jay tells me about a girl he talked to or played a sport with or had any kind of fun with, I immediately create an image of an extremely beautiful girl with a perfect body and a great personality. I tell myself that Jay was having more fun with this girl than he does with me and that he is attracted to her more than he is to me. I tell myself that I am not fun enough for Jay and that he deserves a prettier girl. Even though I know that none of these insecurities are true, my self can't leave me alone and let me enjoy hearing about Jay's day without getting jealous.

Jealousy sometimes lingers for a very long time because the self can sustain it even in the absence of confirming evidence. The self ruminates and ruminates, even imagining in vivid detail where the loved one might be and what he or she might be doing. Fueled entirely by the self, jealousy may build to the point where the individual reacts as if his or her suspicions were true. Nonhuman animals sometimes show a response that resembles jealousy but only in the immediate presence of the rival. I know of no case in which any other animal went berserk simply from imagining its mate's dalliances.

Pride and Shame in Other People

People also feel good or bad because of the fortunes of other people with whom they are associated. People feel good when those with whom they identify are successful but feel badly when those with whom they identify fail or are disgraced. When we have a relationship with another person, that person's successes and failures often affect us. We want our loved ones to succeed and be happy, so we experience empathic pleasure when our friends, children, and family members succeed, and feel unhappy for them when they fail.

But the picture is more complicated than this. People often react emotionally to other people's successes and failures even when they do not have a personal relationship with them and in no way should feel responsible for their behavior. So, for example, people may be elated or devastated depending on whether their favorite sports team wins or loses.[16] Similarly, people feel good when an alumnus of their high school or college, or a resident of their hometown, becomes famous or is recognized for an achievement, even though they don't know the person personally. They may also feel badly when such an individual is revealed to be a mass murderer, child molester, or terrorist, or is otherwise disgraced. Many citizens of Dallas, Texas, felt ashamed of their city for many years after the assassination of President John F. Kennedy, even though there was no sense in which Dallas or its citizens were responsible for what happened.[17] (Lee Harvey Oswald, the assassin, was from New Orleans.)

These kinds of reactions stem from the fact that people incorporate entities such as organizations, teams, cities, and other individuals into their personal sense of self. Once people have included someone or something in their identity, they react emotionally to what happens to these extensions of themselves. So, for example, sports fans incorporate the team in their identity and treat the team's fortunes as their own. Likewise, residents of a particular city derive part of their identity from where they live, leading them to feel good or bad about what happens to their town. If not for the self, people would not take other people's accomplishments and failures personally.

A second complication arises from the fact that, although they might not want to admit it, people do not always want those with whom they are associated to do well. Abraham Tesser and his colleagues have investigated the ways in which people deal with the successes and failures of people who are close to them. When people close to us succeed in areas in which we have no pretensions, we are happy for them and may even experience a boost in our own self-esteem to be associated with such successful people. However, when people who are close to us succeed in an area that is important to our own identity, we may be threatened by their success and try to reduce its threat to our own ego.[18] For example, we may change the importance we place on the domain in which others outperform us, such as when the less athletically skilled of two brothers decides that sports are not important and puts his energy into other things.[19] More disturbingly, research suggests that we may also reduce the closeness of our relationships with people who outperform us in areas that are important to our identity because another person's successes are less threatening to us the less close our relationship is with them.[20] I will return later to ways in which efforts to maintain one's own self-esteem can affect our relationships with other people. For now, the important point is that our emotional reactions to other people are affected by the ways in which their actions reflect on our images of ourselves.

Evaluations by Other People

Some emotions—such as fear, joy, disgust, and surprise—can be observed within the first few weeks or months of life. Other emotions—such as social anxiety, embarrassment, shame, envy, pride, and guilt—do not appear until somewhat later. These so-called self-conscious emotions do not emerge until later because they cannot occur until children acquire the ability to think about what other people are thinking and, specifically, to think about what other people might be thinking about them.

As we have seen, the ability to put oneself in the minds of other people is a feature of the self. Once children begin to develop self-awareness, usually by two years of age, they begin to think about how other people regard them.[21] At first, they are concerned primarily with their parents' and caregivers' reactions, but later the perceptions of teachers, peers, and others become important. Not only do children start to think about how other people see them, but they also begin to feel good or bad about others' judgments of them. Believing that other people view them favorably results in positive feelings, whereas believing that others view them unfavorably results in negative feelings. From then on, people's emotions are affected by how they think other people regard them, and their concerns with others' evaluations exert a strong influence on how they feel throughout their lives.

Perhaps the most common emotional reaction to imagining how one is perceived by others is social anxiety. Social anxiety involves those familiar feelings of nervousness and awkwardness that sometimes trouble people before and during interpersonal interactions.[22] People may feel socially anxious in job interviews, on first dates, when speaking in front of audiences, or even in casual conversations with strangers. People experience social anxiety when they think that they are unable to make the kinds of impressions on other people that they would like to make.[23] When an actor on stage, an adolescent on a date, or a job applicant in an interview feels nervous, his or her anxiety is fueled by thoughts that others will not perceive and evaluate them as he or she desires. An organism without a self cannot feel socially anxious because it cannot imagine that it is being perceived in a particular way by others, much less worry about the kind of impression it is making.

Similarly, embarrassment requires a self. People become embarrassed when they believe that other people have already formed an undesired impression of them.[24] To feel embarrassed, people must be able to take the perspective of others and imagine the impressions others have formed of them. As with social anxiety, the first signs of embarrassment emerge in young children at about the same age as self-awareness. Like other negative emotions, embarrassment serves a useful function by alerting us when our social image may have sustained damage and motivating us to try to repair it.[25] Yet the ability to think about how one is perceived by others leads people to experience acute pangs of embarrassment and to worry more about their social images than necessary. Because of the bias toward false alarms, people tend to be embarrassed more often than is really warranted. Furthermore, many people agonize over embarrassing events even long after they are over. As one individual told me: "Later, I torture myself thinking about what a fool I made of myself. I think about how I could have acted cooler or smarter or said something wittier and not so humiliating. I beat myself up thinking that everyone else is thinking the same way about what happened when, in reality, they have probably forgotten about it and moved on." When the self replays these kinds of incidents in our minds, we may re-experience the unpleasant feelings.

Like many of their perceptions of the world, people's assumptions about how other people regard them are affected by their own self-images. People who do not view themselves favorably are likely to assume that other people also do not find them desirable. Those with a positive self-image take for granted that others like and accept them unless specific events occur to suggest otherwise. As a result, people who have low self-esteem are more prone to experience emotions such as social anxiety and embarrassment than people with high self-esteem because they are more likely to conclude that others form undesired impressions of them.[26] These reactions are caused not only by what actually happens in social interaction but also by people's own views of themselves.

Attributions and Emotion

Thus far, we have seen that people contribute to their own emotional lives by imagining things that may happen to them, interpreting events as threats to their egos, thinking about their relationships with other people, and worrying about how other people perceive them. Once emotions arise, the self contributes to emotional experience in yet another way.

People often analyze their emotional experiences, trying to understand both why they feel certain emotions (Why did I become so angry? Why am I so afraid of applying for a new job?) and why emotion-inducing events occurred in the first place (Why did I do so poorly on this examination? Why did my partner leave me?). One of the most important psychological discoveries of the 1970s was that the attributions that people make for emotion-producing events have a profound effect on their reactions to those events.[27] Contrary to the layperson's view that emotions are caused directly by certain situations and stimuli in the real world, research shows that people's interpretations and attributions play an important role. The same situation can cause two dramatically different emotional reactions depending on how the person interprets it. Concluding, for example, that I wasn't hired for a job because I'm incompetent will create different emotions from concluding that I wasn't hired because the employer was threatened by my high degree of competence and charisma. Our ability to talk to ourselves about what happens to us plays an important role in our emotional lives.

Depression

Much of the evidence of the role that self-attributions play in emotion comes from research on depression. Depression has many causes, some of which are clearly biological, yet the self is often implicated in its onset and progression. How people think about themselves and their lives has a strong influence on whether they will become depressed and, if so, how much difficulty they will have pulling out of it.

Researchers have identified a *depressogenic* way of thinking about bad events that seems to predispose people to depression.[28] People with a depressogenic explanatory style generally believe that bad things that happen to them are their fault and that they consistently behave in ways that create problems for themselves. A typical depressogenic response to a negative event is "I always mess everything up." It is easy to see why a person who thinks about his or her life in this way would be susceptible to depression. This pattern involves not only a pessimistic view of the future but also the belief that one is personally responsible for the bad things that happen.

Many studies have demonstrated a relationship between having a depressogenic explanatory style and depression. People who make these kinds of personal attributions for negative events are more likely to become depressed when undesirable events occur, take longer to pull out of depressive episodes, and are more likely to relapse in the future. For example, students become more depressed after doing poorly on exams if they have a general tendency to attribute bad events to themselves.[29] Other studies using children, prisoners, and women after childbirth likewise show that people's explanations for negative events are related to whether they cope well with negative events or become depressed.[30]

Even when people do not have a chronically depressogenic view of life, the self-attributions that they make for specific events may promote depression in particular instances. Following a failure, trauma, or other undesirable event, people may engage in *behavioral self-blame*, in which they attribute the event to a behavioral mistake or miscalculation on their part, they may engage in *characterological self-blame* in which they attribute the event to some relatively unchangeable aspect of themselves, or they may blame external factors such as other people or society at large. For example, a woman who was raped on a date might conclude that she made an unwise decision to go out with this particular man (an attribution to her behavior); that she is an undiscerning, stupid person who chronically makes bad decisions (an attribution to her character), or that the man or society is principally to blame (an external attribution).

Research shows that the kinds of attributions that people make for bad events predict how they react to those events. One study showed, for example, that people who engage in characterological self-blame for negative events tend to become more depressed afterwards than people who engage in behavioral self-blame.[31] It is often more upsetting to think that a negative event was the result of some unchangeable aspect of one's personality than to conclude that it was an isolated event brought on by a one-time behavioral miscalculation. Other research has shown that, although the degree to which a person blames him- or herself (either characterologically or behaviorally) may predict depression following a negative event, the degree to which a person blames society does not.[32] Clearly, how people think about their role in their problems affects how they cope with them.

Guilt and Shame

People's attributions also determine how they feel about harmful and immoral things that they do. If I attribute accidentally running over your dog to the fact that it darted into the street too quickly for me to stop my car, I may be quite sorry but feel little self-recrimination. If, on the other hand, I think that I hit your dog because I was not being sufficiently careful or I was driving too fast or I am simply an incompetent driver, I may feel very bad about it. The same harmful event may produce different emotional reactions depending on how people talk to themselves about what they have done.

The emotions of guilt and shame have been the center of a great deal of controversy and confusion among psychologists for many years. Writers have disagreed regarding the differences between guilt and shame, and some have argued that they are two labels for the same emotional experience. Recently, however, June Tangney and her colleagues have offered compelling evidence showing that the primary difference between guilt and shame is whether the individual focuses on the negative action or on what it says about him or her as a person.[33] In guilt, the person evaluates a particular action negatively, feels badly for the harm that he or she has caused, and experiences primarily regret. In shame, the person evaluates him- or herself negatively for having done the bad deed and feels primarily ashamed rather than remorseful. In essence, behavioral self-blame for a harmful or immoral action leads to guilt, whereas characterological self-blame for a harmful or immoral action leads to shame. Again, how people talk to themselves about their behavior makes a difference. The same action (for example, cheating on a test) may evoke either guilt or shame depending on whether the person focuses on the behavior (I did a bad thing) or on his or her character (I am a bad person).

This is not a minor distinction because the emotional and behavioral effects of guilt and shame differ greatly. Tangney's research shows that when people feel guilty, they are remorseful and try to undo the damage they have caused by apologizing or reparation.[34] Their focus is on those they have hurt and on constructive solutions to the problem they have created. When people feel shame, however, they feel dejected and worthless, and focus on their own negative feelings and personal predicament rather than the harm they have caused. Their high level of self-focus interferes with feeling empathic toward those they have hurt, and they typically want to shrink away and feel better about themselves rather than come forward to repair the harm they have done. The difference in these two reactions to doing harm depends critically on how people talk to themselves about what has happened.

Making Matters Worse

People make attributions to explain not only the events that cause their emotions but also their reactions to those events. That is, they ask not only why the event occurred but also why they reacted to it as they did. Imagine two people who experience the same emotional reaction to the same traumatic situation. One individual views his or her reaction as a normal response to such a devastating experience, but the other person thinks that his or her reaction indicates a poor ability to cope with stressful events. The second individual's interpretation of the emotion may fuel other emotional reactions such as frustration (What's wrong with me that I can't cope better than this?) or shame (I'm a loser who's incapable of dealing with life). This secondary emotional reaction is caused solely by how the person talks to him- or herself about his or her primary emotional reaction to the situation.

Perhaps the clearest case of this effect occurs when people make a characterological attribution for being anxious (I feel nervous because I'm a neurotic, anxiety-prone person), which may lead them to worry about their "anxiety problem" and cause even more anxiety. In the same way, people can become increasingly depressed about being depressed, angry about always losing their temper, or even happy about being a joyful person. These are not automatic responses to particular events but rather the result of how people think about themselves and the reasons for their reactions.

The fact that people may react emotionally to their emotions means that problems that are fueled by those emotions may get worse depending on how people think about them.[35] When people have problems that are exacerbated by emotions, certain attributions may intensify or prolong the problem because they increase those emotions even further. A good example involves insomnia. We discussed earlier (chapter 2) that insomnia is often caused by intrusive self-rumination. Whatever its cause in a specific instance, one of the best ways to make insomnia worse is to worry about not being able to sleep. Worry brings with it anxious arousal that interferes with sleep even further. Making certain attributions for insomnia may create anxiety (I'm a neurotic mess! I'm so frustrated about being an insomniac! What's wrong with me? Am I going insane?), thereby making it even less likely that the person will fall asleep.

Given that insomnia can be prolonged by this route when people attribute sleeplessness to personal problems or weaknesses, we might be able to reduce it by getting insomniacs to think about their sleeplessness in less upsetting ways. In a study that tested this possibility, researchers randomly assigned chronic insomniacs to one of three experimental conditions.[36] One group received a pill—actually an inert placebo—that they were told would increase their physiological arousal and, thus, make it difficult for them to fall asleep that night. The researchers hoped that, by giving them a nonthreatening explanation for being unable to sleep (It's the pill, not my insomnia problem), participants in this group would not work themselves into an aroused state fretting about their sleeplessness and, thus, would fall asleep more quickly. The participants in a second experimental condition were told that, although their arousal levels were somewhat higher than average, they didn't need to worry because they were still within the normal range. Researchers suspected that this information would also reduce the degree to which participants would ruminate about their sleeplessness, lower their anxiety, and allow them to sleep. The third condition in the study consisted of a control group of participants who simply went to bed as usual with no new attribution or information about their sleeplessness. As expected, participants in the first two conditions fell asleep significantly faster than those in the control condition. Modifying people's self-attributions, either by getting them to attribute their problem to a nonthreatening cause (the pill) or by assuring them that they are normal, reduced anxious arousal and the degree to which insomniacs' self-ruminations kept them awake.

Any problem that is exacerbated by arousal may be fueled by self-attributions that increase the person's anxiety. Stuttering, for example, increases when people are anxious. Most people speak less fluently when they are nervous or upset than they do otherwise. Imagine, however, what might happen if a person begins to worry a great deal about stuttering. The anxiety may, in fact, increase stuttering, creating greater anxiety and even more stuttering in an escalating cycle. Even people who do not normally stutter begin to speak less fluently after they are told that they seem to display an unusual number of speech disfluencies.[37] When people attribute their stuttering to a chronic personal problem, their attributions may create a self-fulfilling prophecy.

Likewise, sexual impotence is often created by anxiety, fueled by the man's fears that he will not perform adequately in bed. If, after an episode of impotence, a man begins to question his sexual ability and worry about it happening again, he may increase the likelihood that he will be impotent the next time he is in a sexual encounter.[38] Again, the problem is self-created by how he thinks to himself about his "problem."

Changing the Self, Changing Emotion

The idea that the self can create, maintain, and exacerbate unpleasant emotions is not at all new. In fact, the crux of this idea can be traced to philosophers in India and China over 2,000 years ago. Taoist and Buddhist sages realized that a great deal of human suffering could be traced directly to the self.[39] What is new is the depth of our understanding about the relationship between self-talk and emotion. Many of the advances in the science of emotion in the past few decades have involved identifying the nature of the self-thoughts that create and sustain emotion.

Along with greater understanding of how the self creates emotions have come psychological treatments and programs designed to change how people think about themselves. For the past 40 years, clinical and counseling psychologists have explored ways of reducing problematic emotions by helping clients modify their self-thoughts. There is now a wide array of effective treatments that focus on restructuring people's attributions and self-beliefs.[40] All of these approaches are based on the idea that most emotions are generated and maintained by how people talk to themselves, and that by modifying people's self-talk we can change their emotions. Even without therapy, people can learn that their unpleasant emotions—their anger, depression, anxiety, envy, jealousy, and shame, for example—are largely the result of how they talk to themselves.

Of course, sometimes it is neither possible nor desirable to change one's thoughts in ways that promote more pleasant emotions. Presumably, a person experiencing normal grief after the death of a loved one would not wish to try to convince himself, even if he could, that he really doesn't care that the loved one has died. However, when people's emotions are based on faulty or catastrophic thinking, particularly troublesome, or overly prolonged, the best strategy is often to challenge the self-thoughts that are keeping the emotion in place.

5 ∷
When Selves Collide

There is a law that man should love his neighbor as himself. In a few hundred years it should be as natural to mankind as breathing or the upright gait; but if he does not learn it he must perish.

—ALFRED ADLER

On the day that I began writing this chapter, 55 police officers were injured in Belfast, Ireland, trying to quell yet another outbreak of violence between Catholics and Protestants, including one who was attacked by a man with a pickaxe. Since the mid-1960s, approximately 4,000 people have been killed and 36,000 injured in what the residents of Northern Ireland, with considerable understatement, call "the Troubles." The attacks, bombings, and assassinations that continue to fracture the Irish peace had their roots during the reign of Henry VIII, when Catholic Ireland came under the rule of Protestant England. The Catholics revolted against their Protestant landlords on several occasions over the years, with a particularly nasty episode of violence after Protestant settlers streamed into the northern part of the country in the 1600s. In the Catholic uprising, rebels killed or expelled several thousand Protestants, including a massacre of 80 Protestant men, women, and children at Portadown. The Protestants regained control of Ireland when William of Orange, a Protestant, defeated King James II, a Catholic, at the Battle of the Boyne. Predictably, laws were then enacted that favored Protestants and disadvantaged Catholics. In 1920, Ireland was split into two separate political units—the Republic of Ireland and Northern Ireland, each of which elected its own Parliament and conducted its own internal affairs. However, the partitioning of Ireland did little to relieve the mistrust and violence between the groups. Catholics and Protestants remained segregated, not only by neighborhoods but also in workplaces, schools, and most social activities.[1] And, every so often, the violence that began hundreds of years ago rears its ugly head once again.

Social conflicts have many historical, political, economic, and psychological causes. Whether we are talking about Catholics and Protestants in Northern Ireland, Israelis and Palestinians in the West Bank, rival gangs in Los Angeles, blacks and whites in many American cities, or the American war against terrorists, the mistrust and animosity that characterize social conflicts can rarely be traced to a single cause. Even so, the self plays an important role in creating and sustaining frictions between groups. Often, people do not fight with one another because something vitally important is at stake but, rather, because something has threatened their identities and egos. In fact, sometimes people fight simply because they see themselves as members of groups that are opposed to one another. Although the roots of such conflicts may lie deep in the past, the groups continue to clash simply because their members regard themselves as rivals.

Previous chapters have focused primarily on ways in which the self creates difficulties for the individual. However, the self can also curse people's interpersonal relationships, leading to mistrust, disagreement, conflict, and aggression that hurt other people as well.

Personal Distinctiveness

The appearance of self-awareness among our prehistoric ancestors dramatically changed how human beings related to one another. Prior to the emergence of self-awareness, people could not consciously distinguish between themselves and others. They couldn't think about themselves and who they were or about how they were similar to or different from other people. Nor could they think about the groups to which they belonged or about the relationships between their own and other groups.

Of course, every sentient organism, even those without a capacity for self-reflection, can subjectively distinguish its own body from its environment.[2] Without a basic ability to distinguish itself from the world through proprioception (what some have called the "sensory" or "ecological self"), an animal might be as likely to eat its paw or tail as its actual food. In fact, self-less animals sometimes make mistakes in this regard. When a dog chases its own tail or a bird struts before its own reflection in a mirror, one gets the impression that the animal cannot distinguish itself from other features of its environment. In fact, not all human beings can do this, either. Infants before the age of about 18 months do not appear able to recognize or conceptualize themselves,[3] and people with certain disorders of the nervous system, including certain kinds of brain damage and some varieties of schizophrenia, lose the ability to distinguish themselves from other people.[4]

Of course, most people know that they are distinct individuals. Furthermore, with their high powers of abstraction and conceptual thought, people can think about the ways in which they are similar to and different from others. It is not just that I know that I am me and that you are you, but I can articulate how we are different from one another. Each person has a complex set of interrelated ideas of what he or she is like. If I ask you to describe yourself, you will likely provide a description of your self-concept—attributes that define who you are, including your physical characteristics (such as your sex, race, height, or hair color), personal and psychological attributes (conscientious, intelligent, impatient), and social roles and relationships (student, parent, wife, Catholic).

Once formed, people's self-concepts strongly influence their behavior.[5] For example, when faced with decisions—of which job to take, who to ask out on a date, or whether to undertake a risky venture—people's choices are greatly affected by how they perceive themselves. Beliefs about their abilities, knowledge, personality, appearance, preferences, and other characteristics make certain choices seem more sensible than others. A man is more likely to dive off a high cliff if he regards himself as a good rather than a poor swimmer, and more likely to ask an attractive woman for a date if he thinks that he, too, is attractive. Even if his beliefs about himself are distorted or inaccurate, his self-concept will influence his decisions. In many ways, people's course in life is affected, both for better and for worse, by how they see themselves.

One aspect of people's self-concepts involves the groups and social categories to which they belong. People define themselves, in part, by their relationships to other people and the larger social world. Their sex, nationality, ethnicity, religious orientation, occupation, and group memberships help to define who they are. Furthermore, people classify other individuals into these kinds of social categories and thereby see themselves as similar to certain people but different from other people.[6]

Once people classify themselves and others into abstract social categories, they use these categories as a basis for perceiving and interacting with other people. We structure much of our social world in terms of groupings of people—of social categories—rather than in terms of the individual people themselves. Identifying herself as a Catholic, a resident of Northern Ireland may immediately react differently to a stranger who is a Protestant than to one who is a Catholic. In doing so, she is reacting not to the person per se but rather to her mental categorization of that person into a group that is somehow different from hers. Similarly, a man may react differently to an individual with white than black skin, or treat men and women differently. In each case, his interactions are influenced by how he categorizes himself (and the other person) rather than by relevant attributes of those with whom he interacts. People's tendency to think about themselves and others in terms of social categories channels the way they perceive and relate to one another.

Identities in Conflict

Seeing groups battle one another across racial, ethnic, religious, and national lines may lead us to assume that conflicts are necessarily rooted in ideological, political, or practical issues. In fact, however, much more is involved. As one observer wrote about the conflict in Ireland (and it could be said about virtually any social conflict), "anyone who studies the Ulster conflict must be struck by the intensity of the feelings. It seems to go beyond what is required by a rational defense of the divergent interests which undoubtedly exist." The members of antagonistic groups rarely fight because they dislike one another on a personal level. In fact, they usually don't even know one another personally! Rather, they are fight simply because they conceptualize themselves as members of opposing groups.

Behavioral scientists have been surprised to discover how little it takes for conflicts to arise between different groups. Evidence suggests that the mere existence of two groups is often all that's needed to create favoritism toward one's own group and animosity toward the other group. In the early 1970s, Henri Tajfel and his colleagues introduced the Minimal Group Paradigm to study the conditions under which members of one group would discriminate against the members of another group.[7] Their initial plan was to devise laboratory groups that were so artificial that their members would not show the characteristic tendencies toward ingroup favoritism and outgroup hostility seen in real groups. With these minimal groups as a baseline, the researchers could then study the factors that lead groups to come into conflict with one another.

Unfortunately, the researchers immediately hit a snag: They found it quite difficult to create a group that was so artificial and minimal that its members did not show ingroup favoritism. No matter how trivial the basis on which members were assigned to their respective groups, the members of the two groups began to favor their own group and discriminate against the outgroup. In studies using the minimal group paradigm, participants are assigned to one group or another on the basis of bogus scores or an absurd criterion. For example, based on their ratings of abstract art, research participants may be told that they are among participants who favored the work of Paul Klee over Wassily Kandinsky, or among those who overestimated rather than underestimated the number of dots in a complex array. In other studies, participants are sometimes assigned to one of two groups completely at random, with the flip of a coin.

Given how they were assigned to groups, participants in these studies have no reason whatsoever to think that the members of their own group (people who like the work of Klee vs. Kandinsky, over- or underestimate dots, or are assigned to their group at random) are in any sense better than the members of the other group. Yet, no matter how trivial the basis of the distinction between "us" and "them," research participants almost always show ingroup favoritism.[8] Despite the fact that the assignment of members to groups is trivial or random, members of these minimal groups begin to perceive their group as "better" than the other group. They like the members of their group better than members of the other group. They rate their own group's members more positively (even if they have had no personal contact with them) and trust the members of their group more than members of other groups (typically viewing outgroup members as inherently untrustworthy). They also favor their own groups when decisions must be made, such as deciding how to divide money or valuable points between the two groups.[9]

You might imagine that these kinds of ingroup–outgroup distinctions would at least require that members work together as a group but, in fact, people display the ingroup bias even if they have never met one another and don't know who the other members of their group are! All that is required to create distinctions between groups is for people to perceive themselves to be a member of a group! Of course, in real life, this minimal intergroup conflict is often fueled by historic, economic, or political issues, as in Northern Ireland or Israel. But the fact that stereotyping, distrust, and animosity can emerge even without practical outcomes at stake may explain why real-world conflicts, which often involve important issues as well, are often so intractable.

The social identity perspective in social psychology focuses on how people incorporate their group memberships into their self-identities and the ways in which people's identities, once formed, influence their behavior toward others. Social identity theory assumes that people put themselves, as well as other people, into social categories in order to make sense of and navigate the social world.[10] People use social categories like black, white, straight, gay, Christian, Buddhist, student, and dropout because these categories are sometimes useful for understanding other people. If we can assign a person to a category, we feel that we know something about that person and, thus, have at least a minimal basis for responding to him or her. We feel that we have learned something about a person, for example, from knowing that she is a gay Buddhist student rather than a straight Christian dropout.

Categorizing people into groups is essential for making sense of the world. We would have a great deal of difficulty dealing with other people if we didn't put at least some of them into categories, thereby giving us a heuristic for interacting with them. If we could not rely on information about a person's group memberships and social categories, we would have to start from scratch each time we met a new person, building our understanding of each person as a unique individual piece by piece. As desirable and egalitarian as it may sound to treat each person uniquely, we don't have the time or mental resources to process information about every person we meet on a person-by-person basis. Anyway, for many purposes, knowing about a person's social categories—that a man you just met is a homeless person or a bank president or a member of the Ku Klux Klan—may provide some useful information, at least for starters.

Problems arise not because people categorize one another into groups but because they are inclined to assume that the categories to which they belong are better than the categories to which they don't belong.[11] We saw in chapter 3 that people egotistically assume that they and the people associated with them are, on average, better than other people, and this bias extends to the groups to which they belong as well. This tendency to overvalue one's own groups leads most people to think that their own race, religion, country, and assorted groups are better than most, if not all, other races, religions, countries, and groups.

Maintaining an embellished view of one's own group typically does not require self-deception as much as selective judgments. People have a great deal of latitude in how they compare their groups to others. As a result, they can almost always make comparisons that will reflect positively on themselves. College students might compare their college not to all colleges in the country but rather to other colleges of a particular size or to other colleges of a particular size in their immediate geographical region. By selectively choosing the groups to whom they compare, people can stack the deck in ways that allow them to believe that their group is better than most, if not all other relevant groups.

Even when another group is undeniably "better" in some sense, people nonetheless can selectively focus on dimensions that allow them to evaluate their own group favorably. For example, people who live in developing nations might admit that their countries do not measure up to the United States in terms of economic and technological progress, yet they regard their country as morally superior. Students at a small, nondescript college might acknowledge that a nearby state university has a more prestigious faculty and better athletic teams, but still view their college as superior because of its friendly atmosphere and small class sizes. There is almost always a way for a group to construe itself as better than other comparable groups.

Walking through life thinking that our own groups are better than other groups has important ramifications. Once people categorize themselves as a member of a particular group or category, they then react differently to members of their group than to members of other groups. And, as we saw, simply conceptualizing oneself as a member of a particular group is sufficient to produce the effect. It is a short step from seeing oneself as a member of a particular group to favoring one's own group over other groups and interpreting events in a way that shines favorably on one's group. If you are Protestant or Catholic, you may have found yourself taking your own group's side as you read about the conflict in Northern Ireland that opened this chapter.

A great deal of research has shown that people from different groups interpret the same events differently, with members of both groups putting a self-serving spin on the evidence. In one of the earliest demonstrations of this effect, researchers had Princeton and Dartmouth supporters watch a film of a particularly rough football game between the two schools. Supporters of each side saw the other team as the provocateur of the on-field aggression and their own team as responding in a justified, measured way to the flagrant misbehaviors of the other. It was if the Dartmouth and Princeton fans were watching different games.[12] Other research has shown that, although voters generally perceive media coverage of presidential candidates to be fair, those who perceive the coverage to be biased believe that it is biased against their favored candidate.[13] In another study, pro-Israeli and pro-Arab students watched the same six news segments about conflict in the Middle East and were asked to rate the fairness of the reports. The pro-Israeli students thought that the news coverage was biased in favor of the Arabs and the pro-Arab students thought it was biased in favor of Israel.[14] Clearly, once people identify with different sides in a conflict, they interpret precisely the same events in radically different ways.

Defining oneself in terms of one's membership in a social category or group has other effects, as well. Once people socially categorize themselves, they perceive that they are more similar to the members of their own group than they are to members of other groups. Of course, members of a particular group may, in fact, be similar. Birds of a feather do tend to flock together. Yet research shows that people overestimate the similarities between themselves and other members of their group while overestimating the differences (and underestimating the similarities) between themselves and members of other groups.[15] To say it differently, you are probably less similar to the other members of your groups than you assume, as well as more similar to the members of rival groups. This bias can lead people to perceive greater distance between themselves and others than is, in fact, the case. Such contrasts can further fuel distrust, discrimination, and conflict.

Viewed from the perspective of social identity theory, a great deal of prejudice, discrimination, and conflict is based in the processes by which people think of themselves as social entities.[16] As people develop their concept of who they are, part of their self-definition includes the social groups and categories to which they belong. Once they have included these categories in their definitions of themselves, it is difficult, if not impossible, for them to avoid viewing and treating their own groups more benignly than other groups.

In one of the best-known social psychological studies of all times, Muzafer Sherif and his colleagues recruited a group of boys of roughly the same age, educational level, and social background to attend a summer camp at Robbers Cave State Park.[17] The boys were assigned to one of two groups (called the Rattlers and the Eagles), which were kept separated for one week to allow the boys to hike, camp, swim, and play sports only with members of their own group. As each group realized that another group was also staying at the camp, suspicion and rivalry began to develop. The perceptions of the group members showed the classic pattern. When asked to describe the members of the two groups, the boys rated the other group more negatively than their own. They also used different standards to judge the actions of the two groups. Behaviors that were regarded as harmless teasing when done by one's own group were viewed as hostile attacks when done by the other. When the researchers then allowed the groups to meet and compete, they reacted toward one another first with coolness, then with insults and open hostility. The camp staff had to intervene to prevent the boys from injuring one another.

The conflict at Robbers Cave arose purely from the fact that some of the boys identified themselves as Eagles and some of the boys identified themselves as Rattlers. There was really no reason for them to dislike or discriminate against one another except for the fact that they belonged to different groups. Given how easily conflict and aggression arose between two virtually identical groups of adolescent boys, is it any wonder that racial, ethnic, and national groups often have so much difficulty getting along?

Some scientists have argued that this tendency to distinguish members of one's own group from outsiders was adaptive in an evolutionary sense.[18] In the march of human evolution, people who were suspicious of other groups probably fared better than those who did not. Given the small number of people on earth at the time, it was probably rare for our prehistoric ancestors to stumble across members of other groups. When members of strange groups were encountered, there was probably no good reason to form social relationships with them. In fact, it was probably not unreasonable to be suspicious of them. Unfortunately, these tendencies that protected the safety of our prehistoric ancestors carry many liabilities in the modern world in which we necessarily interact with members of many diverse groups. Today, people interact with a broad variety of people of different races, ethnic groups, religions, and nationalities, and it is largely in everyone's best interests to get along, if not forge close and cooperative relationships. Constructing a social identity in which we exaggerate the differences between our own and other groups, then cling to the notion that our groups are consistently better than theirs, is a sure path to unnecessary suspicion, prejudice, and conflict.

We distinguish between ourselves and other people on the basis of a virtually endless number of dimensions. However, some such distinctions are more widespread and, thus, problematic than others. We can glimpse which dimensions these are by looking at the personal characteristics that are protected by federal law. Currently, equal opportunity laws in the United States prohibit discrimination based on national origin (including birthplace, ancestry, culture, and language), race, color, religion, disability, sex, and familial status (whether one is single, married, or divorced, for example). Apparently, these are some of the primary categories by which people distinguish themselves from others and, thus, deal inequitably with those who belong to other categories. People don't forge group identities based on eye color, food preference, or shoe size, so we don't need federal laws to protect people against unfair discrimination in these areas. (Of course, there are other characteristics, such as sexual orientation, on which people do unfairly discriminate against others, but these are not yet widely protected under the law.)

What people fail to appreciate is the degree to which the categories they use to distinguish themselves from other people are generally irrelevant and arbitrary. Many people act as if having a different nationality, race, sex, or religion automatically qualifies other people to be viewed and treated differently. Yet the differences typically reside more in our heads than in reality. If we forbade an Irish Catholic and an Irish Protestant to talk about religion and politics, would they nonetheless not find many similarities in their personal values, interests, priorities, and goals? Does not a bigoted white person share innumerable universal human concerns with the black person he or she hates? After all, all human beings want mostly the same things—to live in peace and freedom, protect one's family, have financial security, and so on. We are far more similar as human beings than we are different as members of diverse nationalities, races, religions, sexes, and so on. Yet, the self parses up the social world into "us" and "them" so easily that we think that the differences between us and members of other groups are inherently there rather than creations of our own mental framework. The self turns objectively trivial differences into giant chasms of separation.

Viewing distrust, prejudice, and discrimination as stemming partly from the way people define themselves suggests a possible solution. If hostility between groups arises, at least in part, because people categorize themselves as members of different groups, then perhaps we can reverse the process by having members of opposing groups see themselves as members of a larger, superordinate unit. Instead of "us" versus "them," perhaps we can get members of both groups to see themselves as "we." Such an approach worked to reduce the conflict between the Eagles and the Rattlers. In the Robbers Cave study, conflicts between the groups all but disappeared once the boys worked together on mutual tasks, such as finding a broken water line at the camp, thereby seeing themselves as sharing a common identity.[19]

Sam Gaertner and John Dovidio, two experts in the psychology of prejudice, developed this idea in their Common Ingroup Identity Model.[20] This model suggests that changing people's categorization of ingroups versus outgroups to a common identity that includes both groups will lead them to treat former outgroup members as members of their own group. Several years of research has supported the model. In some experiments, a white participant has interacted with a black individual after being led to view the two of them as either members of the same group or as separate individuals. Other studies have made black and white participants categorize themselves as members of the same group by stressing their shared university affiliation or nationality as Americans. In these studies, blacks and whites evaluate one another more favorably when they are led to think about their common group identity. Getting people to view themselves and members of other groups as members of a larger common group produces more positive attitudes, increases trust and openness, and leads former rivals to treat each other more equally and fairly.[21] As even its proponents admit, the Common Ingroup Identity Model is not a panacea for intergroup rivalries and hostilities. Yet, because it capitalizes on the self's natural tendency to regard members of one's own group favorably, it shows more promise than many alternative approaches.

Personal Relationships

In perhaps the first discussion of the self by a psychologist, William James observed that people's identities include not only things that are unambiguously part of them—such as their personal body and mental states—but also outer aspects of their lives such as their family, friends, ancestors, possessions, jobs, accomplishments, reputations, and bank accounts.[22] You can see that you regard these things as part of "you" by thinking about how you react when a loved one is mistreated or you lose a prized possession or somebody disparages your heritage, occupation, or social status. Threats to these appendages of yourself evoke much the same response as direct attacks on you. You become upset or angry, suggesting that you are treating these external aspects of your life situation as if they were actually you. In the same way, you may feel as proud of what your loved ones accomplish as of your own successes, happy about finding a lost possession, and pleased when someone compliments your new car or shirt. Strictly speaking, none of these things is really you, yet you act as if they are because you have incorporated them into your sense of self. External things, including other people, can be as much a part of your identity as your own body, thoughts, and feelings.

People's most important social relationships involve those whom they have incorporated into their self-concept.[23] Family members, best friends, and romantic partners are incorporated the most; co-workers, team members, and neighbors somewhat less; and mere acquaintances and strangers the least. How people relate to one another depends markedly on the degree to which they include each other in their sense of self. People treat others who encompass part of themselves differently from those who are not seen as part of the self.

Arthur Aron and his colleagues have studied the social and psychological implications of incorporating other people into one's sense of self. To measure the degree to which people include another individual as part of themselves, the researchers devised a simple measure that consists of seven Venn diagrams that overlap to varying degrees. People are asked to indicate which diagram best describes their relationship with a particular other individual.[24] Pick a person in your own life—a partner, friend, or relative, for example—and decide which of the diagrams in figure 5.1 best reflects the nature of your relationship with him or her.

According to Aron's research, which diagram you select indicates the degree to which you have incorporated that particular person into your sense of self. No incorporation of the other person (as in the first pair of nonoverlapping circles) typically means that you have no concern whatsoever for the other person. The other person is irrelevant to your sense of self. At the other extreme (#7), you view the other person as an integral part of who you are.

Compassion requires that we feel at least some connection to other people. When people see themselves as totally distinct from another person, then the other person's welfare is none of their concern. We are unlikely to feel anything whatsoever for an individual who was not incorporated into our sense of self. Given that most people feel a certain amount

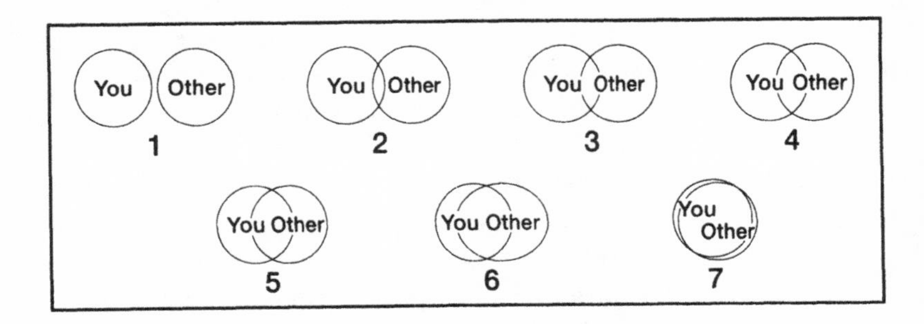

FIGURE 5.1.
Inclusion of Other in the Self Scale.

of empathy and concern for even complete strangers, particularly those in need, it seems that most people's selves incorporate other people, even those they do not know, just a little. The fact that I am affected when I see starving children on television or feel sad for a murder victim's family suggests that I must have incorporated them into my self at least a little (as in fig. 5.1, #2 or #3). However, the fact that I am not as troubled by their plights as I would be if my own children were starving or someone in my own family were murdered suggests that I do not incorporate strangers into my sense of self as much as my own family and friends.

Research shows that people's ratings on this Inclusion of Other in the Self Scale predict the nature of their closest personal relationships. For example, the amount of overlap between the circles correlates with the amount of satisfaction, commitment, and investment that people feel toward their romantic relationships, suggesting that including another person in one's sense of self promotes closeness.[25] Overlap also relates to the number of first-person plural pronouns (such as "we" and "us") that people use when talking about their relationships.[26] Apparently, the more a person incorporates another into the self, the more he or she thinks of the relationship as a single unit rather than as two individuals. People are also more likely to behave selflessly with people with whom they overlap more. Perhaps most impressively, the amount of overlap also predicts how long the relationship will last into the future.[27] More generally, our own research suggests that the degree to which people tend to incorporate others into their selves predicts how kind and forgiving they are toward other people.[28]

By itself, this research might imply that incorporating other people into one's sense of self is a good thing that fosters happy relationships and kindness. But the issue is more complicated. Relational problems can also arise from incorporating other people into one's sense of self too much. A high degree of interdependency (as in fig. 5.1, #6 and #7) indicates that one person's sense of self is based almost entirely on another person. When people have merged their identity with that of another person, they feel that they truly can't live without the other. When their own identity is entirely wrapped up in another person (#7), people literally feel that they would be nothing without them and, from the standpoint of identity, they are right. As a result, they are chronically and heavily invested in the other person's life.

An extreme case of incorporating another person too deeply into one's identity can be seen in cases of relational obsessions such as stalking.[29] A person who makes repeated unwanted intrusions upon another's time and privacy has incorporated the target of his or her attention into his or her sense of self to an inappropriate degree. In less extreme cases, incorporating another person too deeply into one's identity is associated with extreme and unhealthy dependency on the other person.

When we incorporate other people into our sense of self, we infuse those individuals with power to affect how we feel about ourselves. After we perceive a connection between ourselves and another person, we are no longer indifferent to what they do or what happens to them.[30] Most obviously, when people with whom we are linked behave badly, we are implicated by association. The parent struggling with the screaming child in public, the teenager whose father is arrested for embezzlement, and the person whose inebriated spouse vomits at the party—each suffers a threat to his or her own ego and public image at the hands of someone who is symbolically part of the individual. People's reactions to situations such as these are particularly strong because they have incorporated the person into their sense of self. Thus, what happens to the other person is experienced quite personally, almost as if it were happening to oneself. Although they react strongly to their own screaming child, arrested father, or drunken spouse, seeing someone else's misbehaving child, father, or spouse may evoke little response.

That the misfortunes of people we have incorporated into our sense of self affect us personally is probably not surprising. Less obvious is the fact that people's egos can also be threatened when people close to them are successful. Over the past 20 years, Abraham Tesser and his colleagues have studied how people react to the fortunes of people who are close to them. The premise of Tesser's Self-Evaluation Maintenance Theory is that people feel threatened when someone who is close to them outperforms them on a dimension that is important to their own self-identity.[31] Of course, we want our friends, partners, and spouses to do well in life, but mostly as long as they don't outshine us in areas that are important to our own identity. So, for example, a man who doesn't play tennis might be quite proud when his brother wins a major tennis tournament. However, a man for whom tennis-playing ability is important to his self-concept may be ambivalent or even resentful about his brother's success on the tennis court. No matter how gracious his compliments or how much he tries not to feel bad, the man will likely have a negative response to his brother's success.

People do several things to avoid having those who are close to them threaten their egos. First, research suggests that people gravitate toward those who excel in areas that are not central to their own identity.[32] The implications are clear: people's choices of friends and romantic partners are influenced, in part, by their own egoistic desires to maintain positive images of themselves in their own minds. We may like people who share our interests, yet if those interests are central to our own self-concepts, we may prefer not to be friends or lovers with people who outperform us in those areas.

Second, romantic couples may implicitly negotiate domains of expertise so that they do not tread on one another's areas and egos.[33] If they are both in the same profession, they may drift into different subspecialties so that direct comparisons between them are difficult. In other cases, they may do all of their professional activities together so that their individual contributions cannot be contrasted and compared. Couples who go into business together may be using this tactic. In some cases, one partner may decide to abandon the activity and its corresponding identity because of the implicit competition that exists. However they resolve the dilemma, couples must figure out how they can maintain their relationship and protect one another's self-esteem even as both pursue their interests.

Third, people may undermine the successes of other people, even those who are close to them, when others' successes would threaten their own self-esteem. The results of one experiment showed that although participants were more willing to help their friends than to help strangers on a task that was not relevant to them personally, they were less likely to help their friends than they were to help total strangers when the self-relevance of the task was high![34] Participants took subtle steps to sabotage their friends' performance when a strong performance would threaten their own ego.

Fourth, and perhaps most disturbingly, people may distance themselves from those who outperform them in areas that are important to their sense of self. In an experimental demonstration of this effect, research participants learned that another person had performed better or worse than they did in a domain that was either high or low in personal relevance to the participant. When the domain was self-relevant, participants chose to sit farther away from and expressed a lower desire to work with people who performed better than they did on the task.[35]

If Tesser's model is correct—and research suggests that it is—people's relationships are affected by their concerns with evaluating themselves favorably. Our choices of friends and partners, and how we react to those friends' and partners' successes, are affected by our own desire to feel good about ourselves.

⁘ Egotism and Conflict

We saw earlier that people tend to interpret events in ways that reflect favorably on them. They enhance their responsibility for things that go well and minimize, if not deny, their personal responsibility when things go poorly. Fortunately, people often keep these egotistical attributions to themselves, and as long as their thoughts remain private, people feel good about how things turned out and no one else is the wiser.

However, people do not always keep their attributions to themselves. Sometimes, other people ask us directly why something happened. A teacher may ask a student why he failed the test. An angry women may ask her husband, "Why did you yell at me?" A teammate may ask, "Why do you think we lost the game?" If people then voice their egotistical view of matters, views that exonerate themselves or blame other individuals, the interpersonal consequences are almost always negative.[36] And they are particularly negative when one person's egotistical explanations implicate the listener, as when a student blames the teacher for the failing grade, the husband replies that he yelled at his wife because she deserved it, or the athlete pins the team's loss on other team members.

Interpreting events in a self-serving manner creates many problems. Married and cohabiting couples, for example, tend to disagree on the proportion of the domestic chores that each person does. Regardless of whether they do a similar or disparate portion of the housework, each person thinks that he or she does more work than the partner thinks the person does. When researchers asked married couples to estimate the extent to which they and their spouses contributed to 20 domestic activities (such as cleaning the house, taking out the garbage, and caring for children), they found that, in most of the couples, at least one spouse overestimated his or her contributions.[37] Although there was no way for the researchers to know which spouse was telling the truth, it is obviously impossible for two people's contributions to sum up to more than 100% responsibility! However, that's what happened for virtually all of the couples, indicating that one or both people were overestimating the amount of work he or she did around the house.

When one member of the couple believes that the other is taking "too much" credit, resentment and conflict are likely. Each person wants to be recognized for his or her contributions and feels cheated when his or her hard work goes unnoticed. On top of that, it rankles both of them to think that the other person is claiming an unjustified share of the credit. To avoid these conflicts, people need to realize that both their and their partners' perceptions of the relationships are biased in a self-serving manner. By virtue of their partners' normal but unrecognized egotism, their own contributions to a relationship will virtually never be acknowledged as much as they think they should.

A similar effect occurs when things go badly in a close relationship. Who was responsible for last night's argument? Which of us has been most withdrawn lately, and why? Whose fault are our sexual difficulties? Of course, each partner may confess from time to time, admitting responsibility for a particular squabble or relational fiasco. But, more often, each person feels that he or she is ultimately less to blame than the partner. Each person's egotistical biases further fuel the fire as the discussion spreads beyond the initial problem to a debate about relative responsibility. Given the egoistic nature of the self, this is a debate that neither person will win. Even if it finally concludes with an exasperated "Okay, fine, it's my fault," the ostensible perpetrator doesn't believe it and the ostensible victim knows it.

Similar attributional conflicts arise when people work together in groups—on committees, in work groups, on class projects, and on teams of various kinds. As we saw in chapter 3, each member of a successful group tends to believe that they were more responsible for the group's success than most of the other group members.[38] As a result, they feel a greater sense of personal responsibility than they likely deserve and certainly more than other group members grant them. At the same time, members of failing groups feel that they were less responsible for failure than most of the other members were. When members learn of one another's self-serving perceptions, discord and resentment result.

Lest I be accused of pointing fingers, I should note that psychologists and teachers have also been shown to display these kinds of egotistical attributions. When psychotherapists see their clients improve, then tend to attribute the improvement to their own clinical skill. But when therapy goes poorly, psychotherapists tend to blame the client. Similarly, schoolteachers may take more personal responsibility when their students perform well than when the students do poorly, attributing student successes to their teaching but student failures to student stupidity or lack of effort. Most students have had the experience of feeling that their poor class performance was at least partly the teacher's fault and bristled at the teacher's suggestion that the student alone was responsible.

The interpersonal problems that arise from self-serving attributions occur not only because everybody is piqued that others are taking too much credit for the good things that happen but also because egotistical perceptions lead people to believe that they are entitled to greater rewards than they receive.[39] In work groups, committees, teams, and other task-oriented groups, members are often rewarded in proportion to their contributions. If most of the people in a successful group egotistically overestimate their contributions to the cause, then most of the people will also expect a disproportionate share of the spoils. Even if rewards are allocated in an objectively fair manner, virtually everyone will feel that he or she was not rewarded equitably. The natural proclivity to interpret events egotistically makes perceived inequity virtually unavoidable. Given that people generally overestimate their personal contributions to joint efforts, most people will expect a commensurate share of recognition and reward. When it is not forthcoming, virtually everyone will feel cheated, and resentment and conflict will arise.

The Stigma of Self-Importance

The egotistical shenanigans of the self can undermine our relationships with other people in yet another way. Put simply, egotism is aversive to other people. Just consider the words that we commonly use to describe egotistical people. We call them *conceited, vain, haughty, arrogant, stuck-up, pompous,* and *pretentious,* and brand them *blowhards, snobs, narcissists,* and worse. When research participants in one study rated the favorability of 300 adjectives that are often used to describe other people, they rated words that connoted egotism—such as *arrogant, snobbish, conceited,* and *boastful*—among the most unfavorable.[40]

Clearly, we do not like people who overestimate their intellect, ability, importance, appearance, wit, or other valued characteristics. People who think too highly of themselves are disliked, derogated, avoided, and rejected more frequently than people who seem to see themselves accurately.[41] Our tendency to view the world in an egotistical fashion may make us feel good, but it can negatively affect how other people perceive and respond to us.

The interesting question is why people find egotism so aversive and generally dislike and avoid egotistical people. If some big-headed, boastful egotist wants to think that he or she is better than he or she is—or even better than we are—why should we care? Why do we find it so difficult to tolerate egotism when we see it in others?

One possibility is that egotism is often accompanied by the belief that one is entitled to a disproportionate share of recognition, deference, and rewards. People who think they are better than others usually insist they should be treated special. I doubt we are quite as bothered by people who think they are better than they really are as long as they don't expect anything special in return for being so wonderful. Even so, I suspect that we would still dislike them.

Another reason we may dislike egotists is that egotistical behavior sometimes threatens other people's self-images. When a person conveys that he or she is outstanding, the implication is that we are inferior. As a result, egotism sometimes operates as an indirect insult to other people.[42] It's difficult enough not to feel threatened when people really are superior to us on some dimension, but it's particularly exasperating when we feel that the other person is not actually better.

Egotism may also result in negative reactions because people view egotism as misrepresentation. Social norms dictate that people should be who and what they claim to be. All social relationships would be cast into chaos if we couldn't trust people's representations of themselves, their characteristics, and their accomplishments. If I overstate my responsibility for success or convey that I possess more desirable attributes than I have, I have violated the norm that says I must represent myself accurately. Of course, we all fudge from time to time, seeing ourselves as a little too good, and we tolerate a bit of fudging on the part of others. However, when people are too self-aggrandizing, they may be seen as either self-deluded or manipulatively deceptive.

Finally, people seem to believe that self-esteem must be earned. People who are outstanding or successful are entitled to feel good about themselves and their accomplishments. However, by the same token, people are not entitled to enjoy the fruits of successes that they have not earned. In essence, a person who responds egotistically is reaping the emotional rewards of success without having earned them. It's as if the egotist has "stolen" some of the emotional rewards along with the credit.

For all of these reasons, people's natural penchant for egotism can damage their relationships with others. Given how negatively people react to egotism, it is puzzling that people so often behave egotistically. Why are we so willing to risk others' goodwill by being seen as arrogant, stuck-up, or pretentious? Perhaps the best explanation is that, because we believe our own inflated views of ourselves, we don't stop to consider the possibility that other people will regard us as conceited or arrogant. As Calvin (of the popular cartoon *Calvin and Hobbes*) replied after a playmate accused him of being a conceited blowhard, "When you're great, people often mistake candor for bragging." Given that most people truly believe that they are better than they are, they will occasionally be seen by other people as egotistical.

Whatever the reason, our penchant for responding in a self-serving, egotistical fashion can create problems in our relationships with other people. We would all probably like one another a bit more—and be liked more in return—if egotism were not such an intractable part of human nature.

Violent Reactions to Ego Threats

A good deal has been written recently about road rage—acts of violence that arise between drivers in automobiles. I read recently about a man who was trying to merge into a long line of slow-moving traffic on a clogged freeway. He edged up as close as possible to the line of creeping cars, but the first few drivers did not let him in. Although a considerate driver soon yielded to him, the man was already livid at being treated badly by the other drivers. When the traffic came to a full stop, he intentionally rammed one of the cars that hadn't allowed him to merge, then jumped out and pounded on its trunk hard enough to leave large dents. As the other driver started to get out of his car, the irate man knocked him to the ground, screamed obscenities at his wife and children, then jumped back in his own car, made a U-turn across the median, and sped off in the other direction. When he was later apprehended, the man explained that the other drivers had treated him disrespectfully and deserved to be taught a lesson.

Many cases of road rage seem to occur when one driver interprets another driver's behavior as inconsiderate or insulting, even if it has no real consequences. In this example, the man was angry because he was not treated the way he thought he should be treated even though it did not make any practical difference (because the traffic wasn't moving anyway). He had beliefs about who he is and how he ought to be treated, and something about the other drivers not letting him into line violated those beliefs, sending him into a fit of rage.

I suspect that a few moments of reflection will bring to mind occasions on which you, too, reacted angrily, if not aggressively, to events that threatened either your ego or your egoistic view of how you should be treated. Perhaps you weren't behind the wheel of a car at the time (although it seems that many people experience these kinds of reactions while driving). Instead, maybe you were criticized by your partner or boss, kept waiting for an appointment, or publicly insulted. Whether or not you said anything at the time, you were nonetheless boiling inside. Your ego rose up and demanded, "How dare you treat me this way?"

In an exceptionally interesting and controversial article, Roy Baumeister, Laura Smart, and Joseph Boden proposed that violence is a common reaction to events that dispute a person's highly favorable view of him- or herself. They suggested that "when favorable views about oneself are questioned, contradicted, impugned, mocked, challenged, or otherwise put in jeopardy, people may aggress . . . against the source of the threat."[43] Some people seem to interpret other people's rudeness or disrespect as a challenge to their positive self-view, reasoning that "if they regarded me favorably, they wouldn't treat me this way."

There are two things wrong with people's egoistic reading of apparent disrespect, however. The first is that the other person's inconsiderate behavior may have nothing whatsoever to do with you. Those drivers who failed to let the man merge into traffic may have been distracted and not seen him. Or perhaps they had just let some other cars into line and decided that it was somebody else's turn to be charitable. Or maybe they were concerned about inconveniencing the other drivers behind them by holding up the line. Frankly, it seems unlikely that they said to themselves, "that guy trying to merge into traffic is a moron; I'm not going to let him in." Unfortunately, the self's tendency to interpret other people's actions personally—as if they were directed toward us—lead us to err in the direction of inferring disrespect, if not malice, when others have treated us inconsiderately.

The second egoistic error is that, even if another person questions, impugns, or challenges our views of ourselves, what is the good of becoming angry? (I'm setting aside here cases in which a challenge to our favorable self-views has tangible consequences and am focusing only on ego-threatening events that have no direct consequences other than that they challenge our self-views.) Typically, people who react violently to insults or rudeness are not in physical danger and, in fact, they increase their chances of being hurt by challenging the person who "dissed" them. Rather, they are reacting to an affront to their self-image or to their idea of how they ought to be treated. It is as if they regard their mental idea of themselves as a real thing that can be damaged by another person's inconsiderate behavior or disparaging remark. When people react to threats to their egos with anger and aggression, they are treating the image of themselves in their minds as a real thing that needs to be defended. I shudder to think about the amount of violence that has been perpetrated by people who thought that another person disrespected them. A good deal of gang violence falls in this category, as well as many cases of domestic abuse.

It may seem that the people who are most prone to react violently to threats to their self-images are those who have low self-esteem. For many years, we have had a popular cultural image of people (particularly men) with low self-esteem bullying and hurting other people as a way of making them feel better about themselves. (It has never been clear to me why hurting other people would make violent perpetrators feel good about themselves, but that has been the idea.) However, Baumeister and his colleagues offered rather convincing evidence that people with high—not low—self-esteem are more likely to turn violent when their egos are threatened.[44] They explain this finding by suggesting that aggression is a reaction to a discrepancy between one's favorable self-image and the apparent views of oneself by others. Because a given level of negative regard from other people will create a larger discrepancy in people with high than low self-esteem, they will experience a greater threat to their ego and be more likely to react aggressively. The higher people's self-esteem, the greater the range of feedback that may suggest to them that they are not as wonderful as they thought.

Richard Nisbett, Dov Cohen, and their colleagues have provided another angle on the relationship between disrespect and violence.[45] Their work has focused on "cultures of honor" that specify that people, especially men, should defend themselves against affronts to their honor. Although cultures of honor exist all around the world, in the United States it is stronger in the South than in the North. Historically, Southern norms have specified that men should take action when they are insulted. Even today, Southerners are more likely than Northerners to endorse the use of violence in response to affronts by other people even though they are not more likely to endorse violence in general. They are also more likely to denigrate a man who doesn't stand up to insults and affronts. These attitudes are reflected in the fact that homicide rates in the South are greater than in the North only for homicides that result from conflicts, arguments, or insults. Indeed, experimental research has shown that white Southern men showed a greater increase in cortisol (a hormone released during stress) and testosterone (which is released in preparation for aggression) after being insulted than did Northern men.

These regional differences may have arisen from social and economic differences between the South and the North. In sparsely inhabited rural areas in which law enforcement officers are often far away, people may have felt the need to show that they are willing and able to defend themselves. Today, of course, Southerners have no greater need to defend their honor than Northerners, yet the attitudes are slow to change. Affronts to one's ego must be addressed, even at the risk of physical harm.

6 ::

Risking Life and Limb

We let our reputation and good name depend upon the judgement of other men. . . . Merely in order to make them decide in our favour we imperil our peace of mind and way of life in countless ways.
—LA ROCHEFOUCAULD

In February 1836, a small band of Texans converted a Spanish mission in San Antonio into a fort to challenge the armies of Mexican emperor Santa Anna. Although the ensuing engagement was, from a military point of view, an unmitigated disaster, with annihilation of the Alamo's entire force (including folk heroes David Crockett and James Bowie), the battle of the Alamo has held a favored place in American history and lore ever since. One compelling aspect of the story is that the Alamo's defenders knew that they could not fend off Santa Anna indefinitely. Toward the end of the 10-day siege, the Texans recognized that no reinforcements were coming, the Mexicans outnumbered them about 20 to 1, and Santa Anna had declared that it would be a fight to the death. Yet the defenders chose to stay and die even though they probably could have slipped out of the Alamo up until the last day or two.

According to legend, Colonel William Travis explicitly offered his men the opportunity to leave. According to the story, which many historians dispute, Travis drew a line in the dirt with his sword and invited those who wished to defend the Alamo to the death to cross over. All but one of them crossed; even James Bowie, incapacitated by pneumonia, asked to be carried over on a stretcher. Whether or not the line-in-the-dirt episode actually occurred, the point remains that the men stayed in the Alamo even though they had achieved their goal of detaining the Mexican army so that Sam Houston could amass troops elsewhere, most of them were volunteers who had no compelling reason to stay, and they could have abandoned their position and lived to fight another day.

The defenders of the Alamo were clearly willing to die for a cause they regarded as important. Yet one must wonder why they chose to stay at the Alamo beyond the point at which they could achieve no additional good; in fact, it could be argued that nearly 200 men dying in a senseless battle might even reduce the Texans' chances of ultimate success against the Mexicans. So why did they stay?[1]

In the frontier culture of the American South and West in the 1800s, images of toughness, strength, and bravery were highly valued.[2] Within such a culture, men felt compelled to defend their public reputations against suggestions that they were weak or afraid, and each man at the Alamo would have felt implied pressure to fight to the death if he thought it was what his comrades expected him to do. A man who walked away from such a fight would not only find his image irreparably damaged but also would likely find it hard to face himself the next day. The pressure was almost certainly not explicit. It is difficult to imagine the Alamo's defenders prodding one another into staying. ("C'mon, Davy, you ol' yellow-bellied coward. Come on across that line.") Yet the pressure would have been intense nonetheless, particularly if Travis's line-in-the-dirt routine really happened.

The point is not that people risk their lives to defend their principles or pursue important goals; many brave people do that. Nor is the point that people sometimes act braver than they feel; we all do that, as well. And I do not wish to imply that the Alamo's defenders were not fighting for a cause; they clearly felt a deep conviction to stand up to Santa Anna's tyranny. Rather, my point is that the defenders presumably did not really want to wait for the Mexicans to breach the Alamo's walls and viewed their plight as both hopeless and senseless, yet their desire to be seen as brave, or at least not to be seen as cowardly, led them to remain at the Alamo.

As we discussed in chapter 1, one of the self's functions is to allow us to get inside the heads of other people—to imagine what they may be thinking, and particularly to imagine what they may be thinking about us. Indeed, many early analyses of the self (by writers such as William James, Charles Horton Cooley, and George Herbert Mead) stressed this function, and some contemporary theorists also suggest that its primary role is to infer what others might be thinking.[3] As we have seen, the capacity to self-reflect is accompanied by the ability to take other people's perspectives. With the benefit of a self, people can think about how other people perceive them and worry about the impressions they make on others. They can also deliberately behave in ways that convey certain impressions of themselves, even when doing so diverges from the truth or has negative consequences. In part, the men in the Alamo stayed to fight because they could imagine how they would be regarded if they fled. Concerns surrounding their egos and public images were so strong that they held sway over self-preservation. Without in any way diminishing the significance of their sacrifice, it seems clear that the Alamo's defenders stayed to fight because their egos prevented them from leaving.

The defenders of the Alamo were by no means unusual in this regard. Virtually everyone has engaged in dangerous, potentially life-threatening behaviors because they thought that doing so might make a desired impression on other people or bolster their ego.[4] And, often, the ostensible goal of their behavior is far less principled than that of the Texans. In this chapter we examine ways in which the self can lead people to do things that pose risks to their health and well-being, if not their life.

Taking Risks to Make a Point

Accidents are the third leading cause of death in the United States; among people under the age of 45, they are the number one killer.[5] In addition, hundreds of thousands of people are injured each year in accidents that are not fatal. We generally think of accidents as inherently unavoidable (after all, people don't intend to have an accident), but in fact, many so-called accidental injuries and deaths are the direct result of people's deliberately doing dangerous things.

Modern society, like most others throughout history, values boldness. At minimum, most people do not want others to think that they are overly cautious, and often they want to be seen as brave, daring, or risk-taking. As a result, people sometimes do dangerous things for the sole purpose of showing others how brave they are. Of course, in order to convince other people of one's courage, a person must do things that are potentially dangerous, and therein lies the problem.

A few years ago, Kathleen Martin and I surveyed nearly 300 adolescents in the United States and Ireland to find out how many of them admitted taking unnecessary risks in order to impress other people.[6] Given that we had done such things ourselves, the study's findings were not surprising, though they were nonetheless sobering. For example, approximately 25% of both male and female American respondents indicated that they had driven dangerously in order to make an impression on other people. As one woman wrote: "I was speeding while driving with friends because one of the people in the car thought I was an up-tight, overly-safe driver. Although I usually don't speed, I went fast to impress them." One wonders, then, about the number of traffic accidents, injuries, and fatalities that are caused solely by people trying to make an impression. Perhaps this is one reason that the likelihood of a teenage driver's having an accident increases with the number of passengers in the car.[7] The more people in the car, the more reason there is for the driver to speed in order to appear brave, cool, or fun-loving. It is unsettling that the conditions that increase the chance of a self-induced accident also put more people in harm's way.

About a third of the male students in our study also reported doing admittedly stupid stunts simply to make an impression.[8] They reported a variety of hair-raising tales about jumping from high places (bridges, cliffs, second-story windows, roofs of buildings), hanging out of or riding on the tops of moving cars, juggling knives, eating fire, lighting flatulence, and daredevil acts such as jumping over a car on a bicycle and being pulled down the highway on a skateboard. The incidence of these kinds of stunts may have increased with the popularity of the television show and movie *Jackass*, in which the cast engages in a variety of dangerous stunts such as racing down hills in runaway grocery carts, shooting one another with riot-control beanbags, riding golf carts off ramps, and firing bottle rockets that have been inserted in the anus (facing outward, of course).

Ten percent of the men in our study also said that they had gotten into physical fights solely to look brave or cool in other people's eyes. Many of these men did not really want to fight but thought that their public image would be damaged if they walked away. Interestingly, only 3% of the female respondents reported doing dangerous stunts, and only 2% reported fighting for self-presentational reasons.[9] Apparently, women's egos and social images are not as linked to this sort of recklessness as are men's.

I recall a *Far Side* cartoon in which a terrified little dog is shown darting between speeding cars on a busy highway. As he breathlessly reaches his four friends on the other side of the road, one of the other dogs proudly exclaims, "All right! Rusty's in the club!" The cartoon is cute because we know that dogs don't try to impress one another by doing risky things or join clubs that require members to pass dangerous initiation rituals. Human beings, in contrast, are not that smart. Tens of thousands of people are injured and killed each year doing precisely what the dog in the cartoon was doing—taking unnecessary risks to prove themselves to other people. Fraternities are perhaps the most maligned organizations in which members do dangerous things to impress one another, but in fact, people undergo dangerous hazing in military units, athletic teams, marching bands, religious cults, and even professional groups. Initiation may involve being showered in cold water, beaten with wooden paddles, kept awake for days at a time, or forced to consume large quantities of alcohol. Sometimes the consequences are truly disastrous, as when a student at a Midwestern university was permanently paralyzed from the waist down after jumping into a mud pit on the orders of a more senior group member, or the cases in which initiates have died from alcohol poisoning.[10]

Many people wonder why anybody would take such risks simply to join a particular organization, but the issue runs deeper than simply wanting to belong. Often, what is at stake is not simply acceptance by members of the group but one's ego and public image to the world at large. Even if people did not care about being a member of a particular group, they still might consent to dangerous behaviors to show that they are not afraid.

The military particularly prizes courage, and military leaders typically want to be seen as brave. As a result, they sometimes put themselves in unnecessary danger simply to convey the impression of being courageous. For example, during the Southern military barrage during the Battle of Gettysburg, Brigadier General Carl Schurz walked "calmly" up and down the ranks smoking a cigar.[11] Some field generals who have employed such risky self-presentations on the front lines were cut down in mid-stride. In a more bizarre demonstration of fearlessness, the pirate Edward Teach, better known as Blackbeard, would light candles he had put in his beard.[12] Setting one's beard on fire obviously entails a certain degree of risk, yet Blackbeard did so for its intimidating effect.

Although they usually do not resort to behaviors as extreme as Blackbeard's, most people have taken risks to convey images of themselves as daring, fun-loving, a good sport, or part of the gang. We do things that we would never have done if other people were not present and that, deep down, we know are dangerously foolish.

We would not do these kinds of dangerous things if not for the self. Only because we can imagine how we are seen by other people, anticipate how they will react to our behavior, and think about how we want them to view us do we concern ourselves with making impressions on them. Many other animals have impressive automatic displays to convince other animals of their ferocity (hackles rising on a wolf or cat make it appear larger, for example) or attractiveness (the display of a peacock), but they do not deliberately manage their impressions in the wide variety of ways that human beings do. And they certainly don't put their safety and lives at risk just to make an impression unless something very important, such as food or a mate, depends on it. Only an animal with the capacity for self-awareness would, as in the case of one nominee for the annual "Darwin Awards," blow his head off to prove to his friends that he wasn't too "chicken" to put a gun in his mouth and pull the trigger.[13] Whether his friends were impressed is not known.

Risky behaviors decrease with age, probably because behaviors that might be regarded as "cool" for an 18-year-old are viewed as immature and downright irresponsible for a 45-year-old with a job and a family. However, older people are by no means immune to concerns with how they are perceived. Although they are not particularly concerned about fostering an image of being a bold risk-taker, they are often worried about appearing old and infirm. As a result, some older individuals resist using a cane or walker even when they need these devices to navigate safely.[14] When they later injure themselves in a fall, possibly breaking a hip, it would not be an exaggeration to conclude that it was literally a *self*-inflicted injury.

Throwing Caution to the Wind

Not only do people sometimes do unnecessarily risky things to bolster their egos or public images, but they also resist taking precautions when engaging in otherwise reasonable but potentially dangerous activities. Although most people agree that they should wear helmets when riding bicycles and motorcycles, goggles when using power tools, and mouth guards when playing contact sports, many individuals resist taking these kinds of precautions because they are concerned that other people may perceive them as fearful or overly cautious—as a "wuss," "wimp," or "weenie." (My father preferred the label "cream puff," but this may have been idiosyncratic with him.)

These concerns start at a young age. There are reports of young hockey players wearing modified throat guards that provide little protection for their throats but yet conform to the rules that govern youth hockey, thereby showing that they aren't actually worried about their safety. My 7-year-old son resisted wearing kneepads when he skated around the neighborhood because he was afraid he would look like a "sissy."

After a university chemistry professor told me that his students resisted wearing goggles and other protective gear during chemistry labs because they would look overly cautious and "dorky," we decided to conduct a study to see whether people would, in fact, put themselves at risk simply because they were concerned with others' impressions of them.[15] We conducted a study in which research participants were led to believe that they would be working with potentially hazardous chemicals (under the premise that we were studying communication in industrial work groups). Before working with the chemicals, we gave them the opportunity to don an assortment of protective gear, including goggles, latex gloves, face masks, shoe covers, aprons, and surgeons' scrubs. Participants were told to put on whatever items made them feel comfortable, but that we would not insist that they wear them if they did not wish to do so. To determine whether concerns with others' impressions would result in risky behavior, we also led some participants to believe that the other members of their lab group already perceived them as very cautious individuals, whereas other participants thought that the others saw them as average in cautiousness.

The results of our study showed that male participants who believed that the other group members already perceived them as cautious consented to wear significantly less safety gear than those who thought that others perceived them as average in cautiousness. Thus, men who were concerned with appearing overly cautious were willing to place their safety and health at risk to dispel the unflattering impression that they were wimps. Furthermore, men who valued the image of risk-taker wore significantly fewer safety items than men for whom risk-taker was not an important image to cultivate. Given that participants in our study were willing to place themselves at risk to convey an impression of riskiness to complete strangers despite any explicit pressure to do so, one can only imagine the extent to which people do dangerous things in everyday life when the social pressures are more intense.

Female participants in our study wore the same amount of safety gear whether or not they thought other group members viewed them as excessively cautious. The fact that the effect was obtained for men but not for women again attests to the fact that being perceived as a risk-taker is more important to men's social images than women's. People are willing to put their well-being at risk only to the extent that they believe that the conveyed impression is valued by others. As I will explore in a moment, however, women also engage in unnecessarily dangerous behaviors, but they tend to take risks that will make impressions that are culturally valued for women—such as starving themselves to maintain an unrealistically low body weight.

Unsafe Sex

Even with widespread education about AIDS and the push toward safe sex in the past 20 years, a high percentage of sexually active Americans still do not use condoms regularly. If they did, we wouldn't see 1 million teenage girls becoming pregnant each year, and sexually transmitted diseases wouldn't be as rampant as they are. Health educators often suppose that the problem is primarily educational—that people simply don't understand that unprotected sexual intercourse is dangerous or that its risks can be reduced by practicing safe sex. Yet a large percentage of people who don't use condoms certainly know how STDs are transmitted and have heard about condoms, but they nonetheless continue to have unprotected sex with new partners. Why?

As with any complex behavior, unsafe sex results from many factors. One that is relevant to the curse of the self involves the fact that some people are worried that their sexual partner will think badly of them if they request or introduce a condom in a sexual encounter. In the survey of first-semester freshmen that Kathleen Martin and I conducted, 8% of the respondents said they had engaged in unprotected sexual intercourse because they wanted to be seen as cool, laid back, risk-taking, fun, or mature.[16] One woman wrote: "Twice in the last three months I had sex without using a condom. I met this guy and thought I liked him a lot. He knew I was on the pill, so he told me it was ok. When I said I didn't want to get any diseases, he just said, 'Don't worry.' I didn't want to come across in a way to make him not like me, so I gave in."

Some respondents reported that they had unprotected sex even though they had a condom with them at the time! Women reported that they hadn't mentioned the condom because they were worried that the man would think that they were promiscuous or "slutty." ("What kind of a woman carries condoms with her?" one asked.) Men said that they sometimes didn't mention the condom in their wallet because they did not want the woman to think that they had come prepared for or expecting to have sex. Most frighteningly, two research studies found that people who tested positive for HIV (the virus that causes AIDS) sometimes failed to insist on using a condom because they were afraid that their insistence might "give them away" to a new partner!

Intrigued with the idea that people may do blatantly unhealthy things so as not to appear overly cautious or prudish, we started thinking of ways to examine this phenomenon in a controlled laboratory setting. Assuming that the university's ethics approval committee would not allow participants to have unprotected sex in our lab, we devised a somewhat more ethical analogue. After considering several unsanitary, potentially unhealthy behaviors that participants might do in the service of their self, we settled on the behavior of drinking out of a stranger's water bottle. Most people view drinking after strangers as unsanitary, if not downright "gross." Not only do we not know what kinds of diseases the person might have (meningitis can be contracted by sharing drinks, for example), but there's always the potential for "backwash." Drinking after a stranger is something most people would prefer not to do. But would they do it to avoid being seen as uptight, cautious, or prudish?

To find out, we had participants arrive in our lab along with an experimental accomplice who pretended to be another participant.[17] Believing the study was investigating the relationship between personality and taste perception, the participant and accomplice were first shown the participant's scores on a personality test he or she had completed earlier. Two bogus personality profiles were created. Participants in the high-image concern condition were shown a profile that indicated that they were average on most personality dimensions but had scored high on "cautiousness, neuroticism, and obsessiveness." A statement at the bottom of the profile indicated that a high score "is consistent with a personality profile of individuals who avoid risky situations and decisions and tend to worry unnecessarily over small concerns." In contrast, participants in the low-image concern condition received a profile showing that they scored average on all personality dimensions, including cautiousness. Thus, as in our earlier study of people's willingness to wear safety gear while working with dangerous chemicals, some participants in this study believed that the other individual thought that they were very cautious, if not neurotic.

After seeing their (bogus) personality profile, participants engaged in a taste test while observed by the accomplice. The purpose of the taste test was simply to lead participants to want a drink of water. We mixed up some foul-tasting concoctions, such as a mixture of soy sauce, mustard, and concentrated unsweetened Kool-Aid. After the participant had tasted and rated these nasty flavors, the researcher apologized for not having water available for participants to wash out their mouths. On this cue, the accomplice pulled a half-empty bottle of water out of his backpack and offered it to the participant. For half of the participants, he simply said, "that stuff must have tasted pretty nasty. Do you want a drink of my water?" For the other half, his offer was followed by a somewhat challenging statement: ". . . if you're not worried about drinking out of the same bottle as me." We believed that this challenge would make participants even more concerned with not appearing cautious, perhaps increasing their willingness to drink from his bottle to show that they weren't actually squeamish after all.

The results of this experiment showed that participants were more likely to accept the accomplice's offer to drink from his half-empty bottle when they thought that he already saw them as cautious and the accomplice implied that they were afraid of drinking after him. Not only were these participants more likely to take a drink from his bottle, but they actually drank a larger amount. (You need not be concerned about sanitation; all participants actually received a clean bottle half-filled with purified water.)

The dynamics of this study are admittedly not completely analogous to having unprotected sexual intercourse. The health risks of drinking after a stranger are obviously lower than those of having unprotected sex with a new partner. So perhaps it is not surprising that participants who were worried about their image were willing to drink after the stranger. At the same time, however, the participants in our study had no good reason to impress the accomplice. He was not in a position to affect their lives, and they did not anticipate ever interacting with him again. In real-world sexual encounters, the stakes may be much higher as people want to be liked and, often, to pursue a relationship beyond the immediate situation. Perhaps, then, we would see even more risky behavior in real life than in the artificial confines of the social psychological laboratory. Whether or not the study's findings generalize directly to real life, they demonstrate that people are willing to do unsanitary, even unhealthy things when they are worried about other people's impressions of them.

Alcohol, Tobacco, and Other Drugs

If you have used alcohol, tobacco, or illegal drugs, chances are that you did not simply wake up one morning and think to yourself, "I'd like a shot of tequila" or "I wonder where I could find a cigarette?" or "I think

I'll smoke my first joint today." Most people do not have their first experience with cigarettes, alcohol, or other drugs by themselves but rather in a social setting that involves one or more other people. We sometimes hear about people, particularly teenagers, succumbing to "peer pressure," but explicit pressure from others is typically not involved. Instead, people go along with other people who are smoking, drinking, or using drugs because doing so has clear social benefits and they are concerned that refusing to join in the action might have social liabilities. You certainly would not have drunk, smoked, or taken the drug if you thought that every other person present would have hated and rejected you for doing so!

Most people have their first experiences with cigarettes, alcohol, and drugs quite willingly, but underlying their behavior is the desire to be seen as someone who goes along, who fits in. In our research, many respondents indicated that they had used these substances because they wanted to look laid-back, easygoing, or fun-loving. Others said that they did it just to show that they did not object to cigarettes, alcohol, or drugs (presumably not to appear prudish or a goody-goody), or to look mature. Overall, just over half of both male and female respondents indicated that they sometimes drank alcohol for no other reason than to make an impression on others. Similarly, about 25% said that they had smoked cigarettes just to make an impression, and about 10% indicated that they had used drugs for self-presentational reasons (women more than men).[18] Keep in mind that these figures do not reflect the number of college students who said that they had used alcohol, cigarettes, or other drugs but, rather, the percent who explicitly reported that they had done so simply to make an impression on other people.

Not only can a concern with others' impressions lead people to start smoking, but it can also interfere with smokers' willingness to break the habit. Stopping smoking is, of course, quite difficult, and people fail for many reasons. However, some people do not even try to quit smoking because they are afraid of gaining weight.[19] Their concern is not entirely misplaced. Research shows that smokers tend to gain between 4.5 and 8 pounds when they stop smoking, although most of them eventually lose most of the weight that they gain.[20] Even so, the fact that potential weight gain deters many people from breaking the habit shows us how they weigh the pros and cons in their minds. Essentially, people decide that they are willing to risk heart disease, emphysema, and lung cancer in order to avoid gaining a few extra pounds and perhaps making a less desirable social impression. Of course, people don't think through the consequences of smoking this explicitly, yet this is the choice they make.

Enhancing Physical Appearance

Most people think a lot about how other people see them and try to make themselves physically attractive, or at least not unattractive, to others. We devote time and effort each day to making ourselves presentable to other people, and we spend a good deal of money on products, services, and procedures intended to improve our appearance. We may bemoan the emphasis that people place on attractiveness—beauty is only skin deep, right?—yet we cannot escape the fact that our physical appearance influences how other people perceive and react to us and, thus, our social, romantic, and occupational outcomes in life. In light of this, it is not surprising that people think about their appearance and try to make themselves as attractive as they can (however attractiveness is defined within their social groups). What is surprising, however, is the fact that people sometimes risk their health and well-being in order to be attractive.[21]

In Search of the Perfect Tan

The incidence of skin cancer among whites in the United States has at least tripled since 1960; some experts say that it has quadrupled. The increase is due to many things. Compared to the middle of the 20th century, more people now live and vacation in southern latitudes, tanning salons have become more common, clothing styles reveal more skin, and the depletion of the ozone layer has compromised the earth's natural protection from ultraviolet (UV) radiation.[22] Although these reasons are all true, the predominant reason that more people get skin cancer is that they purposefully expose themselves to UV radiation in order to get a tan without protecting their skin adequately.

During the 19th century, fair skin was prized because the aristocrats and professionals who worked indoors had pale skin, whereas farmers and other manual laborers were deeply tanned from spending long days working in the sun. However, when the industrial revolution moved much of the working class into factories and only professional people had the money and leisure time to vacation in sunny places, suntans became associated with wealth and status.[23] For many years, no one recognized the health risks of excessive exposure to the sun, but with mounting evidence, the word got out that tanning can give you cancer. Unfortunately, the warnings did relatively little to deter many people from seeking the perfect tan.

Like the other unhealthy behaviors discussed in this chapter, tanning stems from our ability to imagine ourselves through other people's eyes. If people could not imagine how others saw them, they would not go out of their way to be tanned. Indeed, my own research shows that the strongest predictors of how much people work on being tan involves the degree to which they are motivated to be attractive and believe that having a tan enhances their attractiveness to other people. Despite warnings against getting too much sun, the desire to be attractive may override rational concerns with health. Skin cancer is a disease that many people give themselves.

Given that tanning is linked to the desire to be attractive, we wondered whether people might be dissuaded from excessive tanning if they were warned about the negative effects of tanning on their appearance. To answer this question, Jody Jones and I asked university students to read one of three essays about tanning.[24] One essay stressed the health risks associated with excessive exposure to the sun (particularly skin cancer), a second essay stressed the negative effects of the sun on physical appearance (such as wrinkling, premature aging, and scarring), and the third essay simply described the process by which tanning occurs without mentioning any hazards. After reading one of these essays, the participants completed a questionnaire about their attitudes toward tanning and their tanning plans for the coming summer.

Overall, the essay that described the negative effects of tanning on appearance led to the most unfavorable attitudes toward tanning and to the strongest intentions to use sunscreen in the future. Essentially, participants seemed more concerned that the sun might make them look bad than that it might give them cancer! Surprisingly, however, the essay that dealt with the effects of tanning on appearance was least effective for participants who were most concerned about their appearance. Participants who were invested in being attractive appeared to dismiss the notion that tanning might ultimately make them look worse.

Some people seem to be obsessed by tanning. These tan-insatiable individuals are as brown as they are ever going to get, yet they keep working on their tans. To study these tan-insatiable people, researchers approached individuals who were sitting in the sun at parks and swimming pools and gave them a short survey.[25] The survey included questions about their tanning attitudes and behavior, sunscreen use, and the importance they placed on looking good, as well as a brief measure of obsessive tendencies. Results showed that the belief that being tanned improves one's appearance, paired with a tendency toward being obsessive-compulsive, is associated with tan insatiability. Apparently, people who believe that tanning helps them make a better impression on others and who cannot stop thinking (i.e., obsessing) about how they are being perceived are most likely to overtan. Again, this pattern implicates the self because obsessive people have difficulty not talking to themselves about the object of their obsession, in this case a tan.

The Quest to Be Thin

Given that the American prototype of an attractive person tends to be one who is reasonably fit and trim, people understandably think that they will make a better impression on others by working on their weight and physique. In many ways, this interest in watching one's weight is beneficial. I suspect that Americans would quickly become more even more overweight than they already are if everyone suddenly became unconcerned about what he or she looked like. Here, then, is a case in which the ability to self-reflect promotes our health and well-being. Even so, it can also lead to behaviors that are decidedly unhealthy.

Although some people need to lose weight for medical reasons, research suggests that over half of the people who are on a diet at any given time have no health-related reason to watch their weight, but rather are dieting solely in an effort to look better. In other words, most dieting is driven by efforts to look good rather than to be healthy.[26] In fact, dieting may lead to overtly unhealthy behaviors. At minimum, unnecessary dieting may lead to mild malnourishment. People who diet unnecessarily don't eat quite enough to keep their bodies functioning optimally, and they end up with less energy and lower resistance to disease than they otherwise would have.

But the problems can be more serious. Many people resort to dangerous diet regimens, diet aids, and yo-yo dieting. They try diets that, that despite helping them lose weight, do not provide adequate nutrition and may upset critical balances in the body. They may also use untested dietary supplements and diet suppressors, or go on and off diets as their weight goes up and down in a dangerous yo-yo pattern.[27]

Even more seriously, excessive weight loss can be life-threatening, as in the case of eating disorders. Although many causes of anorexia and bulimia do not involve self-generated concerns with making good impressions on other people, research suggests that a very high percentage of women with eating disorders are excessively—or, more accurately, obsessively—concerned with their appearance and others' impressions of them.[28] Women with eating disorders have great difficulty stopping their internal self-talk about weight, appearance, and food. We do not see other animals starving themselves to make an impression because they do not self-reflect about their weight and others' impressions of them.

Overexercise and Underexercise

People also think they can improve their appearance through physical exercise. Like maintaining a healthy weight, physical exercise is obviously healthful as long as it isn't taken too far. Unfortunately, the self-motivated effort to maintain a positive social image leads some people to exercise too often, too long, or too hard. In our own research, 10% of the men and 30% of the women admitted that they had overexercised because they wanted to make a good impression. Some people overexercise to reap the benefits of appearing trim, fit, or strong.[29] Other people overexercise because of the positive social benefits of being seen exercising.

Runners, for example, will run faster and longer than feels comfortable to them when they run with other people. Thus, they may push themselves too hard because they do not want to appear unable to keep up with the others. One study showed that runners who were jogging in a park ran faster when people along the running path were watching them than when they thought they were alone.[30] Similarly, male weight-lifters often lift more weight than they should when other people are watching. In one of our studies, 27% of the men admitted that they had lifted too much weight explicitly to make an impression.[31] As one male respondent told me, "I was lifting free weights with my friends, and I purposefully tried to lift more weight than I usually do, and I also did more repetitions to prove that I was stronger than my friends. I paid for it the next day, though." Another man reported lifting too much weight to impress the women's aerobics class when it walked through the weight room. It's not clear whether the women even noticed him struggling with the weights, but he certainly noticed his strained back when he tried to get out of bed the next morning. Such efforts to wow other people with one's strength can result in pulled muscles, strained backs, neck problems, and even stress fractures. Only about 3% of the women in our sample reported overlifting to make an impression, presumably because they do not believe that lifting excessively heavy things will improve other people's perceptions of them.

Many people need to exercise and even want to exercise, yet they do not do so because of how they think they look to other people while exercising. People who think they look fat, scrawny, misproportioned, or unfit may worry about others seeing them exercise or even being seen in certain kinds of exercise clothing. As a result, they are reluctant to be seen bouncing around an aerobics class, swimming at the local pool, jogging in a public place, or lifting weights among the jocks.[32] Their self-created concerns may deter them from healthful and enjoyable activities.

Fleeing the Curse of the Self

We have seen that people create a great deal of their own distress by ruminating over the past and worrying about the future (chapter 4). Most of the emotions that we create for ourselves are unpleasant, and people understandably want to get rid of them as quickly as possible. People usually prefer to change the situation that is causing their distress, but when they can't change the situation, they may simply try to escape the bad feeling itself. Given that self-talk maintains these unpleasant emotions, one solution is to quiet the self. No self-thought, no emotion, no problem.

Psychologist Roy Baumeister has conducted a fascinating investigation into the ways that people escape the burden of selfhood, which he describes in his book *Escaping the Self.*[33] Some of these strategies are used by nearly everyone. People who want to escape the aversiveness of self-reflection may watch mindless television, listen to music, read, exercise, shop, sleep, meditate, or have sex. Assuming that the person is not so self-absorbed that escaping the self is impossible (for example, when one is grieving), these diversions can decrease self-thought by focusing one's attention on other things. Some of the pleasure of these sorts of activities comes from their ability to quiet the self.

Sometimes, though, people take more extreme steps to quiet or escape the self. Part of the appeal of thrill-seeking experiences is to escape the self's recriminations. When people are bungee-jumping, riding on a roller coaster, skydiving, or rock-climbing, so much of their attention is usurped by the immediate situation that no cognitive resources are available to allow them to think about the past or the future. Of course, some people find such experiences so terrifying that the self is locked in obsession about the present ("I'm terrified to jump out of this plane"), but even that kind of temporary gut-wrenching fear is sometimes preferable to distressing, chronic self-talk about one's personal shortcomings, failures, occupational stresses, relational problems, and otherwise miserable life.

Most mundane efforts to escape the self, even those that entail a certain amount of calculated risk, are often beneficial. Given that human beings are saddled with a mind that talks to them more than necessary and inflicts upon them a great deal of unnecessary unhappiness, they need a way to shut it off from time to time. Unremitting self-reflection is unpleasant, stressful, and exhausting. If the self had an on-off switch that allowed people to turn their self-reflection off when it became unruly and back on again when it was needed, they would not need to seek behavioral ways to escape the self. But, given that no one has yet discovered such a switch, it is probably good that people have figured out ways to diminish their self-reflection from time to time. Without these self-escapes, many people would be even more unhappy, stressed out, and desperate than they already are. Even so, some self-escaping tactics can create as many problems as they solve.

Losing the Self in Alcohol

People often drink alcohol in order to relax, such as at the end of a stressful day at work or at a party where they feel awkward and uncomfortable. The relaxing effects of alcohol derive from at least two processes. First, alcohol has a direct depressive effect on the central nervous system, lowering physiological arousal and relaxing the muscles. These direct effects do not require mediation by a self; even rats will become relaxed, if not intoxicated, after ingesting alcohol.

More important for our purposes, alcohol also interferes with the cognitive processes that are involved in self-reflection. This should not be surprising given all of the obvious ways in which alcohol impairs thinking, judgment, and memory. Even so, the self-muting effects of alcohol help to account for why people try to "drown their problems" in alcohol. Clearly, the problems have not really gone away (much less "drowned"), yet they don't often seem as imposing because alcohol renders the person less capable of thinking about them.

In two experiments, Jay Hull and his colleagues demonstrated that alcohol consumption can lower self-awareness.[34] In these studies, participants consumed either alcohol or tonic water, all of them believing that they were drinking a mixture of vodka and tonic. (A squirt of lime juice in each drink made it impossible for participants to distinguish the alcoholic from the nonalcoholic drinks.) After allowing time for the alcohol to be absorbed into the bloodstream, participants gave a three-minute speech on "What I like and dislike about my body and physical appearance."

Although participants in both conditions spoke approximately the same number of words, analysis of their speeches revealed that participants who had consumed alcohol used a lower proportion of sentences that referred specifically to themselves, as well as a smaller number of first-person pronouns (*I, me, mine*) than participants who drank only tonic water. The researchers interpreted the effect of alcohol on first-person pronouns as indicating that the alcohol had diminished participants' self-awareness. Importantly, this effect was not due to participants' expectancies regarding which beverage they had consumed, thus eliminating the possibility that it was due to a placebo effect.

In another study, male social drinkers were given bogus feedback indicating that they had performed either very well or very poorly on an intelligence test; in reality, the scores they received were unrelated to their actual intelligence. Then, under the guise of a second study, the participants were allowed to drink as much of several varieties of wine as they desired as they rated the taste of each one. Men who were generally high in their tendency to think about themselves (those who scored high on a measure of dispositional self-consciousness) drank significantly more wine when they had received failure feedback than when they had received success feedback on the intelligence test. Presumably, they drank more wine to quiet their recriminating self-thoughts after failure. In contrast, men who generally did not think much about themselves to begin with (those who scored low in dispositional self-consciousness) did not drink more wine after failure than they did after success. Given that they were not prone to self-ruminate anyway, they did not need to lower their self-awareness through alcohol after doing poorly on the test.[35]

So, we know that alcohol can lower self-awareness and that people sometimes use alcohol to mute their self. Could this process account for some cases of alcoholism? Might some alcoholics become addicted to alcohol because it helps them turn down the volume of their inner self-talk? To find out, researchers studied men who had recently completed an alcohol detoxification program.[36] The researchers reasoned that, if people drink alcohol to reduce self-awareness after stressful events (such as failure), recovering alcoholics who experienced stressful life events should relapse at a higher rate than those with fewer stressful events. Furthermore, this effect should be particularly pronounced for alcoholics who are prone to self-reflect a great deal because they are the ones who should most wish to escape self-related thinking after stress or failure.

Three months after completing the detoxification program, 70% of the highly self-conscious men who had experienced predominately negative life events had relapsed, compared to only 14% of those who had experienced primarily positive events. Thus, among men who were high in the dispositional tendency to be self-conscious, negative events were associated with relapse. Furthermore, men who scored low in self-consciousness did not relapse at different rates depending on whether they had experienced positive or negative events. About 40% of these men started drinking again regardless of whether their lives following treatment for alcoholism were positive or negative. These studies suggest that alcohol treatment programs should include a component that helps alcoholics learn to control their self-chatter. People may learn to substitute other, less destructive ways of quieting the self for the bottle, or could be taught practices such as meditation that help to reduce self-reflection.

Although studies have shown that people may not think about themselves as much or as deeply after they have ingested alcohol, sometimes the opposite effect occurs. Rather than allowing them to escape the self, alcohol may bring the curse of the self upon them with full force. Drinking alcohol sometimes locks people into an unpleasant state of self-focus, magnifying their problems in their minds and leading them to wallow in self-pity. In these instances, alcohol can increase depression, self-recrimination, and feelings of despair.

How can we explain the fact that alcohol can have both of these effects, sometimes turning the self down (if not completely off) and sometimes turning it up full blast? Current thinking suggests that alcohol produces a cognitive narrowing of attention in which people's awareness becomes focused primarily on whatever is most salient to them, and other things are more or less ignored. When intoxicated, people cannot spread their attention around as easily as when they are sober and instead focus on only a small number of things. This effect, which is called *alcohol myopia*, can produce quite different effects depending on the person's psychological state.[37] If the inebriated person is focused on an interesting conversation, lively party, or loud concert, for example, troubling self-thoughts may be reduced. But if the person is drinking alone after a recent romantic breakup or other personal setback, alcohol myopia may lead to excessive self-focus. When people who are depressed or dejected drink alone, they often dwell excessively on their difficulties and end up "crying in their beer." My guess is that when people drink to escape the self, they generally expect that drinking will make them feel better. Sometimes, though, they are already so focused on themselves that alcohol myopia takes them more deeply inward, turns up the self-chatter, and makes them feel worse.

Beat Me, Hurt Me, Help Me Lose My Self

Masochism has been a puzzle to psychologists and lay people alike because it goes so strongly against the general tendency for people to avoid pain. Most of us cannot easily understand why anyone would want other people to hurt or humiliate them.

Roy Baumeister, who conducted one of the few scientific studies of masochists, concluded that masochism is, at its heart, a way of escaping the self.[38] Pain is perhaps the most effective way to eliminate abstract thoughts about oneself. When people are in physical pain, their attention is rooted to the physical sensations and, perhaps, to thoughts of how to make the discomfort end. But people in pain are not likely to ponder their shortcomings, failures, worries, regrets, or self-worth. As pain increases, people find it increasingly difficult to engage in abstract self-thought, focusing them instead on the concrete here and now.

Masochists are not the gluttons for punishment that many people imagine. Rather, they generally seek mild pain, accompanied by humiliation and control at the hands of another person, but they are typically very careful to avoid severe pain and injury. They select their partners carefully and typically have agreed-upon signals by which to indicate if the pain becomes too severe. Masochists don't want to experience excruciating pain, just enough discomfort to keep their attention on the pain and off abstract thoughts about themselves.

Rather than being psychologically maladjusted, masochists tend to be surprisingly normal people. In fact, Baumeister reported that masochism appears to occur most frequently among those who are successful and well-to-do.[39] This fact makes sense if masochism reflects an effort to escape the stress and aversiveness of self-reflection. People with the highest status and power often need to escape the burdens of the self because they are chronically overwhelmed by their authority and responsibility.

The Ultimate Escape

Like masochism, suicide is a puzzle to many people. Given the exceptionally strong motive to survive that we observe in all animals, why would a person try to take his or her own life? And, why are human beings the only animals that purposefully kill themselves? Other animals may sacrifice themselves to protect their young, and lemmings are known to follow one another into the sea, but these behaviors do not resemble the desperate actions of a suicidal person. Only human beings purposefully kill themselves for no other reason than to end their life.

Baumeister suggests that people who attempt suicide are not trying to kill themselves as much as they are trying to escape painful thoughts and feelings about themselves and their lives.[40] A person in the throes of despair who is contemplating suicide would presumably settle happily for a pill that eliminated self-awareness over the final act of killing him- or herself. Other animals do not kill themselves because they are not pestered by the distressing self-thoughts and feelings of existential hopelessness that plague many human beings.

Attempting suicide can provide a means of escaping the curse of the self in two ways. Most obviously, a person who successfully kills him- or herself has effectively solved the problem of a rampaging self that is inflicting intolerable misery. However, even when a suicide attempt is unsuccessful (as they usually are), the simple act of trying to kill oneself may help the person to escape the self for a while. As Baumeister observed, "An unsuccessful attempt at suicide may be a successful attempt at escape."[41] Simply thinking about and planning a suicide may reduce aversive self-awareness even if the person is not ultimately successful at killing him- or herself.

Thinking about killing oneself produces a state of concrete thinking that minimizes the sort of abstract self-thoughts that create despair. When people are thinking about suicide, they think in rigid, narrow, and concrete ways. As they plan their death, they focus intently on mundane details of the act. Because concentrating on plans for the suicide mutes higher level thoughts about the past and the future, people often achieve a feeling of emptiness, numbness, or even peace. People who have attempted suicide often report experiencing a sense of detachment or release as they made their plans, which was a vast improvement over the despair that prompted them to consider suicide in the first place.[42]

The Paradox of the Self

As we discussed earlier, human beings' capacity for self-reflection presumably evolved because it conferred a distinct advantage in the struggle to survive and reproduce. Paradoxically, the same mental process that enhanced our prehistoric ancestors' reproductive success is also responsible for many of the most dangerous and destructive behaviors in which people engage. The same self mechanism that allows people to see into the future in order to anticipate the negative consequences of their behavior ("Perhaps I shouldn't eat the rotten food with the slimy green mold growing on it") also prompts them to do potentially disastrous and self-destructive things in spite of those consequences ("but my friends will think I'm cool if I eat it").

How can the self be so reasonable and helpful yet so foolish and dangerous at the same time? As we have seen, the human self evolved under conditions that were far different than those in which people live today.[43] It is quite plausible that the environmental and social conditions of prehistoric Africa did not offer many opportunities for people to use their ability to self-reflect in ways that were harmful to themselves. For example, people who lived their entire lives within a single clan may have had little reason to impress other clan members in dangerous and arbitrary ways. In contrast, people in modern societies regularly change social groups and must reestablish their social identity each time. Furthermore, as we mentioned in chapter 4, prehistoric people living in an immediate-return environment were probably less troubled by self-reflection than are people today. With little reason to look more than a couple of days ahead, our prehistoric ancestors did not worry much about their distal futures.[44] As a result, they would have had less of a need to escape aversive self-thought through dangerous activities. Perhaps the selves of prehistoric people were more of an unmitigated blessing and less of a curse than the selves of people today.

7 ∷ Religion and Morality

The very purpose of religion is to control yourself, not to criticize others.
—THE 14TH DALAI LAMA

Siddhartha Gautama, born around 563 B.C.E., was the son of the ruler of a small Indian state just inside the border of present-day Nepal. As a young man, Siddhartha became intrigued with the problem of human suffering, and he left his family on a spiritual quest in an effort to understand why people suffer and how the human condition may be improved. Forsaking the comforts of his life as a prince, he lived as a wandering mendicant, practicing yoga, meditation, and asceticism. After six years of subjecting himself to extreme fasting and other forms of bodily mortification, Siddhartha concluded that he was no more likely to find the answers he was seeking through self-denial than through the comforts of his princely life back home. He thus came to advocate a lifestyle between the extremes of austerity and extravagance, something he would later call *The Middle Way.*

After meditating all night near the town of Gaya, Siddhartha experienced a series of insights that finally provided the answer to his search. Among them was the realization that people suffer, in part, because they cling to the idea that they have a self that must be protected and preserved. In his doctrine of *anatman*, or "no self," Siddhartha proposed that the self has no fixed or independent existence but rather is a temporary composite of concepts, feelings, and perceptions. This surprisingly modern view of the self became a core tenet in the philosophy that Siddhartha taught for over 40 years and that we know today as Buddhism.[1]

Siddhartha, better known as the Buddha (Pali, for "one who is awake"), was not the only moral philosopher or religious visionary to talk about the self. In fact, despite their many differences in doctrine, ritual, and practice, all major religious traditions share the conviction that the self is a problem. Various religions construe the nature of the problem a bit differently, but they concur that the self is an impediment—perhaps the chief impediment—to spiritual realization, religious practice, and moral behavior, and that a spiritual person must take steps to neutralize the self's negative effects.[2] The notion that the self is a "curse" can be traced to earliest written records in Hinduism, Taoism, and Buddhism, and it is likely that indigenous religions held this view even earlier. The major religions of the West—Judaism, Christianity, and Islam—have likewise confronted the problem of the self. Whatever one's personal religious orientation and beliefs—theist, pantheist, atheist, or agnostic—the fact that religious visionaries throughout history have wrestled with the problems created by the self is intriguing.

Spiritual Insight

Most religions agree that the self creates three special problems. First, most religions teach that the self interferes with spiritual realization and insight. Of course, various traditions construe spiritual insight in different ways. For some, it involves hearing the voice of God, being touched by the Holy Spirit, or accepting Jesus as one's savior. For others, it may involve enlightenment to the true nature of reality, perceiving the natural way of the Tao, reaching nirvana, or seeing visions. Regardless, most religions regard the inner monologue of the self as a hindrance to making contact with the divine and attaining other spiritual goals. The self's ongoing chatter not only creates "noise" that drowns out the perception of the divine, but it distorts reality in egocentric ways that obscure people's perceptions of ultimate reality.

According to the teachers of almost all religions, spiritual truths are difficult to discern as long as the individual is caught up in an inner self-driven monologue of worrying, planning, and remembering. That "still small voice" that religious practitioners seek cannot shout over the hubbub of one's self-chatter. The *Hua Hu Ching*, an early book of Taoist thought, says that conceptual thinking blocks "perception of the Great Oneness. . . . Those who live inside their egos are continually bewildered."[3] Similarly, St. John of the Cross insisted that contemplatives must "lose the radical self-centered awareness of our being, for it is our own self that stands in the way of God."[4] When asked why we don't see God clearly, Sri Ramakrishna, a Hindu master, replied, "Maya [illusion] is nothing but the egotism of the embodied soul. This egotism has covered everything like a veil."[5]

Second, most religions assert that the self can interfere with spiritual transformation. Most traditions teach that spiritual insight, salvation, redemption, or enlightenment require a radical change in the individual. Most liken the change to a rebirth, regeneration, or transformation in which the person acquires "a new heart and a new spirit."[6] Jesus proclaimed that "Except a man be born again, he can not see the kingdom of heaven,"[7] clearly recommending a rather dramatic personal transformation. Indigenous religions that involve an intense spiritual quest or initiation process often view the individual who returns from such an experience as a totally different person from the one who existed beforehand.[8] Repentance, also a mainstay of many religions, involves not only confession of past sins but also a vow to turn away from one's old identity to become a new person.

People often resist these personal transformations because they cling tightly to their existing identities even when new views and lifestyles would be more desirable and functional. Psychological research attests to the lengths that people will go to preserve their existing identities and to resist changes in their self-images, roles, or lifestyles.[9] Religious writers have recognized that this resistance may lead people to shrink from the changes that are needed to capitalize on spiritual experiences. A hard-and-fast commitment to a particular image of oneself stifles personal transformation.

Emmet Fox explains that this concern with self-imposed rigidity was the basis for Jesus's admonition during the Sermon on the Mount that people should "swear not at all"—not by heaven, by the earth, by Jerusalem, or by one's own head. According to Fox, Jesus was not warning his audience against cursing, as is often assumed, but rather against making vows that they will or will not do certain things in the future.[10] When a person swears to do or to refrain from doing something, this self-imposed rule restricts the person's ability to be influenced by changing circumstances and divine will. According to Fox, Jesus was suggesting that an ego-driven determination to conduct oneself in a particular way may override ongoing guidance from God. Thus, binding commitments to other people, and to oneself, are to be avoided.

According to various religions, the self stymies spiritual insight in yet a third way. All spiritual paths require a certain amount of effort and hard work. Typically, practitioners must pray or meditate, worship, perform rituals, study scriptures, and sometimes go on pilgrimages or spiritual quests. Religious teachers through the centuries have warned that spiritual seekers will be distracted from their quest by egoistic concerns. Seekers' self-centered hedonism may lead them to stray from the spiritual path or abandon it altogether. Put simply, people will talk themselves out of doing what is required for spiritual fulfillment.

According to many spiritual traditions, the goal for the religious practitioner is to distinguish these desires of the personal ego-self from those of the "true self," which many religions conceive as an aspect or manifestation of the One (God, Allah, Tao, Brahman, or Great Spirit). Most spiritual traditions suggest that people are much more than the small, earthbound, psychological self that they imagine themselves to be and should heed the True Self rather than the personal ego. The Upanishads, written in India between the 4th and 8th centuries B.C.E., made this distinction between the psychological ego and a person's true transcendent "self:" "Like two golden birds perched on the selfsame tree, intimate friends, the ego and the Self dwell in the same body. . . . As long as we think we are the ego, we feel attached and fall into sorrow. But realize that you are the Self, the Lord of life, and you will be freed from sorrow. When you realize that you are the Self, supreme source of light, supreme source of love, you transcend the duality of life and enter into the unitive state."[11]

Sogyal Rinpoche, a contemporary Buddhist master, made the same point: "Two people have been living in you all your life. One is the ego, garrulous, demanding, hysterical, calculating; the other is the hidden spiritual being, whose still voice of wisdom you have only rarely heard or attended to."[12] Such views suggest that the self-centered desires of the ego stand in opposition to people's inherent spiritual nature.

By interfering with the detection of Truth, resisting changes that are needed for transformation, and focusing the person on the hedonistic desires of the ego rather than the "big picture," religious traditions around the world teach that the self throws numerous roadblocks in the way of spiritual attainment.

Sin and Immorality

Most religions also blame the self for sinful thoughts and behaviors. The self is inherently inclined to make the individual selfish, self-centered, and thus sinful. When people are selfish and self-centered, they are likely to act without regard for the well-being of other people or divine will. Most religions teach that the spiritual person is selfless.

The link between the self and morality appears early in the Bible, for example. In the story from Genesis, God told Adam and Eve that they could eat the fruit of any tree in the Garden of Eden except the "tree that gives knowledge of what is good and what is bad." However, when tempted by the serpent to eat fruit from the tree, Eve ate it and gave some to Adam as well. When they had eaten the fruit, Adam and Eve suddenly realized for the first time that they were naked, and covered themselves with clothing made from leaves. When they encountered God that evening, they were banished from the garden because "they have the knowledge of what is good and what is bad."[13]

Although the story of Adam and Eve is often interpreted as one about the origins of sin, it can also be seen as a myth about the beginnings of human self-awareness. The tree of knowledge had conferred upon Adam and Eve self-awareness (which is why they suddenly realized they were naked), as well as the ability to distinguish right from wrong. An animal without a self can have no concept of morality; it does what it does without self-evaluation or regard for moral principles. We implicitly recognize this when responding to the misdeeds of animals; no matter how bad or unpleasant an animal's behavior may be, few people characterize an animal's behavior as immoral or the animal itself as sinful. Only by having a self that allows reflection on the implications and morality of one's behavior can a creature be said to be good or evil. Viewed in this way, the story of Adam and Eve draws a close link between self-reflection and the capacity for sinfulness.[14]

In most religions, self-centeredness and pride—creations of the ego—are singled out as particularly evil attributes. Within Christianity, pride is included among the "seven deadly sins" (along with greed, envy, anger, lust, gluttony, and sloth), and numerous spiritual writers have warned about the sinfulness of pride.[15] In Proverbs, we find that "God is stern in dealing with the arrogant, but to the humble He shows kindness."[16] The Catechism of the Catholic Church suggests that pride is "a sin against God's love," and that "hatred of God comes from pride."[17] St. Catherine, who lived in the 14th century, also described the perils of pride in no uncertain terms, warning particularly about the evils of pride among powerful people: "And who is hurt by the offspring of pride? Only your neighbors. For you harm them when your exalted opinion of yourself leads you to consider yourself superior and therefore to despise them. And if pride is in a position of authority, it gives birth to injustice and cruelty, and becomes a dealer in human flesh."[18]

Archimandrite Dionysios, an Eastern Orthodox cleric, stressed the importance of squelching the self when he said that "A man without ego is a man with God."[19] Jesus echoed the same sentiment when he said that "whosoever shall exalt himself shall be abased; and he that shall humble himself shall be exalted."[20]

Admonitions to abandon pride also pervade other traditions. The *Tao te Ching* recommends that followers of the Tao diminish self-importance:

> Achieve results, but never glory in them.
> Achieve results, but never boast.
> Achieve results, but never be proud.[21]

Rumi, the Sufi mystic, was a bit more blunt: "Put your vileness up to a mirror and weep. Get that self satisfaction flowing out of you!"[22]

In brief, most religious and spiritual systems view the self as an impediment to spirituality and morality, although they don't always state it in quite those terms. Not surprisingly, then, all religions offer their adherents ways to counteract the negative influences of self. In fact, religion itself might fruitfully be regarded as a system for counteracting the deleterious personal and social effects of self-awareness and egoism. Although many religious practices seem to fulfill this function, they can be classified roughly into two categories: one that tends to be associated with Western religions and one that tends to be associated with Eastern and indigenous religions.

The Western Solution: Controlling the Self

The major religions of the West—Judaism, Christianity, and Islam—confront the problems that are created by the self by admonishing believers to change the nature of who they are. Although differing in specifics, these traditions seem to agree that people can transform their sinful selves through faith, devotion, rituals, divine intervention, or diligently following moral commandments. Western religions try to strengthen and purify the self so that the person will obey moral directives and live ethically.

Judaism, for example, is based on adherence to moral laws. Actions are considered to be of primary importance, and proper beliefs are assumed to follow from behaving morally. Thus, Jewish life stresses strict adherence to the Law (particularly the Torah) regarding the observance of the Sabbath, regular attendance at synagogue, celebration at annual festivals (such as Passover and Yom Kippur), and dietary rules. Kabbalah, the mystical face of Judaism, asserts that a person's personality becomes increasingly refined and Godlike the more that one devotes him- or herself to religious study: the more one studies Kabbalah, the more divinely inspired one becomes. The emphasis of Judaism is largely on exercising one's own volition to behave in moral ways that please God.[23]

Although many scholars believe that Jesus's original teachings were more akin to the mystical traditions of the Sufis or Taoists than to the litany of the organized church,[24] modern Christianity is based largely on a system of moral rules that believers are expected to follow. Christians aspire to change the old, sinful self into a new and spiritually improved one. According to St. Paul, Christians must "put off . . . the old man, which is corrupt according to the deceitful lusts; and be renewed in the spirit of your mind; and that ye put on the new man, which after God is created in righteousness and true holiness."[25]

In some Christian denominations, this change from the old to the new person occurs in a conversion experience in which a radical spiritual and personal change is assumed to occur. According to this view, by making a conscious decision to "accept Jesus," the person is transformed. Then, after conversion, Christians are admonished to use Jesus as the ultimate role model for how they should behave. In recent years, members of Christian youth groups have displayed the letters *WWJD*— What would Jesus do?—to remind them and others to follow his example. Whatever their beliefs about faith and conversion, all Christian denominations emphasize that believers should become more Christlike.

Islam also relies on a combination of belief and religious practice, using personal volition to transform the individual. Islam is based on the Shahada or Muslim testimony of faith ("There is no true god but Allah, and Muhammad is the messenger of God"), which once declared with conviction and sincerity, allows the individual to start fresh as a new person. Muslim religious life is dominated by behaviors such as praying (five times a day), giving support to the needy, fasting from dawn until sundown during the month of Ramadan, and making a pilgrimage to Makkah (Mecca) at least once in one's lifetime.[26] From a psychological standpoint, the goal is to change the nature of the person's old self, replacing it with a new, holier one.

As world religions, Judaism, Christianity, and Islam differ in important respects. Yet they share the belief that people may become less sinful and more holy by intentionally changing themselves through actions of faith.

The Eastern Solution: Quieting the Self

The major Eastern religions—Hinduism, Buddhism, and Taoism—as well as many indigenous religions, adopt a rather different approach to solving the problem of the self. Rather than trying to change or control the self as the Western religions do, these approaches try to reduce the problems created by the self by quieting it down or even getting rid of it altogether. These religions have moral precepts that should be followed, but their guidelines are usually viewed as temporary crutches to be used only until the self is eradicated. The assumption is that, once the egocentric self disappears, the person will naturally behave in a moral way.

Dampening the Self

The approaches that have been used to reduce the self's influence fall into two general categories. The first involves self-quieting practices such as meditation and yoga, which are an essential aspect of Hinduism, Buddhism, and Taoism. In these practices, the goal is typically to stop self-relevant thinking, leaving the mind empty to perceive spiritual insights or to see the world as it really is.[27] Meditators enter a state of consciousness in which the self is much quieter than in ordinary life, reducing the degree to which their view of reality is contaminated by their concepts, judgments, attachments, and desires.

Sometimes meditators combine these self-quieting techniques with a deliberate effort to pay attention to their immediate experience. In walking meditation, meditators not only reduce their self-talk but also concentrate on the process of walking or the stimuli around them.[28] Similarly, Hindus and Buddhists sometimes arrange their temples and other meditation settings in a way that stimulates the senses. The sounds of tingling bells and chanting, scents of incense or fruits, and sights of flickering candles stimulate hearing, smell, and vision, gently drawing the person's attention away from inner self-talk and toward the outer world. Similarly, mindfulness practices train individuals to pay close attention to everything that they experience without internal comment or judgment.[29] Paying mindful attention to one's physical actions or sensations helps to minimize the intrusion of self-reflection. Meditations that are based on repeating a mantra also help to keep one's self quiet by focusing the person's attention on the sound of the mantra.

A second category of self-obliterating practices takes the opposite approach from meditation. Rather than quietly calming the mind, the practitioner subjects him- or herself to sensory overload. The chanting used by Hindus, Buddhists, and many indigenous groups serves this purpose. Typically, the chants are based on religious teachings, but as important as the content of the chant is its effect on self-reflection. The ongoing, rhythmic drone of the chanting stifles self-directed thought. If you have ever been somewhere that was so noisy that you "couldn't hear yourself think," you have experienced the effect of loud, droning sounds on the self. In religious practice the music and chants are often (but not always) soothing rather than frenetic, so the dampening of self-thought may be accompanied by relaxation and peacefulness.

Many cultures throughout history have used various forms of dancing, typically accompanied by drumming or chanting, in their religious practices. These dances have various purposes depending on the tradition, but they often induce a trancelike state in which the dancer is assumed to be susceptible to divine influence. The dancing of the whirling dervishes—Sufi mystics who dance and spin themselves into selflessness—is a well-known example.[30] Most indigenous religions—those practiced, for example, by Native Americans, Africans, and Aboriginal Australians—use dancing and drumming in their religious ceremonies. Presumably people find it quite difficult to think about their worldly identities when dancing in such a manner. In Voodoo, prolonged dancing and drumming help to induce states of selflessness in which participants are believed to be temporarily taken over by spirits.[31] Similarly, the stifling heat, steam, and aromas of Lakota sweat lodge ceremonies help to cut off conscious thought.[32]

Although an emphasis on quieting the self is most commonly associated with Eastern and indigenous religions, it can also be seen in aspects of Western religion. Many teachers in Judaism, Christianity, and Islam have advocated the abolishment of self-reflection as a path to spiritual realization. Early in the development of Christianity, meditation was far more commonly practiced than it is among Christians today. Jesus likely practiced meditation, and the meditative tradition carried on for some time after his death. It is known that the Desert Fathers—hermit Christian monks of the 4th century A.D.—practiced meditation.[33] Furthermore, the

Islamic Sufis regard the self as a barrier to spiritual fulfillment and employ practices to obliterate it.[34] Today, certain Christian denominations, including the Society of Friends (Quakers), use self-quieting silence in their services so that worshipers will be open to "the God within."[35] John Main, a Benedictine monk who learned meditation from a Hindu swami as a young man, repopularized the idea of Christian meditation as a means of stilling the self and opening oneself up to divine influence in the 20th century.[36]

Zen

Perhaps no approach has focused as directly and intentionally on practices designed to quiet the self as Zen. Although Zen is typically regarded as a sect of Buddhism (i.e., Zen Buddhism), in its pure form, Zen may be aligned with any religion (there are, in fact, Zen Jews and Zen Christians, for example) or with no religion whatsoever. At its core, Zen simply involves an ongoing commitment to live life in the present without unnecessary intrusion by the self. A primary goal of Zen (although goals are technically antithetical to Zen) is to do whatever one is doing with full and complete attention and no self-commentary.[37] As we have seen, few people do this naturally because their minds continually are abuzz with self-generated thoughts. Instead of focusing on the here and now, they fret over what's already happened, how things are going, and what's to come.

According to Zen, the way out of this mess is to loosen the self's grip. The reason we think and imagine and fret so much is that we are egoistically trying to look out for ourselves. In moments of pure rationality, we know that we can't reasonably expect things to happen the way we want, that life has no obligation to conform to our desires, and that all of our internal self-talk usually does more harm than good in helping us get what we want out of life. Yet we act as if life should always be to our liking and become egoistically upset when it is not. Our chronic preoccupation with what we want creates the mental ruminations that, if unchecked, ruin the quality of our daily lives. As Zen master Hui-Hai said to a student who was having difficulty seeing his path in life, "Your me is in the way."

Zen relies heavily on meditation to achieve the mental conditions necessary for this uncluttered approach to life. Through practicing sitting meditation or *zazen* (pronounced zah-zen), people learn to let distracting self-focused thoughts come and go without obscuring the present moment.[38] The goal of zazen is not necessarily to stop one's thoughts, although they do become less frequent and intense with practice. Rather, the goal is to see that one's self-thoughts are not reality, and thus they should not attract more than passing attention. Once a Zen student understands this, he or she finds it increasingly easy to let thoughts pass through the mind without evoking an emotional reaction. The mind begins to still, and the self's chatter subsides. The result is a state of quiet awareness, without comment or judgment, of whatever happens to be right here, right now. Zen suggests that, as we still our impetuous ego and quiet our minds, people achieve a quiet acceptance of each moment as it is, resulting in a less cluttered and confused experience of life.

Zen masters are also known for their use of the *koan* (pronounced ko-ahn), a seemingly inexplicable question or story that confounds rational interpretation. Imagine that your venerable master relates the following story and expects you to respond:

> The priest Nan-ch'üan found the monks arguing about a cat. He held up his hand and said, "Everyone! If you can say something, I will spare this cat. If you can't say anything, I will cut this cat in half." No one could say a word, so Nan-ch'üan cut the cat in two. [Being a compassionate Buddhist monk, it seems likely that Nan-ch'üan only pretended to bisect the cat.] That evening, Chao-chou returned from outside, and Nan-ch'üan told him what happened. Chao-chou removed a sandal from his foot, put it on his head, and walked out. Nan-ch'üan laughed and said, "If you had been here, the cat would have been spared."[39]

For most people, the most obvious conclusion after hearing such a koan is that your master has lost his mind. Not only is the behavior of the principal characters, Nan-ch'üan and Chao-chou, incomprehensible, but the master also seems to think that the story means something.

Zen masters insist that there is a message in such tales, but it is not amenable to rational inspection and analysis. The purpose of the koan is to break down the student's normal, habitual way of thinking about the world and him- or herself.[40] Recall from chapter 3 that much of what people regard as reality is based, in part, on their ongoing stream of self-talk and interpretation. In assigning students to study koans, Zen teachers hope to bring their students' rational, self-guided interpretations to a screeching halt. Hakuin, the Zen master who popularized the use of koans, explained that "If you take up a koan and examine it persistently, your spirit will die and your ego will be destroyed."[41] There comes a point at which the self simply gives up trying to decipher the koan, which leaves the student open to a new way of seeing the world and him- or herself.

In the nearly 2,000 years since it emerged as a blending of Buddhist and Taoist thought in China, Zen (or Chan, as it is known in China) has accumulated an extensive tradition of beliefs, rituals, and practices, many of which are peripheral to the essence of Zen itself. People who resonate to esoteric rituals or religious beliefs can find them in some sects of Zen Buddhism. But, people can also have their Zen plain if they wish. Many Westerners have come to "secular Zen" as a lifestyle without the religious trappings simply as a way of reducing the degree to which their lives are dominated by the self.

The Mystical State

Many people regard the term *mystic* with either awe or skepticism because it conjures up an image of a powerful visionary with special spiritual and psychic abilities. In fact, mysticism is somewhat more mundane, even if the mystical state itself may inspire awe in those who experience it. Many writers prefer to use the terms *peak experience, transcendent experience,* or *unmediated consciousness* rather than mystical experience to remove the magical, mysterious connotations.

Mysticism refers to practices that aim to obtain direct knowledge or first-hand experience of reality without the use of thoughts or reasoning.[42] Mystics try to attain a clear vision of reality, unblemished by thoughts, concepts, or opinions about it, and thus experience ultimate reality firsthand. Most religious traditions have branches that include a mystical component. In theistic religions, the objective is to have a direct encounter with the divine (e.g., God, Allah, Brahman, Great Spirit). In nontheistic religions, such as Taoism and Buddhism, the practitioner aspires to experience the underlying essence of the world as it actually exists. In either case, the goal is the direct experience of the world and oneself as they really are, as opposed to how we typically think they are.[43]

The assumption that underlies mysticism is one that we have encountered throughout this book: people do not normally experience the world as it "really is." Rather, their experience is contaminated by the concepts, labels, ideas, and opinions that they automatically impose on everything they encounter. Under normal circumstances, people cannot help but to see the world through these mental filters, many of which are maintained by their ongoing self-talk. As we have seen, people find it virtually impossible to step outside themselves and see the world in an impartial fashion. Not only do their egocentric, egotistical tendencies distort the truth, but their beliefs and opinions about themselves and the world also channel their perceptions in particular ways. We have discussed at length how people talk to themselves as they go through life, adding a running commentary to whatever they encounter. The result is that they rarely ever have a view of the world that is not overlaid with self-talk.

The solution, according to the mystical traditions, is to stop the self from interfering with one's direct experience. By inhibiting self-talk, one's ongoing interpretations and judgments are stopped, thereby revealing reality without obstruction by conscious thought. The Yacqui shaman, Don Juan, explained it to his apprentice Carlos Castaneda this way: "The first act of a teacher is to introduce the idea that the world we think we see is only a view, a description of the world. . . . A teacher . . . aims at stopping that view. Sorcerers call it stopping the internal dialogue, and they are convinced that is the single most important technique that an apprentice can learn."[44]

Various mystical traditions promote different means of stopping the internal dialogue of the self, but the most common is undoubtedly meditation. Other traditions, including many indigenous ones, stop the self by overstimulating it, using chanting, singing, dancing, and even sex. More extreme are traditions that overwhelm the self by requiring people to withstand rigorous, stressful, and sometimes painful procedures.[45] Fasting, certain yogic practices, living burial, and physically painful procedures (such as incisions and handling hot objects) all have the capacity to narrow the person's focus of attention (as we discussed in the context of masochism in chapter 6). Other people have used psychoactive drugs such as peyote, cannabis, and LSD to induce transcendent experiences. In the United States, members of the Native American Church incorporate peyote into their ceremonies as a means of inducing mystical experience. In the case of using hallucinogens, however, it is never clear which aspects of the resulting experience are due to stopping the self (as in a true mystical experience) and which are due to the direct hallucinogenic effects of the drug.[46]

For our purposes, the important thing about mysticism is what it teaches us about how the self influences people's perceptions of the world. When mystics successfully turn self-reflection off, they experience a world that is somewhat different from the one they experience in their ordinary state of consciousness. Regardless of their religious backgrounds, mystics the world over report similar experiences. They may interpret their experiences in ways that are consistent with their religious and cultural beliefs, but their reports share a great deal in common.[47]

First, mystics invariably report perceiving that everything is a unified whole. When the concepts, categories, and labels they normally use to classify objects and events are silenced, people experience the world as an undifferentiated unity. This oneness also includes the individual him- or herself because, with the self no longer operating as usual, people lose their sense of unique identity and thus feel that they are a part of the harmonious integral whole that they perceive. Experiencing the underlying oneness of the world often leads mystics to assert that they and the universe are one or that they feel they have merged with God.

Second, mystics typically report a shift in their experience of time. They may say that time stopped or that they were outside of time, in eternity. This transcendence of time is not as strange or magical as it may at first sound. In many ways, our sense of time arises from the fact that we consciously monitor the passage of time and think about ourselves in a temporal framework (what we did yesterday, what we will do later today). I suspect that if asked during any waking moment, you would generally have a pretty good idea of what time it is.

When we are neither deliberately monitoring the passage of time nor thinking about past or future, time seems to stand still or pass more quickly than when we are watching the minutes tick by. When people lose themselves (or more accurately, lose their self) in an engrossing activity, as when in a flow experience, they may have no sense of time passing. Only when self-reflection returns do they realize that time has elapsed, making it seem in retrospect that it flitted by in an instant. People sometimes say that "time passes quickly when you're having fun," but it may be more accurate to say that time is simply immaterial when we don't monitor it. While engaged in an engrossing activity and the self is quiet, we have little or no sense of time passing, which is precisely what people report during a mystical experience.

Third, people who enter the mystical state usually report positive emotions such as peace, love, and joy. These emotions are due in part to a sense of awe or wonder about the specialness, sacredness, or mystery of the experience. They typically have the conviction that they have perceived something new about the world and that their experience is somehow more "real" than the world they normally inhabit. This peacefulness may also result from the fact that, without self-talk to stir up negative emotions, the mystical experience is free of tension.

Finally, the individual in a mystical state loses some or all of his or her sense of personal identity. Upon returning to their normal state of consciousness, mystics report that they had ceased to exist as a separate entity during their mystical experience. Abraham Maslow, the noted humanistic psychologist who studied people who had such experiences, described their experience with terms such as *ego-transcending, self-forgetful, egoless, unselfish, desireless,* and *detached.*[48]

Although controversy remains, most experts have concluded that all mystical experiences share these features, which are roughly the same in all cultures and religions throughout history.[49] Of course, people interpret what they have experienced in line with their belief systems. Taoists report that they have experienced the Tao; Christians, Jews, and Muslims that they have encountered God; Buddhists that they have become enlightened to the nature of reality, and so on. Although mystics' interpretations tend to be phrased in spiritual terms, we could just as easily say that mystical experience involves a new perception of physical rather than spiritual reality. That is, if stopping the self allows mystics to glimpse the world with less intrusion by their self-thoughts, they could be said to have a clearer view of physical reality.

Researchers in the new field of *neurotheology* have begun to study the changes in the brain that accompany mystical and other kinds of religious experiences.[50] Their findings suggest that mystical states are associated with the disengagement of neural circuits in the frontal and temporal lobes of the brain that generate self-awareness and mark the passage of time. In addition, electrical activity changes in portions of the parietal lobes that orient people spatially and allow them to demarcate the boundary between themselves and the external world. Because the brain can no longer tell where the person ends and the world begins, the individual feels him- or herself to be endless and interconnected with all things. There is also evidence that hyperstimulation, such as produced by prolonged dancing or chanting, affects the parts of the brain that allow people to distinguish themselves from the world.[51] Together, these data suggest that, in order for people to have a mystical experience, the regions of the brain that mark the distinction between self and world must be quiescent. The fact that mystical states often involve positive emotional experiences also implicates brain regions that control emotion, such as the amygdala.

People will interpret the results of these studies differently depending on their personal beliefs. Nonbelievers will conclude that mystical experience is a normal, though perhaps uncommon, state of consciousness that results from certain patterns of brain activity. If people can cause certain neuronal circuits to shut down through mediation or other activities, they will have unitive experiences in which they feel one with the world or think they sense God's presence. Believers, on the other hand, will insist that the direct experience of ultimate, transcendent reality creates particular changes in the brain, just as the experience of ordinary reality does. After all, they argue, every experience is mediated by brain activity, and that is true whether we are experiencing the smell of pizza, the sensations of sex, or oneness with the divine.

Maslow concluded that virtually everyone is able to have mystical or peak experiences. If a fundamental aspect of the transcendent experience involves simply quieting, if not eliminating, self-talk, it seems likely that most people have experienced such states either spontaneously or after training in meditation or similar practices. As I noted earlier, the flow experience contains elements of the mystical state. Maslow observed, however, that some people find experiences of this sort frightening, and thus avoid, suppress, or deny them. People who try to be extremely rational, who think that their experience indicates that they are losing touch with reality, or who wish to be unemotional may find peak experiences unsettling if not downright frightening.

No one sustains this kind of selfless vision of the world permanently, but the experience typically deeply affects those who experience it even briefly. The perception of oneness often changes people's sense of identity from that of a self-contained individual to part of a larger cosmic whole. People also tend to emerge from mystical experiences with a more positive, optimistic outlook on life, increased feelings of peace, and a more patient, compassionate, and altruistic approach to other people.[52] In seeing such changes, religious individuals are apt to infer that the person has had a direct experience with the divine. Nonreligious people, in contrast, may conclude that unmediated consciousness has given them a new perspective on themselves and the world, and that this realization has led to changes in how they approach themselves, other people, and life in general. Whatever one's interpretation, fostering one's ability to quiet the self and experience this state appears to alleviate some of the curse of the self.

8 ::

The Self Out of Control

Lack of will power has caused more failure than lack of intelligence or ability.
—FLOWER NEWHOUSE

Most people know at least one person like Alan, the brother of one of my friends. For the 30 years that I've known him, Alan's life has been a series of missteps, bad decisions, and bungled opportunities. Although he was undoubtedly capable of doing well in school, he never put enough time and effort into his schoolwork to accomplish more than barely passing grades. After graduation, Alan and his girlfriend got married because she was pregnant, but their relationship was rocky from the start owing to Alan's difficulty in controlling his temper. Through the years, Alan held a series of unsatisfying jobs, all of which he eventually lost because he either quit impulsively in a huff or was fired for not showing up for work. Even though his employment was uncertain, Alan bought almost everything he wanted and accumulated a rather large debt, which he tried to eliminate again and again through gambling.

The noteworthy thing about Alan is that he brought most of his troubles on himself. His problems arose from his failure to control himself effectively. Alan's life was a series of fiascos because he either couldn't or wouldn't make himself study, practice safe sex, control his temper, be a responsible employee, live within his means, and resist the lure of gambling. Although his case may be extreme, most of us can identify with at least some of the difficulties Alan had managing his behavior. Which of the following events have created problems that undermined your success, happiness, and personal well-being?

- You had trouble maintaining your desired weight because you overate.
- You were swamped by excessive debt because you bought things that you could not afford.
- You overindulged in alcohol, cigarettes, or drugs.
- You had trouble controlling your anger.
- You procrastinated on important tasks at school or work.
- You failed to keep a secret that you should have kept.
- You violated your moral standards.
- You behaved sexually in an unwise or irresponsible manner.
- You broke a promise you had intended to keep.
- You got into trouble because you acted impulsively.

Many of the problems that undermine the quality of people's lives involve failures of self-control. Most people would strongly endorse the idea that they should eat reasonably, live within their means, avoid addictions, control their anger, complete their work on time, keep secrets, follow their moral standards, be sexually responsible, abide by their promises, and otherwise reign in impulses that might get them into trouble. Yet most of us have violated some of these tenets, not because we intended to do harm but because we could not make ourselves do otherwise.

However, most people have also shown that they can, at times, exercise magnificent self-control. Sometimes they successfully maintain their diet and lose weight (at least for awhile), resist buying things they can't afford, conquer their dependence on cigarettes or alcohol, control their anger, meet deadlines at school and work, guard others' secrets, stand up for what they believe, resist imprudent sexual urges, keep their promises, and hold other undesired impulses in check. In fact, sometimes we see examples of self-control that seem almost superhuman, as when human rights activists fast for their cause or a bystander dives into a swollen, freezing river to rescue someone. Even Alan, the poster child for poor self-control, has undoubtedly controlled himself many times in his life.

We have, then, the paradox of an organism that can sometimes exert firm control over itself, even at great personal risk, but at other times cannot make itself behave in even minimally acceptable ways. Why is it that we can sometimes control ourselves quite successfully, but at other times seem to live at the mercy of our impulses?

Self-Regulation

Perhaps the greatest advantage of having a self is that it allows people to regulate their own thoughts, feelings, and behavior.[1] Because they can see into the future and anticipate the consequences of their actions, people can take steps to behave in ways that facilitate their well-being. The self not only allows people to behave intentionally in ways that move them toward important goals, but it also permits them to override impulses that they know are not in their best interests.[2] Other animals cannot do this. All organisms possess internal mechanisms by which they regulate themselves automatically, but human beings are unique in their ability to control themselves intentionally.

For example, we may purposefully control our attention, as when parents force themselves to listen to their child's rambling account of a trivial matter, a student makes himself pay attention to a boring lecture, or a sleepy driver forces herself to pay careful attention to the highway. We may also try to control our thoughts, such as when we do not want to dwell on some upsetting matter or are trying not to be distracted from our work by extraneous preoccupations. We may also control our emotions as we shrug off a disappointment, suppress our anger, or hide our glee at a rival's misfortune. And, perhaps most important, we often control our behavior, either by making ourselves do something we prefer not to do or by making ourselves resist compelling urges. Without a self, we would have no possibility of purposefully controlling our attention, thoughts, emotions, or behavior. Armed with the capacity to evaluate and control ourselves, we are not puppets of our genetics and circumstances to the same extent as other animals.

Two features of the self are key to human beings' ability to regulate ourselves intentionally. The first is our ability to imagine ourselves in the future. By thinking about the likely consequences of their actions, people can deliberately choose to behave in ways that are beneficial in the long run. As we will see, many failures of self-control occur because people do not adequately transcend the current situation to imagine how things will turn out later.

The second is our ability to talk to ourselves. People typically control themselves by telling themselves to do or not to do certain things.[3] From the time they are very young, children learn to do as they are told, and other people's instructions, orders, and encouragement motivate and guide them to behave in particular ways. As the self emerges, children develop the ability to tell themselves to do things as well. At first, their self-instructions are often audible. A child starting to touch an object that he has just been told to leave alone may say out loud, "No! Don't touch!" At times, even adults revert to spoken language for self-control, as when a woman overtly warns herself to control her temper ("Calm down; it's no big deal") or a man reminds himself aloud of a grammatical rule ("Let's see, it's '*I* before *E* except after *C*'").

As children grow, their self-generated instructions become internalized, and they learn to control their behavior by talking to themselves in their own minds.[4] Researchers believe that this sort of private speech is essential for deliberate self-control. Through private speech, people remind themselves of their goals ("I need to stop watching TV and work on that presentation I have to give tomorrow"), plan ahead for upcoming self-control opportunities ("Remember not to lose your temper when Mr. Smith criticizes your idea"), give themselves instructions for particular actions ("I think I'll include in my presentation mention of Fred's involvement"), assess their progress toward their goals ("Hmm, I need to hurry to get this finished by midnight"), and comment on their performance ("Well, it's not perfect, but it'll do"). The ability to talk to ourselves is essential for planning our actions, staying on course, and judging whether or not we have been successful.

In many instances, the self is up to the task of regulating our attention, thoughts, emotions, and behaviors. We have all learned how to restrain certain undesirable behaviors, such as overeating, swearing, procrastination, excessive anger, oversleeping, leaving the toilet seat up, and other vices and bad habits. And, we have also learned how to make ourselves do things that we would often prefer not to do, such as compromising, paying our bills, cleaning the house, flossing our teeth, and going to work when we'd rather stay in bed. Yet not all efforts to control oneself are successful, and some are miserable failures. Most people who want to lose weight have tried dieting on many occasions, smokers typically try several times before they break the habit (if they ever do), and many people finally despair of ever changing the behaviors that create problems for them. This is not to say that self-initiated change never works; it clearly does. But the self is, at best, an imperfect control mechanism. Like Alan, all of us sometimes have trouble controlling ourselves.

Psychologists and other researchers have devoted a good deal of attention to self-regulation.[5] Although we do not yet have a complete understanding of precisely how people manage themselves through willpower and effort, we have a reasonably clear idea of the necessary ingredients for successful self-control. Four primary things are needed in order for people to control their own behavior. They must adequately monitor themselves, have clear goals, mentally transcend the immediate situation to imagine the long-term consequences of their behavior, and have sufficient self-control strength to override impulses that go against the desired behavior. If any of these elements are weak or missing, people will be unlikely to control themselves as effectively as they desire.

Self-Awareness: Monitoring What One Is Doing

To control their behavior purposefully, people must consciously and deliberately monitor what they are doing.[6] As long as their self is engaged and they are consciously thinking about their behavioral goal—to eat less, stop chewing their fingernails, control their anger, or whatever—people often control themselves rather effectively. But as soon as the self is distracted from the goal, either by external events (a lively party or a good movie, for example) or by other self-thoughts (such as daydreams or worries), the undesired behavior may appear unbidden. So, despite my sworn conviction not to overeat at the party, I may get caught up in the frivolity and mindlessly consume massive quantities of junk food. I can resist chewing on my fingernails as long as I'm monitoring myself, but when I lose myself in a good book, I may mindlessly gnaw them to the quick. Although I'm determined to control my temper, problems may distract me from my goal and so I lash out at a minor frustration. Deliberate self-control is possible only if the person actively monitors his or her behavior.

For many years, psychologists debated whether people's behavior is determined most strongly by aspects of the situation they are in or by characteristics of the person him- or herself. On one hand, a person's behavior is almost always affected by the situation in which the person finds him- or herself—its familiarity, the presence or absence of other people, the norms and rules that are in effect in the situation, the possibility of rewards and punishments, the physical setting (such as its color, lighting, temperature, and size), and so on. On the other hand, a person's behavior is also determined by internal, personal factors such as the person's personality characteristics, beliefs, attitudes, values, and goals. The advocates of one extreme position, the behaviorists, argued that the situation reigned supreme; and advocates of the other extreme, the psychoanalysts, argued that what happened inside the individual was paramount.

Undoubtedly, almost every behavior is influenced by both situational and personal factors, and it now seems absurd to have ever thought that only one answer is correct. Even so, it does appear that people are sometimes influenced primarily by the situation but at other times are affected more strongly by internal psychological factors, including their deliberate efforts to control themselves. Not until the 1970s did researchers begin to develop a cogent way of thinking about the fact that behavior is sometimes under personal, internal control whereas sometimes it is not. In the early 1970s, two social psychologists, Thomas Shelley Duval and Robert Wicklund, proposed a theory that identified self-awareness as the critical variable that determines whether behavior is influenced primarily by the situation or by the inner workings of the person.[7] When people are self-aware and consciously thinking about themselves, Duval and Wicklund suggested, they are more strongly influenced by their personal standards, attitudes, and characteristics than when they are not self-aware, in which case they either react automatically, mindlessly, and habitually or else are affected primarily by features of the situation in which they find themselves.

This intriguing proposition was supported in hundreds of experiments. Studies showed, for example, that people's privately held attitudes were related to how they behaved only when people were induced to think about themselves.[8] When they were not self-aware, however, people reacted out of habit or were influenced by the situation. In fact, some studies showed that people with diametrically opposing attitudes would behave in precisely the same way when they were not self-aware![9] People do not purposefully control their behavior in ways that are consistent with their attitudes, values, and goals unless they are self-focused and monitoring themselves. Self-control requires self-awareness.

The importance of self-awareness to self-control helps to explain many instances in which people do things that are out of character. Afterwards, we may wonder why we acted uncharacteristically, in opposition to the goals we wanted to accomplish or contrary to our personal values. Later we may think, "I wasn't myself; I don't know what got into me," which raises the question of what it is that gets into people when they act in these ways. When people aren't themselves, whose self are they?

Perhaps the best answer is that when people act out of character, they often aren't anybody's self—not even their own! Because their self was not actively engaged in monitoring their actions, they were not operating under self-control. Being on autopilot, factors other than their personal goals and values influenced their behavior. People can exercise deliberate self-control only when they actively monitor what they are doing.

The term *deindividuation* refers to a temporary loss of self-awareness in which the self goes into standby mode, to use a computer metaphor.[10] It's as if the conscious self has "powered down," leaving the individual subject to the influences of the situation and personal habit. People who are in a deindividuated state have a diminished ability to think about themselves and, as a result, do not monitor or regulate themselves as they normally do. Failing to monitor themselves sufficiently allows impulses that were previously held in check by deliberate self-control to emerge. Research shows that people often behave in uncharacteristically dishonest, cruel, and antisocial ways when they are deindividuated.[11] At other times, however, deindividuation can release people's inhibitions to act in a positive, prosocial fashion.[12] Sometimes people refrain from expressing kindness, love, and caring because they fear rejection or they do not want to appear softhearted. However, if they become deindividuated and their attention is diverted from themselves, they may not control their prosocial urges and, thus, may act more compassionately. So, turning off the self is not always a bad thing, although the costs often outweigh the benefits.

Many things can lead to a deindividuating loss of self-awareness. What deindividuation-producing events have in common is their ability to draw people's attention away from themselves and toward external stimuli.[13] For example, deindividuation sometimes occurs in large, unruly crowds in which people's attention is focused on stimulating, arousing, or emotion-producing events. A protestor in a civil disturbance may have the urge to hurl bricks and invectives at the police but controls those urges until the distractions of a rioting crowd draw his attention away from thinking about his values. At that point, he may mindlessly join the melee. Experimental research shows that anything that diminishes a person's sense of individuality can induce deindividuation, including darkness, wearing the same uniforms as everyone else who is present (particularly if one's face is covered), and particularly large groups.[14]

The degree to which people in a large group will maintain versus lose self-awareness depends in part on the relative sizes of any subgroups that may exist within the larger crowd. For example, a rioting throng being corralled by police consists of two subgroups—rioters and police—and the relative number in each group helps to determine the self-awareness of the individuals involved. Researchers have devised a rough formula to express the effect of group size on the self-awareness of any given individual. Put simply, the self-awareness of the members of a subgroup is related to the self-attention ratio—the size of the other subgroup divided by the total number of people present.[15] For example, imagine singing a duet on stage in front of an audience of 100 people. There are two people in your subgroup (you and the other singer) and 100 people in the other subgroup (the audience). According to the formula, your self-awareness is equal to the ratio of the number of people in the other subgroup (100) to the total number of people present (102); thus, your self-attention ratio would be .98, which indicates that you would probably be quite focused on yourself. (In fact, you might say that you felt very "self-conscious" while on stage.) Compare this to a situation in which you are performing with a chorus of 60 singers in front of an audience of 10. Your self-attention ratio would be only .14 (that is, 10/70). Lost in the crowd, you would not be particularly self-aware.

If self-control requires self-awareness, and if the self-attention index reflects how self-aware people in a group are likely to be, then people ought to be more likely to lose control—to become deindividuated—in situations that are characterized by a low self-attention ratio. To examine this possibility, Brian Mullen analyzed 60 instances in which blacks were lynched by whites in the United States between 1899 and 1946.[16] For each case, Mullen calculated the self-attention ratio based on the number of victims and the number of lynchers in the group, and also judged the atrocity of the event. (Obviously, all lynchings are atrocities, yet some are particularly heinous by virtue of their cruelty.) As predicted, the self-attention ratio was inversely related to the atrocity of the lynching. Mobs that, according to their self-attention ratio, were less self-aware perpetrated particularly atrocious crimes. Or, to say it differently, many of these events may have been less atrocious, if they had occurred at all, had the ratio of potential lynchers to potential victims been lower, thereby making the lynchers more self-aware of what they were doing.

Self-awareness is absolutely essential for effective self-control, but, ironically, too much self-awareness can sometimes interfere with a person's ability to control his or her responses. Some of the problems that people try to fix through self-control are caused by too much self-reflection to begin with. When this is the case, paying even more attention to oneself inevitably backfires.[17] For example, if a man is impotent because he thinks too much about his sexual performance, no amount of additional self-thinking will help him control the problem. Likewise, deliberately trying not to be an insomniac won't help one fall asleep, and telling oneself not to obsess over the breakup of a relationship is not useful because doing so keeps you thinking about the breakup. In each case, the problem itself is exacerbated by self-thinking, so it won't be relieved by monitoring oneself more closely.

Goals and Standards

People cannot exert self-control—to eat sensibly, study for a test, control their temper, practice safe sex, or drive safely, for example—unless they have an explicit goal. Some failures of self-regulation occur not because the self has failed but because the person did not have a clear idea of what he or she was trying to achieve. Self-control requires the existence of goals that the person desires to meet, along with clear standards for judging whether or not those goals are met.[18] A person on a diet should have both a clear goal and standards regarding what he should and should not eat. A student facing an evening of homework needs an ultimate goal as well as a standard regarding what she ought to accomplish that evening. A marathoner must have goals for her performance in the big race and standards regarding how much training is needed to achieve it. Sometimes people appear to lack self-control because their goals or standards are not clear in their own minds.

More often, however, people have a clear goal about the behavior they want to control (and corresponding standards for assessing its attainment), but it conflicts with other goals.[19] For example, a man on a diet may decide in advance to eat lightly at tonight's party and to avoid calorie-laden alcoholic drinks altogether. His goal and standards are quite clear. However, he may also desire to have fun at the party, join in the festivities, and avoid letting other people know he is dieting. When he later becomes immersed in the party, these competing goals may sabotage his goal of dieting, so that he gorges himself and gets drunk. In retrospect, the man probably feels that he lost self-control, but in fact, he lost control only with regards to the goal of dieting. His self may have successfully helped him to meet other goals, such as having a great time at the party. Many failures of self-regulation occur because one urge or goal overrides another. This suggests that people who are trying to control a particular behavior should consider whether doing so conflicts with other goals that they may have.

Sometimes self-control breaks down because a person's initial decision to act (or refrain from acting) in a particular way is initially motivated by a particular goal, but later on, another, competing goal becomes more important and causes the person to change his or her mind. For example, Annie may decide to donate blood for the first time. However, once she arrives at the blood center and sees the needles and bags of blood, the goal of avoiding pain may become more important to her than the goal of donating blood. As a result, she changes her mind and decides to leave without donating. She did not follow through on her initial intention because other considerations overrode it. In retrospect, Annie might feel that she had "changed her mind" rather than "lost self-control," but other people may perceive that she was unable to exert sufficient control over herself to follow through on her initial intention.

In other cases, people do not control their behavior as they intended even though they have not changed their mind about the desirability of doing it. Rather, they perform a behavior contrary to their goals even as they are telling themselves at the time that they shouldn't do it! Such actions, in which people intentionally and freely behave contrary to their better judgment are called *akratic actions*.[20] (*Akrasia* comes from a Greek word that refers to a weakness of will or a deficiency in the power of self-control.) Akratic actions may be the most common variety of self-control failure. They are particularly interesting because they occur even though the person is telling him- or herself not to do them at the time. A rational analysis of the situation tells the person that it is better not to behave in these ways, yet he or she persists nonetheless. Clearly, the problem in akratic actions does not involve the absence of a goal.

Transcending the Immediate Situation

Part of what has happened to the person who overeats despite his intention to eat sensibly, the person who succumbs to an unwise sexual temptation, or a person who tells off the boss—indeed what often happens whenever people do not regulate themselves effectively—is that their behavior is controlled by the immediate situation and their long-term goal (of losing weight, being faithful, or keeping one's job) takes a back seat. In many instances, effective self-control requires that a person forgo compelling urges in the present situation in order to achieve important long-term goals.[21] The dieter must resist the siren's song of the junk food in the present situation in order to achieve the long-term goal of losing weight. The spouse who is tempted by the offer of an extramarital fling must fully consider the possible long-term implications of a dalliance. The employee must consider the consequences of shouting at the boss in order to resist the urge to express his or her anger.

Self-control often fails because the person does not adequately transcend the immediate situation. In the abstract, the person sincerely wants to behave in a particular fashion because doing so will have long-term benefits or avoid long-term costs. However, a situation may arise in which the self's ability to contemplate the future is overwhelmed by compelling stimuli in the immediate situation. For example, the student may be committed to studying for tomorrow's test and have every intention of exerting the self-control needed to study sufficiently. But when roommates invite her to join them at the local pub the night before the test, the immediate situation is far more compelling than the imagined future that the self conjures up. A married individual may be sincerely committed to the notion of fidelity yet be seduced when the stimuli in the situation cut off reasonable self-thought about the future. Employees know that shouting at their boss is unwise, yet a particularly frustrating interaction with him or her may override any thoughts about the long-term consequences of doing so. Had individuals in such situations been able to keep the long-term implications of their behavior in mind, they might have been able to resist the urges that were pulling on them.

The difficulty of transcending the immediate situation is compounded because the value of any particular goal decreases the further the goal is in the future. A potential reward that could be received soon exerts a stronger pull on behavior than the same reward in the distant future.[22] Likewise, potential costs and punishments seem worse when they might happen soon than when they might happen later on. Because both rewards and punishments are discounted by delay, the lure of immediate gratification often overrides the pain of future negative consequences. As a result, behavior is often determined primarily by a person's assessment of the consequences of the action in the near future (what economists and decision-theorists call the "local utility" of the action) and less by the overall consequences of the action in the long run (the "global utility").

For every choice a person makes, there is a time horizon in the relatively near future that defines the "local" period of time that the person views as "the present situation." Consequences that might occur within this window of time are given inordinate weight when people decide how to behave. Possible consequences beyond this local time frame are given little, if any consideration. At one extreme, sometimes the local time horizon is virtually zero, and the person considers only the immediate consequences of his or her actions. We usually describe behaviors that occur with a very brief local time horizon as impulsive or shortsighted. At the other extreme, sometimes a person's time horizon is very far in the future, encompassing his or her whole life or even longer. In such cases, present decisions may be affected by possible consequences that will occur way down the road, such as when a person decides to recycle to keep the earth viable for his or her grandchildren, or a religious person's behavior is constrained by beliefs in an afterlife.

For over 30 years, Walter Mischel and his colleagues have studied the strategies that people use to control themselves and the factors that affect their success at self-control.[23] In many of their studies, research participants are asked to decide whether they want to obtain a less valued outcome right now or wait to receive a more valued outcome in the future. For example, in the standard delay-of-gratification paradigm, children might be shown a small pile of M&Ms and a large pile of M&Ms and told that, if they will wait until the researcher returns in a few minutes, they will receive the large pile of M&Ms. However, they are also told that they may eat from the small pile at any time while they are waiting if they wish. However, if they eat any of the candy before the researcher returns, they will forgo the large pile. The researcher then leaves the room for a half hour or so and the child is observed.

This research has shown that the ability to delay gratification depends greatly on people's use of transcendence strategies that allow them to look beyond the immediate situation and put it in context with their longer-range goals.[24] For example, people can better resist the temptation to settle for the immediate, less valued reward if they distract themselves from it. In fact, children who are particularly effective at self-control may actually cover their eyes so that they cannot see the reward they are trying to resist. In contrast, children who focus on the immediate sensory properties of the present reward, such as how delicious it will be, have more difficulty resisting it.[25]

In addition, people trying to resist temptation may talk to themselves about the merits of the larger, more distal reward ("Boy, it sure will be nice to have that big pile of M&Ms"). As long as they keep the distal reward in mind, they are able to hold out longer.[26] Similarly, in everyday life, people may bolster their motivation to continue working on difficult tasks by reminding themselves of the long-term payoffs of doing so.

Transcending the situation does two things that help people control their behavior. It reduces the saliency and appeal of rewards in the immediate situation, and it leads the person to consider consequences that lie outside the local time frame. Together, these two effects allow people to forgo attractive rewards now for the possibility of greater rewards in the future. Only by using self-talk to project oneself into the future to imagine the long-term consequences of one's actions can people adequately control themselves.

Self-Control Strength

Tracey is trying to lose weight, both because his doctor says that it will lower his blood pressure and because he detests how he looks carrying an extra 30 pounds. Tracey has made a commitment to himself to watch what he eats, with the goal of trying to lose two pounds a week for the next few months. He has not only this long-range weight-loss goal but a number of short-range ones as well, such as refusing to eat any junk food whatsoever. For three weeks, Tracey has steadfastly maintained his diet and resisted his urges to splurge on junk food, but one evening a particularly strong craving for ice cream arises. He fights his urge at first, reminding himself that he has committed himself to diet and repeating to himself all the reasons that he should forgo a raid on the freezer. He may even try psychological strategies for dampening the urge by imagining how much better he'll look and feel in a few weeks if he can stay on his diet. So far, Tracey has exercised impressive self-control. However, when he opens the freezer to get ice cubes for his diet cola, Tracey spies the half-gallon of ice cream and, still telling himself that he really should not eat it, removes the carton from the freezer, heaps a large helping in a bowl, douses it with chocolate syrup and cherries, and feasts, all the time thinking that he shouldn't be eating it.

Tracey's effort at self-control successfully incorporated the first three ingredients discussed above. He monitored his behavior throughout the whole episode, so we cannot attribute his lapse to a failure to pay attention to his self. Furthermore, he had a clear goal about what he wanted to achieve and a clear plan for how to achieve it. And he transcended the situation by thinking about the long-term consequences of eating versus not eating the ice cream. Yet, despite all of this, he still failed to exercise self-control. In everyday language, we might say that he simply didn't have enough willpower or self-discipline to resist. Tracey himself might well feel that he was overcome by a powerful urge that he simply could not withstand.

The fourth factor underlying successful self-control—self-control strength—is the least understood. Many failures of self-control occur because people do not have the psychological energy needed to make themselves behave as they desire.[27] People may monitor their behavior, have clear goals and standards, and transcend the immediate situation, yet still not have the brute psychological strength or willpower to control themselves.

Typically, when people fail to control themselves as they desire, they feel that their powers of self-control are overwhelmed by an irresistible impulse. The dieter who splurges on chocolate chip cookies, the abstaining smoker who breaks down and lights a cigarette, and the person who strikes his or her spouse in anger usually blame their lapses on an overpowering urge that they could not inhibit. Although we cannot doubt that people who lose self-control are indeed responding to an urge of some sort, the strength of this impulse depends to a large extent on how they talk to themselves about the situation at hand. They are, in part, creating the urge to which they are responding. Thinking to oneself about the situation in certain ways energizes the undesired urge, whereas thinking about it in other ways may reduce the urge and enhance self-control.

In the research discussed earlier on how children resist the urge to grab small amounts of treats (usually M&Ms, pretzels, or marshmallows) in favor of receiving larger amounts in the future, one of the most important determinants of self-control was how a child talked to him- or herself about the desired objects. Children who thought about abstract qualities of the objects—imagining marshmallows as fluffy clouds, for example—were much more successful at waiting for the larger reward than children who thought about their appealing qualities, such as the delicious, mouth-watering taste of those M&Ms.[28] Successfully controlling one's impulses often involves using mental "cooling operations" that focus attention away from the features of the situation that would undermine self-control. These cooling operations help to reduce the power of the urge, thereby requiring less self-control strength to fight it. Because the amount of self-control strength needed to control oneself is inversely related to the power of competing impulses to behave in other ways, deliberately turning strong temptations into mild ones through cooling operations helps to maintain self-control.

Perhaps this is why people have greater success controlling themselves if they do so early in a sequence of temptations when the impulse is not yet too strong.[29] Imagine a person with a sweet tooth who finds peanut-butter-and-chocolate concoctions of all kinds virtually irresistible. Putting a plate of these goodies in front of this person would invite disaster because the impulse to indulge would be so strong that a large amount of self-control strength would be needed to override it. Less self-control strength would be needed to resist the same goodies if they were still in their package in the cabinet, and even less self-control strength would be needed to resist the urge to drive to the store to buy some. The lesson is clear: people who are trying to exercise self-control should focus their efforts on the first line of defense. It is far easier for a person with a sweet tooth to avoid buying goodies than to resist eating them once purchased, and it is easier for a spendthrift in debt to leave his or her credit cards at home rather than to resist using them once at the mall.

Self-Control Depletion

Sometimes the self-control reservoir seems full, and people feel in full control—masters of themselves. At other times, the reservoir is nearly empty, and people seem unable to muster even simple acts of self-control. In the case of severe depression, for example, a person might be unable to will him- or herself to get out of bed in the morning. Clearly, people sometimes have more of the psychological energy needed to control themselves than they do at other times.

We do not understand the precise nature of the psychological energy or strength that energizes self-control, but researchers have learned a bit about factors that deplete and restore it.[30] Perhaps the most obvious factor that depletes self-control strength is physical and mental fatigue. We have all had the experience of losing control over things when we were very tired that we might have handled more successfully had we been rested. People are far more likely to lose control and to behave in undesired ways when they are tired. Thus, it is no surprise that people are more likely to break their diets, get into arguments, behave aggressively, and engage in other impulsive behaviors as the day wears on than when they first get out of bed.[31] Moreover, it also seems that one's storehouse of self-control strength can be replenished by a good night's sleep. Events that were pushing the person over the edge at bedtime usually seem more manageable in the morning. Negative emotions also lower people's ability to self-control, which helps to explain why people lose control—of their emotions, their eating, their addictions—when under stress. In contrast, positive emotions seem to facilitate self-control.[32]

Perhaps the most surprising thing about self-control strength is that it can be depleted by previous acts of deliberate self-regulation. Each time a person controls him- or herself, self-control strength is temporarily weakened—as if some of it were used up—making subsequent efforts to control oneself more difficult. In some ways, the self can be compared to a muscle that must rest after being used to regain its full strength. Just as using a muscle excessively without allowing it time to recover temporarily decreases the muscle's ability to lift heavy objects, repeatedly exercising self-control without allowing self-control strength to replenish results in a diminished ability to self-regulate.[33] Of course, the self is not actually a muscle, and self-control strength and physical strength are quite different things, so the metaphor takes us only so far. Even so, research documents that self-control is an expendable resource that, like a muscle, can be depleted temporarily. Just as running a long distance diminishes one's ability to run far in the near future, exerting control over oneself may temporarily lower one's ability to control oneself.

In many studies of self-control depletion, participants are induced to exert self-control over a behavior, and their ability to control another behavior is then tested. For example, participants might be asked to eat radishes while resisting a plate of freshly baked chocolate chip cookies, work on difficult math problems, or try to control their thoughts. Afterwards, their ability to exercise self-control is assessed in a different domain, such as persisting on difficult anagrams or completing a difficult figure-tracing task. The results consistently show that participants who had to exert self-control on one task subsequently had more difficulty controlling their behavior in other domains than participants who had not had to control themselves on the first task.[34] For example, when participants in one study were instructed to avoid thinking about a white bear, they subsequently found it more difficult to stifle their expressions of amusement while watching a humorous videotape.[35] In another study, participants who worked to control their emotional reactions to upsetting pictures later showed reduced endurance on a physical task.[36] In yet another experiment, resisting the temptation to eat chocolate chip cookies led participants to perform more poorly on a figure-tracing task.[37] In each instance, exerting self-control seemed to deplete something that the participants needed to control their behavior later.

At present, researchers do not understand the nature of the energy—what I have been calling self-control strength—that helps people control their thoughts, emotions, and behaviors. The studies just described clearly show that efforts to control oneself draw upon the same reserve of willpower no matter what type of control is being exerted. In fact, simply making choices and decisions also depletes self-control strength. Even when people are not asked to control their behavior, they show signs of self-depletion when they must make difficult decisions.[38] So, both self-control and decision making seem to be drawing on the same expendable resource, but, again, we do not understand precisely what it is.

Everyday examples of self-depletion abound. The woman who exerts a great deal of control to work hard during the day may have few psychological resources left to deal with frustrations at home that evening. The man who is trying not to smoke may have trouble staying on his diet because resisting cigarettes depletes the self-control strength he needs to fight the urge to eat. The executive who makes important decisions all day long may have trouble deciding what to eat for dinner.

Situations in which the proverbial straw breaks the camel's back may also reflect self-depletion. People sometimes reach a point at which previous stressors and efforts to control themselves have depleted their self-control strength to the point that they have none left. They could control their reactions to the earlier stresses with their declining reserve of self-control strength but, at last, they lose control. Suddenly, a minor stressor evokes a catastrophic reaction that is out of proportion to the precipitating event. The harried parent at dinner calmly cleans up the toddler's spilled milk, trying to take the accident in stride. The child's request to be taken to the bathroom depletes self-control strength further as the resigned parent not only must interrupt his or her dinner but also has to exert effort to avoid becoming disgusted by bathroom matters in the middle of eating. Trying to remain patient during the child's slowness in dealing with his or her bathroom urges, then trying to wipe the bottom of a squirming toddler requires even more self-control. By the time the parent returns to the dinner table, his or her self-control strength may be dangerously low. It might then take only one further small event to cause total parental meltdown. Suddenly, the child's refusal to eat its carrots may provoke an overblown response.

Importantly, it is not the mere unpleasantness of these events that depletes people's ability to control themselves. Researchers have taken great pains to be certain that the self-depletion effect is not caused simply by frustration or other negative emotions. After all, we would not be surprised that people who were frustrated or in a bad mood (by being asked to eat radishes rather than cookies, for example) might make less of an effort to control themselves later. Yet research has shown that, above and beyond whatever effects negative feelings have on people's willingness to control their behavior, merely engaging in a prior act of self-control depletes people's self-control strength.[39]

Trait Differences in Self-Control

Alan, whom we met at the beginning of this chapter, is one of those people who seem to be chronically low in self-control strength. Other people, in contrast, are paragons of self-control, rarely failing to do what they should and typically resisting doing what they shouldn't. Most of us fall somewhere in between, generally controlling ourselves reasonably well yet suffering occasional lapses.

People who possess greater self-control strength live quite different lives from those who seem chronically unable to control themselves. Walter Mischel and his colleagues have followed the children who participated in their early research for many years, in some cases until the participants were in their thirties. This research found that, compared to children who had difficulty controlling their impulses when they were 4 years old, children who successfully controlled themselves at age 4 were judged more adjusted and mature as adolescents.[40] They managed stress better, dealt more effectively with frustration, and were seen as more socially competent by other people. Perhaps most striking was the fact that high school students who had demonstrated greater self-control as 4-year-olds scored significantly higher on the S.A.T.—the college admissions exam—than high schoolers who lacked self-control when they were age 4. (In fact, self-control at age 4 predicted S.A.T. scores better than the children's intelligence when they were 4!) Apparently, a high degree of self-control helps children and adolescents perform better in school and master their schoolwork more successfully. Furthermore, children who had greater self-control at age 4 became adults who were less aggressive and more interpersonally skilled. Research using other measures of self-control has also shown that college students who have a good deal of self-control handle frustration better, have fewer problems with alcohol, are less likely to have emotional problems, and earn higher grades. They also approach problems with other people in a more constructive and accommodative manner and, not surprisingly, have happier and more stable relationships.[41]

Fighting Self With Self

Western culture holds the view that people ought to have the self-discipline to make themselves behave as they should, avoid moral lapses, and overcome their personal difficulties. Many people think that self-control typically ought to be sufficient for people to stop smoking and overeating, overcome their fears, control their temper, leave abusive spouses, succeed in school and at work, and get over various kinds of losses (such as deaths and romantic break-ups). We expect people who stumble in life to "pick themselves up by their bootstraps" and, if they don't, we may conclude that they simply aren't trying hard enough.

However, it is rarely that easy. Although people often control themselves successfully, the process of self-regulation may derail at many points.[42] As we have seen, in order to regulate effectively, people must monitor themselves, have clear goals, transcend the immediate situation to consider long-term ramifications, and possess adequate self-control strength at the moment. A person's ability to exert self-control is only as strong as the weakest of these links in the chain of events that underlie self-control.

Furthermore, the self did not evolve to exert the amount of control that we require of it in modern life. To begin with, our lives are filled with far more choices and decisions than the lives of the individuals in whom the modern self first appeared. Spending their entire lives in the same clan, wandering the same territory, planning only a day or two ahead, and practicing the same cultural traditions, our prehistoric ancestors would not have confronted the innumerable choices that modern people must make every day. Whether we are talking about major, life-changing choices such as the selection of colleges, jobs, mates, and houses, or minor choices such as what to have for dinner, the brand of cereal to buy, or which TV show to watch, our selves are massively overtaxed compared to those of primitive people or, for that matter, people is many nonindustralized cultures today.

In addition, we must force ourselves to do far more "unnatural" things each day than our prehistoric ancestors did—from making ourselves wake up before dawn to the sound of an alarm clock to commuting on crowded highways to our job to performing personally unimportant tasks at work to spending our evenings chauffeuring our children to practices and meetings. My point is not that our modern lives are worse than those of prehistoric humans but, rather, that our lives require a far greater amount of self-control. As a result, we sometimes push our efforts to control ourselves past the self's ability to respond. The result is not only occasional failures of self-regulation, some of which are disastrous, but also a chronically low level of self-control strength. The self presumably evolved because it allowed people to look toward the future and regulate their behavior accordingly. But it did not evolve to handle the decisions, choices, and acts of unnatural self-control that we require of it. Perhaps the surprising thing is that self-control works for us as well as it does.

Not only do we sometimes expect too much of the self, but our efforts to control our behavior sometimes backfire because the self itself is part of the problem. One good example involves instances in which people deliberately try not to think about something. People often want to make themselves stop dwelling on memories about the past or expectations about the future because those thoughts are distracting, distressing, or unacceptable to them. People who have experienced traumatic events, who are worrying about the future, or who are simply distracted by their self-chatter understandably want to stop thinking, and often try to do so by force of will. ("I'm going to make myself not think about it"). But the futility of fighting self with self in this way should be apparent. In order to make ourselves stop thinking about ourselves, we must think about ourselves! The Taoist philosopher Chuang-tzu described attempts to use the self to reduce the influence of the self as "beating a drum in search of a fugitive." The approach to solving the problem assures that the problem will not be easily solved.

Not only is it difficult, if not impossible, simply to will oneself to stop thinking of things that one cannot stop thinking about, but Daniel Wegner and his colleagues have shown that trying not to think about something typically increases how much the person thinks about the forbidden topic. In some of their studies, research participants were told to ring a bell every time they had a thought about a white bear. Some participants were told to try not to think about white bears, whereas other participants were not prohibited from thinking about them. The results showed that participants who actively tried not to think about bears actually thought more about them, as reflected in how many times they rung the bell, than participants who didn't try to stop thinking about them. To make matters worse, once they were told they could stop suppressing thoughts about bears, participants who had earlier tried to resist bear-related thoughts had a particularly large number of thoughts about white bears.[43] Trying to stuff one's thoughts into a dark mental closet results in a rebound effect in which they come flooding back to consciousness.

A similar problem arises when people monitor themselves closely in an effort to avoid performing some undesired behavior. In order to monitor oneself adequately, a person must think about the unwanted action a great deal. However, because monitoring one's behavior makes the undesired behavior more cognitively available in awareness, the chances of performing the unwanted behavior may actually increase.[44] I'm reminded of a friend who, when he broke up with his romantic partner and became involved with another woman, was terribly afraid that he would accidentally call the new woman by the old partner's name. He fretted over this possibility for quite a while and even devised mnemonic tricks to be sure that he didn't make the dreaded mistake. Of course, all of this thinking about the former partner simply kept her name primed in his memory and, as you have probably guessed, he did indeed blurt it out on a very inopportune occasion.

Attempting to stop thinking about something promotes an ongoing preoccupation with the object of the unwanted thought. Wegner has suggested that this process may underlie the development of certain obsessions.[45] When people purposefully try not to think about certain topics, they may ironically start to obsess about them. And, in trying even harder to expunge the unwanted thoughts, they may further fuel the obsession. Evidence suggests that efforts to suppress thoughts about sexual topics, for example, may lead to a preoccupation with sex.[46]

Facilitating Self-Control

Purposeful control over oneself is an essential feature of human behavior. In fact, human beings would not be recognizably human if they could not deliberately control themselves. Yet our thoughts, emotions, and behaviors are not always amenable to self-control and, in fact, trying to control oneself sometimes makes matters worse. However, if one understands the nature of self-control and the conditions under which it is likely to fail, a person can take deliberate steps to avoid self-control catastrophes.

First, although the success of self-control is limited by a person's self-control strength at any given moment, research suggests that it is possible for people to compensate for depletions in self-control strength.

Imagine a college student trying to study for an important exam at 3 o'clock in the morning. As hard as he tries, he can't seem to will himself to stay awake, and he falls asleep at his desk. By all accounts, his reserve of self-control has been depleted to the point at which he can no longer force himself to study. He would likely maintain that he just couldn't stay awake. But, imagine that, at just the moment that he is falling asleep, he is offered $10,000 to stay awake until dawn. My hunch is that he could, in fact, exert sufficient self-control to stay awake a few more hours—and longer if necessary—to claim the money.

In almost all instances in which people feel as if they can't make themselves do something they should or can't resist doing something they shouldn't, providing additional incentives will suddenly increase their self-control.[47] (Of course, there may come a point where no amount of incentive will suffice, and people will fail at self-control even at the threat of death.) Reminding oneself that one could likely exercise self-control if necessary to win $10,000 may be sufficient to show that one is not really a hapless pawn who is powerless to resist the seemingly uncontrollable impulse tugging at one's sleeve.

Second, we must be aware of instances in which trying to exert self-control will be useless or, worse, detrimental. Not all behaviors can be changed directly by force of will and some may even get worse if we try. In general, any problem that is exacerbated by self-attention cannot be solved easily through deliberate self-control. So, for example, insomnia, stage fright, impotence, excessive blushing, and test anxiety are not responsive to direct self-control at the time they are occurring because each gets worse when people focus attention on themselves. This does not mean that people cannot develop strategies in advance to help them deal with these kinds of problems, only that they can not force themselves to fall asleep, reduce stage fright, increase sexual responsivity, stop blushing, or eliminate test anxiety through sheer self-control or willpower.

Finally, we should consider the possibility that many problems may be reduced by not trying to control ourselves, at least not directly. Sometimes, when people give up trying so hard to control themselves by force of will, they find that they automatically and naturally respond in the desired fashion. For example, instead of trying to suppress unwanted thoughts, which only makes them stronger and more frequent, people can just let thoughts arise but without attending to them. Mindfulness and meditation practices that teach people to let thoughts pass through their minds while paying only bare attention to them typically cause the progression of unwanted thoughts to slow down. Similarly, once we know that a problem such as test anxiety, excessive blushing, choking under pressure, or sexual impotence is the result of too much self-focused thinking, giving up all efforts to eliminate the problem may paradoxically help it go away.[48] And, even if it doesn't disappear entirely, at least we won't make it worse by trying to exert self-control.

9

Bringing Out the Best in the Self

The true value of a human being can be found in the degree to which he has obtained liberation from the self.
—ALBERT EINSTEIN

Twice during the 20th century, movements arose in American psychology in response to what some saw as an overemphasis on the maladaptive, dark, and seedy side of human behavior. The first was the humanistic movement of the 1950s, championed by Carl Rogers, Abraham Maslow, and others who reacted against the unflattering and pessimistic views of human nature promoted by psychoanalysis and behaviorism. Freud's psychoanalytic theory portrayed human beings as seething cauldrons of unconscious urges and conflicts (mostly involving sex and aggression). Behaviorism portrayed them as hapless slaves to the rewards and punishments in their environments—intelligent rats pushing levers in the Skinner box of life. As a counterweight, humanistic psychologists stressed the human potential for growth and positive experiences, and turned their attention toward understanding how people become well adjusted, productive, and fully functioning.

A second reaction to the morbid fascinations of mainline psychology arose in the 1990s in the form of the positive psychology movement. Looking at the topics that seemed of greatest interest to behavioral researchers, one could not help but sense a fascination with the dark side of human existence. As a result of this focus, psychologists had learned a great deal about topics such as aggression, depression, anxiety, rape, self-deception, manipulation, and psychopathology but knew far less, if anything, about topics such as hope, wisdom, compassion, love, forgiveness, and selflessness. The advocates of the positive psychology movement insisted that we should be at least as interested in understanding why people behave well as why they behave badly, and they initiated a movement to explore the beneficial aspects of human behavior.

At first blush, a book called *The Curse of the Self* would seem to be the antithesis of humanistic and positive psychology's emphasis on the brighter side of human existence. As I admitted at the outset, the portrayal of the self offered in this book has been a bit lopsided, focusing primarily on aspects of the self that create personal and social problems and paying less attention to its many benefits. Yet understanding how the voice in our heads undermines our well-being is intimately linked to understanding how people can become more well-adjusted, compassionate, caring, forgiving, and content. They are two sides of the same coin.

As I have noted throughout the book, I am not suggesting that the self is bad or that it ought to be eradicated. Rather, the same ability to self-reflect that makes us wonderfully human and underlies the best features of civilization also creates havoc by fostering selfishness, suffering, troubled relationships, disastrous decisions, and behavior that is dangerous to ourselves and to other people. The self is at once our greatest ally and our fiercest enemy, and many of the biggest struggles that people face in life are directly or indirectly the doing of the self. Even so, I am not suggesting that the self is nothing but a curse, that human beings are incontrovertibly "bad," or that our situation is hopeless. Rather, I believe that the realization that human beings come equipped with a mental apparatus that, despite their best efforts, can create serious personal and social problems will help us live saner, happier, more caring lives.

The core of the problem is that the self evolved through millions of years to help us meet the challenges of living as prehistoric hunters, gatherers, and scavengers. At the time, the self was an outstanding evolutionary adaptation. For the first time, people could think consciously about themselves and their lives, allowing them to plan, act intentionally, and solve problems better than any other creature on earth. But, in a relatively short period of time (at least on an evolutionary scale), this new ability to self-reflect led people to create for themselves a world that was so dramatically different from the one in which the self evolved that the ability to self-reflect was no longer an unmitigated blessing. These changes led to many improvements in the quality of human life, but they also turned the self into a liability. So, there is nothing wrong with the self or those of us who possess one. We are simply doing the best we can to live in modern society with a brain that was designed to be used tens of thousands of years ago!

Rather than being a message of gloom and doom, this realization can have very positive effects. To begin with, the insight that many of our problems, mistakes, and misbehaviors stem from the inherent nature of the self should lead us to cut everyone, ourselves included, a little more slack than we usually do. After all, we are all in this boat together, doing the best we can, using psychological equipment that isn't perfectly suited for the job. The mere realization that we are equipped with a mental apparatus that, despite our best intentions, creates many problems is a big first step. Sometimes we can avoid dangers simply by knowing that they are there.

In addition, understanding how the self creates problems may equip us to deal better with them. When resisting the curses of the self, knowledge is power. This final chapter focuses on using our knowledge about the self to create positive changes in our lives. We will examine four solutions to the curse of the self, each one an ingredient for exorcising the demon without harming ourselves.

Solution 1: Quieting the Self

We have seen that the self's ongoing chatter lies at the heart of its curse. Most people obsessively self-reflect as they remember, rehash, regret, worry, scheme, and ruminate incessantly, their everyday lives accompanied by the self's ongoing patter. As we have seen, this inner monologue distracts them from life in the real world, maintains unpleasant emotions (such as worry), and creates a variety of problems such as test anxiety, insomnia, and impotence. Because virtually everyone's mind runs along in this fashion, most people regard this obsessive thinking as normal and do not realize how unnecessary and harmful much it really is.

Contrary to how it may seem, most of people's inner self-talk does not help them to anticipate problems, cope with difficulties, or improve the quality of their lives. True, the chatter deals mostly with problems of the past and future, but rarely does this kind of rumination actually help people to improve their lives. Think of all the times that you have replayed upsetting past events in your head—a conflict with another person, a humiliating experience, a stupid mistake, a traumatic event. In how many of those times did rehashing the experience actually help you to understand or cope with it? And, in those rare cases in which self-reflection was ultimately helpful, was all of your rumination useful or did you analyze and agonize more than necessary? Now think of all the times that you have thought about a potentially upsetting event in the future—an upcoming public presentation, important test, unpleasant visit to the doctor, possible dangers to yourself or loved ones. How many of those times did imagining and rehearsing horrible scenarios in your head actually help when the event actually occurred? For that matter, how many times did the event you imagined even happen and, if it did happen, did it transpire the way you imagined it? If you are honest, I suspect that you will conclude that you have wasted a great amount of time, energy, and emotion on the past and future ruminations of the self.

I am not saying that there are never good reasons to reflect on the past or plan for the future. Clearly, the self evolved because projecting oneself into the past and future had adaptive value. We would not want to stop the self's inner monologue entirely even if we could. Just as the hassled parent wouldn't wish the overly chatty or whiny child to be struck permanently mute, we should not want our self to cease operations entirely. Even so, most people would benefit markedly from learning to quiet the self, just as the beleaguered parent would benefit from having a child who chattered and whined just a bit less.

I initially had trouble accepting that most of my self-thoughts were useless, if not destructive. I was one of those people who place a high value on thinking, intellectualizing, planning, and figuring things out. In fact, I prided myself on the fact that I rarely "wasted" time because, no matter what else was happening, I was always thinking, planning, and solving problems. However, having seen the difficulties that excessive rumination causes and having experienced firsthand the improvement in one's quality of life when the self quiets down, even just a little, I have to admit that I was as wrong as I could be.

People's selves can be an unpleasant, sometimes unbearable burden, and most people resort to various diversions that help them to escape, temporarily, the incessant noise in their heads. Some common escapist activities are relatively benign. People may lose themselves in mindless television (even endless channel-surfing may be a wonderful self-silencer) or a good book, go shopping, listen to music, or take a long bath. Part of the appeal of rigorous and extreme recreation activities—such as parachuting, hang-gliding, mountain biking, rock-climbing, white-water kayaking, and extreme sports—is that they help to quiet the self. Of course, certain escapes, such as the excessive use of alcohol and other self-numbing drugs, spawn problems of their own.

Escapist behaviors usually get a bad rap, being regarded, at best, as a waste of time, and worse, as unhealthy or dangerous habits (of shopping, watching TV, or rock-climbing, for example). Yet such activities are probably beneficial to the well-being of people who spend too much time in the grip of the self. Occasional respites from the burden of selfhood, as Roy Baumeister calls it, are healthy. In fact, I suspect that most people would be far more preoccupied, tense, and unhappy if they did not engage in escapist activities from time to time.

If these kinds of escapist tactics have a drawback, it is that they are not always available. If your chattering self is distracting you from focusing on an important task while you are at work, you may not be able to quiet its babble by watching your daytime soaps, listening to music, sipping vodka, or having sex in your office. Thus, many people have found it beneficial to develop ways of quieting their self more-or-less at will. I can think of few more important skills than to learn how to minimize the intrusion of the self. If I had my way, all high school students would learn to do so in a life skills course and later receive booster classes in college and in the workplace. Many approaches exist to help people quiet their inner chatter, but most of them share an emphasis on keeping one's attention rooted in the present situation and, thus, off of self-thought as much as possible. It is, of course, necessary to make mental trips to the past and future from time to time. But the goal should be to step out of the present moment and into one's mind only when necessary.

As noted in chapter 8, people cannot stop thinking simply by trying because deliberate effort requires self-thought. Thus, any successful attempt to still the self must come in through the back door. The most popular approach to quieting the self is meditation (which we discussed in chapter 2). Meditation comes in a number of varieties to suit almost any taste—transcendental mediation, zazen, insight meditation (vipassana), mindfulness meditation, guided imagery, and so on. Despite their differences, all meditation practices share an emphasis on reducing unnecessary self-talk. Many meditation techniques are couched within a particular philosophical or spiritual tradition, and many newcomers to meditation are turned off by the tradition that they first encounter. From the standpoint of quieting the self, however, they are probably all effective, and one's choice is a matter of personal preference. If one's goal is to quiet the self, no philosophical baggage whatsoever is necessary to practice meditation.

Readers who are interested in learning these techniques have a wide variety of books, tapes, CDs, classes, and Web sites from which to choose. Meditation practice is perhaps the best way to learn to reduce one's self-chatter "on demand."

Solution 2: Fostering Ego-Skepticism

A second aspect of the curse is that, as it chronically intrudes into our experience of life, the self makes it difficult for us to discern reality from self-made fiction. Our perception of the world, including other people and ourselves, is almost always some amalgam of real, objective events and our subjective interpretations of them. We generally think that our reactions are responses to actual events in the real world, but in fact our self always plays a role in construing the world we perceive. The real and self-spun worlds are fused so tightly that we rarely realize that our experience is tainted by the self.

Everyone is naturally, inherently, and incontrovertibly egocentric. No one can see the world from any perspective other than his or her own nor fully escape the tendency to perceive the world through the filter of his or her own self-interest. As we have seen, most people are more egocentric than they need to be to protect their own well-being and their egocentrism often harms other people. And, even when we recognize that our views may be contaminated by our egoistic perspective, we have extreme difficulty separating the actual events from our interpretations.

The solution is to develop a healthy sense of ego-skepticism—to recognize that one does not always have an accurate view of the world and to be skeptical of one's own interpretations of events. Of course, everyone thinks that his or her perceptions and beliefs are accurate and that other people's are distorted. And, as we discussed (chapter 3), people overestimate how egocentric other people are while underestimating their own egocentrism. But, we all can't be right, and it would be rather odd if our own personal views were consistently more objective and unbiased than other people's. We must recognize that we each have a one-sided view of things (even when we think we don't) and that our views are, on average, probably just as wrong as anybody else's. You may find the conclusion that your perceptions, beliefs, and opinions are, on average, no more accurate than other people's difficult to accept. The fact that you find this claim unsettling, if not downright wrong, shows how deeply our natural egocentrism is rooted.

In our battle against our personal egocentrism, it helps to realize how unique each of us is. Once we grasp that we are very unusual, we can begin to see how idiosyncratic our perspective on the world must be. You can see your uniqueness quite clearly if you compare yourself to the "average" person in the world. Are you a typical person whose views represent an unbiased human perspective? Or are you so atypical that your notions about the world are quite unusual?

A few years ago, Stanford University professor Phillip Harter forwarded an e-mail message he had received that described what the population of the world would look like if it were reflected in a single village of only 100 people. This insightful description of the world was so provocative that this message was forwarded and reforwarded until Dr. Harter became somewhat of a minor celebrity even though, as Harter has protested thousands of times, he was not the author of the piece. Even so, it was so intriguing that others independently checked and updated the numbers in the message. Here's what they show.

Imagine that we could shrink the earth's population to a village of precisely 100 people. If we held the existing ratios of types of people in this village the same as it is on earth, the population of this village would consist of 60 Asians, 12 Europeans, 13 Africans, and 15 from the entire Western hemisphere, only 5 of whom would be from North America. Furthermore, 80 of these 100 inhabitants of the village (i.e., 80%) would be nonwhite, and 67 would be non-Christian. (I suspect that most readers are already feeling rather atypical.) Only 2 of the 100 residents of the village would have a college education, and only 4 would own a computer. A quarter of them would live in substandard housing, 13 would suffer from malnutrition, and 17 would be unable to read. The vast majority of the village's wealth—89% to be exact—would be owned by only 20 residents; the remaining 11% would be divided, rather unequally, among the remaining 80 residents.

Perhaps you see my point. You are such an atypical human being, from the standpoint of the human population of the world, that you should be very reluctant to assume that your views are the right ones. Only if you are a nonwhite, non-Christian Asian without a college education and no computer could you even begin to think and speak for people at large, and even then, you would likely differ from others in this group so substantially that you could not be said to have the inside road to truth, either. All of us are entitled to our opinions. However, for any of us to conclude that our opinions are right and everyone else's in the village are wrong reflects staggering egocentrism.

Many people worry that taking ego-skepticism too far may result in paralyzing uncertainty or a complete loss of self. If we can't trust our own view of reality, would we not be riddled with doubt and unable to know what to think or do? If we insist on certainty in life, the answer is probably yes. But if we simply act on the basis of our best judgments, all the while knowing that our views and the information on which they are based are fallible, then we will be able to do just fine, without the burden of insisting that we are always correct.

Solution 3: Reducing Egotism and Ego-Defensiveness

To make matters worse, people's perceptions are not only egocentric but also egotistic. As we have seen, people have a tendency to spin the facts to reflect as positively on themselves as possible. The defensiveness that egotism spawns is a source of a great deal of distress and dysfunction. Events that threaten our egos—that show us to be less capable, desirable, or ethical than we see ourselves—are usually upsetting. Furthermore, trying to protect our ego against onslaughts against it often makes us defensive, unpleasant, and sometimes aggressive. A great deal of conflict, both in personal relationships and in society at large, stems from battles between egos.

Simply trying, by force of will, not to be defensive when one experiences failure, criticism, rejection, or some other ego-deflating event is rarely effective. We may hide our defensive reaction from others, which may be a step in the right direction, but inside we are probably hurt, anxious, angry, and resentful. And we may carry those feelings for a long time to come, fueled by the self's tendency to keep such events alive in our minds.

Aside from learning to quiet the self when it starts dredging up ego-threatening interpretations of events, two other strategies may be useful in reducing egotism. The first is to recognize that the ego is really nothing more than a mental idea or image we have of ourselves. At its core, then, ego-defensive reactions are simply efforts to protect an image or self-thought. Viewed dispassionately, it would not seem to be a particularly good use of emotional energy to defend a mental image as if the image were actually us.

It is true that events that threaten our egos and make us feel badly about ourselves sometimes have real and important consequences, as well. If you are fired from your job, fail an important exam, or are dumped by your romantic partner, you may face potentially unpleasant changes in your life situation. People naturally experience negative emotions to such events, and I am not suggesting that those reactions are necessarily undesirable. (Even so, I would argue that some of those negative feelings actually serve no useful purpose.) However, in addition to the real-life implications of such events, your ego takes a blow. You feel hurt, defensive, depressed, or angry, and may begin to question yourself. This aspect of your reaction is largely unnecessary. You have enough real problems to face to waste much time or energy protecting a mental image of yourself. Many people find it useful simply to remind themselves that threats to their egos have no real implications and to turn their attention to dealing with the tangible outcomes of negative events.

A second, more general approach to reducing ego-defensiveness is to foster an ongoing attitude of self-compassion. Just as people may have compassion toward other people, to whom they react in a caring, kind, and responsive fashion, they may also have compassion toward themselves. Kristin Neff, who has studied self-compassion, suggests that people benefit from adopting a kind, understanding, nonjudgmental, and accepting attitude toward themselves. An attitude of self-compassion does not involve self-pity, self-indulgence, or self-centeredness. Rather, it involves accepting the fact that one is not perfect and, thus, will invariably experience failures, setbacks, and losses. When unhappy times arrive, self-compassion involves being gentle with oneself—acknowledging and addressing one's shortcomings without undue self-criticism. Essentially, self-compassion involves approaching oneself with kindness, concern, and forgiveness, recognizing that we are, after all, only human.

Self-compassion reduces egotism because it lowers the degree to which events threaten the ego. If you treat yourself with kindness and respect when things go wrong, your ego will not be battered by life's circumstances and, thus, will have no need to defend itself. It will not need to distort the sometimes ugly truth to preserve your feelings and self-esteem, and it will not cause you to suffer over the common but largely inconsequential setbacks that you experience. Self-compassion provides a bubble of emotional safety within which you can perceive yourself and your life's circumstances clearly without fear of self-condemnation.

Having self-compassion does not imply that a person never feels badly for his or her misdeeds. Nor does it suggest that people should simply accept their shortcomings without trying to improve. We may feel remorse about doing wrong (at least up to a point), and we may work to improve ourselves. But we may deal with failures, mistakes, and transgressions with compassion toward ourselves, and without defensiveness or self-hatred.

Solution 4: Optimizing Self-Control

Pragmatically, the greatest benefit of possessing a self is that it permits people to exert deliberate control over their thoughts, feelings, and actions. Not only would many complex behaviors be impossible without self-control, but self-control lies behind the major advances in human civilization. Although many problems remain, it seems safe to say that people treat one another better, on average, than they ever have. The incidence of slavery has greatly diminished over the centuries (although by no means disappeared), advantaged well-to-do nations feel a responsibility to help less developed ones, basic human rights are endorsed by all but a few governments, and democracies in which citizens have a say in their own government are more common than ever. People who live in civilized societies not only try to maintain certain standards of personal conduct but insist that other societies do as well. Even when atrocities such as infanticide, genocide, and terrorism occur, the widespread outcry at least demonstrates a degree of awareness and sensitivity that was not widespread in other times. These changes in how people try to treat one another reflect the self's ability to judge itself, imagine a better future, and control people's baser impulses. Ironically, then, the self may be one of our best weapons against the self. We can, within limits, resist many of our egocentric and egoistic inclinations. However, using the self to control the self is, as we saw in chapter 8, only partially effective.

The optimal approach to self-control may be somewhat different from what people usually imagine. Self-control is typically viewed as requiring Herculean effort to resist overwhelming impulses or to force oneself to behave in ways that one resists. And, in many cases, this is precisely how self-control feels. The smoker trying to resist the temptation to smoke and the unmotivated student trying to make herself study are pouring all of their willpower into thwarting their natural inclinations.

But there is another, less effortful approach to self-control. Many of the urges that one is trying to combat emerge from how one is thinking to oneself about the issue at hand. Self-talk fuels many of the urges that one must then use self-control to resist. A man who has trouble controlling his temper may not realize that he often creates his own anger by thinking about situations in particular ways. Taking preemptive steps to quiet or change his self-talk, reduce the demands of his ego, or interpret events in more benign ways would be a far more effective remedy for a bad temper than trying to contain his hotheaded reactions after he is already enraged. Exerting self-control by practicing self-quieting, fostering ego-skepticism, and lowering ego-defensiveness in advance will do far more good than trying to exert willpower after situations get out of hand.

We must be careful not to feed the self as we try to change or control it. Many efforts to change ourselves are predicated on the belief that successful living requires people continually to set goals for themselves that they then pursue with all their might. Books, tapes, and courses will help you to "Take charge of your life," "Develop personal power," or "Achieve all of your goals." There is nothing inherently wrong with figuring out what one wants out of life and making reasonable, strategic decisions to increase one's chances of attaining it. But if we are not careful, these kinds of efforts to take charge of our lives will feed the self and strengthen its curse.

For one thing, chronically setting and pursuing goals can lead to a situation in which the purpose of life today is always the achievement of some goal tomorrow. Today simply becomes a means to some future end, leading us to forget that the only life we really have is the one going on right now. The self's ability to project into the future keeps us focused on the distant prize and distracts us from living fully today. Accompanying this future orientation are the self's reflections and ruminations about how things are going with respect to our goals. So, we feel good or bad today not because something important has actually happened but, rather, because we feel good or bad about our progress toward some future goal.

Furthermore, we often do not achieve the goals we set for ourselves. Our business was not as successful as we had planned, we didn't lose as much weight as we wanted, our new relationship did not pan out as we hoped, we were not accepted into the college of our choice. These "failures" invariably upset us, sometimes for quite a while afterwards. What we typically do not appreciate is how we set ourselves up for failure by our goals and expectations. Someone once said that "expectation is premeditated resentment." The solution may be to have goals, but not to become too attached to them.

Thus, the bottom line on self-control is a mixed message. Purposeful control over oneself is an essential aspect of human behavior, and people are often effective in changing their thoughts, feelings, and behavior in positive ways. However, many of the processes that make the self an occasional curse are not amenable to conscious and deliberate change. And, often, trying to change or control oneself can create more problems than it solves if such changes are not pursued carefully.

Moving Beyond the Self

I have heard people envy their pets because cats and dogs seem to be untroubled by the concerns that preoccupy most human beings. One gets the sense that our cats and dogs (and birds and horses and goats) are generally far more relaxed and content than their owners ever are. The only nonhuman animals that show signs of psychological problems are those that have suffered at the hands of human beings, such as pets that have been mistreated and wild animals in captivity.

Looking at one's apparently carefree cat sleeping soundly while its master tosses and turns in bed worrying about the day ahead may make one wish to go back to a time before the evolution of self-awareness. Yet such a wish is as shortsighted as it is impossible. Without a self, we would be no more than intelligent apes, without the capacity for philosophy, education, government, education, and all of the other accoutrements of civilization. And, perhaps most important, we would lack the ability to control our own behavior. In light of the self's many redeeming qualities, I doubt that many people would choose to trade places with an animal that does not have a self or, if it were possible, to excise their self and everything that it entails. In any case, like it or not, we are stuck with our selves and cannot go back to the state of mind that existed before the appearance of self-awareness.

If we cannot return to a time before self, the only way to go is forward, to a state of mind in which we use our self when needed but are not slave to its every egocentric, egoistic, and egotistical whim. We may be able to move toward such a nonegoic state by successfully combining the four solutions I have listed: quieting the self, fostering ego-skepticism, reducing egotism and ego-defensiveness, and developing optimal self-control.

For the nonegoic person, the normally boisterous self becomes relatively quiet, the babble replaced by an inner stillness. Because the self has subsided somewhat, the person feels (and appears) generally calm, attentive, and content. Without interference by the self, the person stays focused on the reality of the here and now and discounts whatever superfluous commentary and judgments the self may offer from time to time. Distinguishing clearly between what is real and what is self-talk, the nonegoic individual tends to have a more accurate, insightful view of what happens around him or her. The person also avoids the biases of the ego, as well as becoming excessively attached to idiosyncratic points of view that stem only from his or her own limited range of experience. Self-control, then, becomes easier as the person tends to respond naturally without a great deal of inner conflict. Put simply, the self of the nonegoic individual is no longer a curse to the same degree as the self of the egoic individual.

Of course, the individual who typically functions in a nonegoic state still has a fully functioning self that permits the normal range of human self-reflection. Without a self, the person would be unable to remember where he parked his car, plan a friend's birthday party, or think about herself in abstract, symbolic terms when needed. So, the nonegoic self still operates but in finely tuned and optimal fashion, as needed, rather in the clumsy, hyperactive fashion that it does in most people.

Of course, no one functions in the nonegoic state at all times, so it is useful to think of people being spread out along a continuum of egoism. At the egoic end of the continuum are people who live most of their lives in their heads—planning, scheming, worrying, regretting, and so on. At the other, nonegoic end of the continuum are people who spend most of their time in the nonegoic state, moving into self-awareness and egoism only as needed. The rest of us lie somewhere in between.

In my view—and here I step far beyond the research literature on which this book rests—our personal and societal well-being requires that we begin to foster nonegoic ways of living. Given that so many personal and social ills can be traced directly to the way that the self inherently operates, we must train the self to behave. In doing so, we are redressing the fact that we modern humans are living in the 21st century with a mental self that evolved to suit the needs of people who lived in small nomadic bands on the prehistoric plains. Partly because the self was so good at what it did, we have created a cultural and technological environment that has rendered the self less functional than it once was. The new and very unnatural environment that human beings have created is so recent (at least in the span of human evolution) that the self has not had nearly enough time to catch up.

The only solution is to take steps that help us—individually and collectively—to avoid the pitfalls of the egoic self. Because we have a self, we can decide to do things to minimize its totalitarian control over our lives and to make it work for us rather than against us. Practices for reforming the self have existed for thousands of years, probably ever since someone first realized that the self is sometimes a curse. Our advantage now is that behavioral science has helped us understand this curse—and how it may be exorcised—more fully than ever.

NOTES

CHAPTER 1

1. E. Larson, *Summer for the Gods: The Scopes Trial and America's Continuing Debate over Science and Religion* (Cambridge: Harvard University Press, 1998).

2. Ibid.

3. R. W. Mitchell, "Subjectivity and Self-Recognition in Animals," in *Handbook of Self and Identity*, ed. M. R. Leary and J. P. Tangney (New York: Guilford, 2003).

4. M. R. Leary and J. P. Tangney, "The Self as an Organizing Construct in the Behavioral Sciences," in *Handbook of Self and Identity*, ed. M. R. Leary and J. P. Tangney, 3–14 (New York: Guilford, 2003).

5. J. Jaynes, *The Origin of Consciousness in the Breakdown of the Bicameral Mind* (Boston: Houghton-Mifflin, 1976).

6. S. Epstein, "Integration of the Cognitive and the Psychodynamic Unconscious," *American Psychologist* 49 (1994): 709–24.

7. J. A. Bargh and T. L. Chartrand, "The Unbearable Automaticity of Being," *American Psychologist* 54 (1999): 462–79.

8. J. A. Bargh, "The Automaticity of Everyday Life," in *Advances in Social Cognition*, ed. R. S. Wyer, 10: 1–61 (Mahwah, NJ: Lawrence Erlbaum, 1997); Bargh and Chartrand, "The Unbearable Automaticity."

9. R. F. Baumeister, T. F. Heatherton, and D. M. Tice, *Losing Control: How and Why People Fail at Self-Regulation* (San Diego: Academic Press, 1994).

10. S. Epstein, "The Self-Concept Revisited: Or a Theory of a Theory," *American Psychologist* 28 (1973): 404–16; H. Markus and E. Wurf, "The Dynamic Self-Concept: A Social Psychological Perspective," *Annual Review of Psychology* 38 (1987): 299–337.

11. R. F. Baumeister, "The Self," in *The Handbook of Social Psychology*, ed. D. Gilbert, S. T. Fiske, and G. Lindzey, 680–740 (New York: Oxford University Press, 1999).

12. T. D. Wilson and K. J. Klaaren, "'Expectation Whirls Me Round': The Role of Affective Expectations in Affective Experience," in *Emotion and Social Behavior*, ed. M. S. Clark, 1–31 (Newbury Park, CA: Sage, 1992); T. D. Wilson, D. J. Lisle, K. Kraft, and C. G. Wetzel, "Preferences as Expectation-Driven Influences: Effects of Affective Expectations on Affective Experience," *Journal of Personality and Social Psychology* 56 (1989): 519–30.

13. N. Humphrey, "Nature's Psychologists," in *Consciousness and the Physical World*, ed. B. D. Josephson and V. S. Ramachandran, 57–75 (New York: Pergamon Press, 1980); N. Humphrey, "Consciousness: A Just-so Story," *New Scientist*, August 19, 1982, 474–77; N. Humphrey, *The Inner Eye* (London: Faber & Faber, 1986).

14. G. G. Gallup, Jr., "Self-Awareness and the Emergence of Mind in Primates," *American Journal of Primatology* 2 (1982): 237–48; Mitchell, "Subjectivity and Self-Recognition"; see, however, D. J. Povinelli and C. G. Prince, "When Self Met Other," in *Self-Awareness: Its Nature and Development*, ed. M. Ferrari and R. J. Sternberg, 37–107 (New York: Guilford, 1998).

15. F. B. M. de Waal, *Chimpanzee Politics: Power and Sex Among Apes* (New York: Harper and Row, 1982).

16. J. Goodall, *The Chimpanzees of Gombe: Patterns of Behavior* (Cambridge, MA: Harvard University Press); F. B. M. de Waal, "Deception in the Natural Communication of Chimpanzees," in *Deception: Perspectives on Human and Nonhuman Deceit*, ed. R. W. Mitchell and N. S. Thompson, 221–44 (Albany: State University of New York Press, 1986).

17. M. Lewis and J. Brooks-Gunn, *Social Cognition and the Acquisition of Self* (New York: Plenum, 1979); J. Kagan, "Is There a Self in Infancy?" in *Self-Awareness: Its Nature and Development*, ed. M. Ferrari and R. J. Sternberg, 137–47 (New York: Guilford, 1998).

18. G. Strawson, "The Self," in *Models of the Self*, ed. S. Gallagher and J. Shear, 1–24 (Thorverton, UK: Imprint Academic, 1999).

19. R. Barbeito and H. Ono, "Four Methods of Locating the Egocenter: A Comparison of Their Predictive Validities and Reliabilities," *Behavior Research Methods and Instrumentation* 11 (1979): 31–36; L. Mitson, H. Ono, and R. Barbeito, "Three Methods of Measuring the Location of the Egocentre: Their Reliability, Comparative Locations, and Intercorrelations," *Canadian Journal of Psychology* 30 (1976): 108.

20. Strawson, "The Self."

21. T. E. Feinberg, *Altered Egos: How the Brain Creates the Self* (London: Oxford University Press, 2001); W. M. Kelley, C. N. Macrae, C. L. Wyland, S. Caglar, S. Inati, and T. F. Heatherton, "Finding the Self? An Event-Related fMRI Study," *Journal of Cognitive Neuroscience* 14 (2002): 785–94.

22. M. F. Robinson and W. Freeman, *Psychosurgery and the Self* (New York: Grune & Stratton, 1954), 18.

23. D. T. Stuss, "Self, Awareness, and the Frontal Lobes: A Neuropsychological Perspective," in *The Self: Interdisciplinary Approaches*, ed. J. Strauss and G. R. Goethals, 255–78 (New York: Springer-Verlag, 1991).

24. J. A. Mangels, R. B. Ivry, and N. Shimizu, "Dissociable Contributions of the Prefontal and Neocerebellar Cortex to Time Perception," *Cognitive Brain Research* 7 (1998): 15–39; Stuss, "Self, Awareness, and the Frontal Lobes."

25. U. Neisser, "Five Kinds of Self-Knowledge," *Philosophical Psychology* 1 (1988): 35–59.

26. G. G. Gallup, Jr., "Chimpanzees: Self-Recognition," *Science* 167 (1970): 86–87.

27. G. G. Gallup, Jr., "Self-Recognition in Primates," *American Psychologist* 32 (1977): 329–38; Gallup, "Self-Awareness and the Emergence of Mind"; G. G. Gallup, Jr., and S. D. Suarez, "Self-Awareness and the Emergence of Mind in Humans and Other Primates," in *Psychological Perspectives on the Self*, ed. J. Suls and A. G. Greenwald, 3: 3–26 (Hillsdale, NJ: Lawrence Erlbaum, 1986).

28. J. Lethmate and G. Dücker, "Investigation of Self-Recognition in the Mirror by Orangutans and Some Other Types of Ape," *Zeitschrift für Tierpsychologie* 33 (1973): 248–69; H. L. Miles, "ME CHANTEK: The Development of Self-Awareness in a Signing Orangutan," in *Self-Awareness in Animals and Humans*, ed. S. T. Parker, R. W. Mitchell, and M. L. Boccia, 254–72 (New York: Cambridge University Press, 1994); Mitchell, "Subjectivity and Self Recognition."

29. Mitchell, "Subjectivity and Self-Recognition."

30. Povinelli and Prince, "When Self Met Other."

31. M. R. Leary and N. Buttermore, "The Evolution of the Human Self: Tracing the Natural History of Self-Awareness," *Journal for the Theory of Social Behavior* 33 (2003): 365–404.

32. C. Sedikides and J. J. Skowronski, "The Symbolic Self in Evolutionary Context," *Personality and Social Psychology Review* 1 (1997): 80–102; C. Sedikides and J. J. Skowronski, "On the Evolutionary Foundations of the Symbolic Self: The Emergence of Self-Evaluation Motives," in *Psychological Perspectives on Self and Identity*, ed. A. Terrer, R. B. Felson, and J. Suls, 91–117 (Washington, DC: American Psychological Association, 2000); C. Sedikides and J. J. Skowronski, "Evolution of the Symbolic Self: Issues and Prospects," in *Handbook of Self and Identity*, ed. M. R. Leary and J. P. Tangney, 91–117 (New York: Guilford, 2003).

33. Leary and Buttermore, "The Evolution of the Human Self."

34. R. G. Klein, *The Human Career: Human Biological and Cultural Origins*, 2nd ed. (Chicago: University of Chicago Press, 1999); R. G. Klein and B. Edgar, *The Dawn of Human Culture* (New York: John Wiley, 2002).

35. D. B. Dickson, *The Dawn of Belief* (Tucson: University of Arizona Press, 1990); Klein and Edgar, *The Dawn of Human Culture*.

36. Leary and Buttermore, "The Evolution of the Human Self."

37. S. Mithen, *The Prehistory of the Mind* (London: Thames and Hudson, 1996). This period has also been called the "human revolution" [T. W. Deacon, "The Neural Circuitry Underlying Primate Calls and Human Language," *Human Evolution* 4 (1989): 367–401]; "cultural explosion" [P. Boyer, "Evolution of the Modern Mind and the Origins of Culture: Religious Concepts as a Limiting-Case," in *Evolution and the Human Mind: Modularity, Language, and Meta-Cognition*, ed. P. Carruthers and A. Chamberlin, 93–112 (Cambridge: Cambridge University Press, 2000)]; and "dawn of human culture" [Klein and Edgar, *The Dawn of Human Culture*].

38. R. K. White, "On the Evolution of Human Socio-Cultural Patterns," in *Handbook of Human Symbolic Evolution*, ed. A. Lock and C. R. Peters, 239–62 (Oxford: Oxford University Press, 1996), 242.

39. Bargh and Chartrand, "The Unbearable Automaticity."
40. L. Martin, "I-D Compensation Theory: Some Implications of Trying to Satisfy Immediate-Return Needs in a Delayed-Return Culture," *Psychological Inquiry* 10 (1999): 195–208.

CHAPTER 2

1. S. Duval and R. A. Wicklund, *A Theory of Objective Self-Awareness* (New York: Academic Press, 1972).
2. J. Blachowicz, "The Dialogue of the Soul with Itself," in *Models of the Self*, ed. S. Gallagher and J. Shear, 177–200 (Thorverton, UK: Imprint Academic, 1999).
3. Plato, *Collected Dialogues*, ed. E. Hamilton and H. Cairns (New York: Pantheon, 1961).
4. Blachowicz, "The Dialogue of the Soul."
5. J. Jaynes, *The Origin of Consciousness in the Breakdown of the Bicameral Mind* (Boston: Houghton-Mifflin, 1976).
6. Ibid.
7. Ibid.
8. K. Jaspers, *Origin and Goal of History* (New Haven, CT: Yale University Press, 1953).
9. H. Pashler, "Attentional Limitations in Doing Two Tasks at the Same Time," *Current Directions in Psychological Science* 1 (1992): 44–48.
10. C. F. Bond, "The Next-in-Line Effect: Encoding or Retrieval Deficit?" *Journal of Personality and Social Psychology* 48 (1985): 853–62.
11. J. D. Wine, "Test Anxiety and Direction of Attention," *Psychological Bulletin* 76 (1971): 92–104.
12. R. F. Baumeister, "Choking Under Pressure: Self-Consciousness and Paradoxical Effects of Incentives on Performance," *Journal of Personality and Social Psychology* 46 (1984): 610–20.
13. R. F. Baumeister and C. J. Showers, "A Review of Paradoxical Performance Effects: Choking Under Pressure in Sports and Mental Tests," *European Journal of Social Psychology* 16 (1986): 361–83.
14. Baumeister, "Choking Under Pressure"; J. L. Butler and R. F. Baumeister, "The Trouble with Friendly Faces: Skilled Performance with a Supportive Audience," *Journal of Personality and Social Psychology* 75 (1998): 1213–30; B. P. Lewis and D. E. Linder, "Thinking About Choking? Attentional Processes and Paradoxical Performance," *Personality and Social Psychology Bulletin* 23 (1997): 937–44.
15. R. F. Baumeister, T. F. Heatherton, and D. M. Tice, "When Ego Threats Lead to Self-Regulation Failure: Negative Consequences of High Self-Esteem," *Journal of Personality and Social Psychology* 64 (1993): 141–56.
16. Baumeister, "Choking Under Pressure."
17. K. S. Courneya and A. V. Carron, "The Home Field Advantage in Sport Competitions: A Literature Review," *Journal of Sport and Exercise Psychology* 14 (1992): 13–27.
18. R. F. Baumeister and A. Steinhilber, "Paradoxical Effects of Supportive Audiences on Performance Under Pressure: The Home Field Disadvantage in

Sports Championships," *Journal of Personality and Social Psychology* 47 (1984): 85–93; see, however, B. R. Schlenker, S. T. Phillips, K. A. Boniecki, and D. R. Schlenker, "Championship Pressures: Choking or Triumphing in One's Own Territory?" *Journal of Personality and Social Psychology* 68 (1995): 632–43.

19. E. F. Wright, W. Jackson, S. D. Christie, G. R. McGuire, and R. D. Wright, "The Home-Course Disadvantage in Golf Championships: Further Evidence for the Undermining Effect of Supportive Audiences on Performance Under Pressure," *Journal of Sport Behavior* 14 (1991): 51–60; S. L. Beilcock and T. H. Carr, "On the Fragility of Skilled Performance: What Governs Choking Under Pressure?" *Journal of Experimental Psychology: General* 130 (2001): 701–25.

20. S. Epstein, "Integration of the Cognitive and the Psychodynamic Unconscious," *American Psychologist* 49 (1994): 709–24; S. Franquemont, *You Already Know What to Do* (New York: Tarcher/Putnam, 1999).

21. Franquemont, *You Already Know.*

22. R. D. Wilson and J. W. Schooler, "Thinking Too Much: Introspection Can Reduce the Quality of Preferences and Decisions," *Journal of Personality and Social Psychology* 60 (1991): 181–92, Exp.1.

23. Wilson and Schooler, "Thinking Too Much," Exp. 2.

24. T. D. Wilson and D. Kraft, "Why Do I Love Thee? Effects of Repeated Introspections About a Dating Relationship on Attitudes Toward the Relationship," *Personality and Social Psychology Bulletin* 19 (1993): 409–18.

25. R. E. Nisbett and T. D. Wilson, "Telling More Than We Can Know: Verbal Reports on Mental Processes," *Psychological Review* 84 (1977): 231–59.

26. Ibid.

27. L. G. Lundh and J. E. Broman, "Insomnia as an Interaction Between Sleep-Interfering and Sleep-Interrupting Processes," *Journal of Psychosomatic Research* 49 (2000): 299–310; H. Hall, D. J. Buysse, P. D. Nowell, E. A. Nofzinger, P. Houck, C. F. Reynolds, and D. J. Kupfer, "Symptoms of Stress and Depression as Correlates of Sleep in Primary Insomnia," *Psychosomatic Medicine* 62 (2000): 227–30.

28. M. D. Storms and R. D. McCaul, "Attribution Processes and Emotional Exacerbation of Dysfunctional Behavior," in *New Directions in Attribution Research*, ed. J. H. Harvey, W. J. Ickes, and R. F. Kidd, I: 143–46 (Hillsdale, NJ: Lawrence Erlbaum, 1976).

29. W. H. Masters and V. E. Johnson, *Human Sexual Inadequacy* (Boston: Little, Brown, 1970); D. J. Abrahamson, D. H. Barlow, J. G. Beck, D. K. Sakheim, and J. P. Kelly, "The Effects of Attentional Focus and Partner Responsiveness on Sexual Responding: Replication and Extension," *Archives of Sexual Behavior* 14 (1985): 361–71.

30. C. R. Snyder and S. J. Lopez, eds., *Handbook of Positive Psychology* (New York: Oxford University Press, 2002).

31. M. Csikszentmihalyi, *Flow: The Psychology of Optimal Experience* (New York: HarperCollins, 1990).

32. P. Jackson, *Sacred Hoops* (New York: Hyperion, 1995), 4.

33. E. Tolle, *The Power of Now* (Novato, CA: New World Library, 1999).

34. S. L. Shapiro, G. E. R. Schwartz, and G. Santerre, "Meditation and Positive Psychology," in *Handbook of Positive Psychology*, ed. C. R. Snyder and S. J. Lopez, 632–45 (New York: Guilford, 2002).

35. R. Ellwood, *Finding the Quiet Mind* (Wheaton, IL: Quest, 1983); J. Kabat-Zinn, *Wherever You Go, There You Are* (New York: Hyperion, 1994); H. Gunaratana, *Mindfulness in Plain English* (Boston: Wisdom Publications, 1991).

36. M. C. Dillbeck and D. W. Orme-Johnson, "Physiological Differences Between Transcendental Meditation and Rest," *American Psychologist* 42 (1987): 879–81; J. Miller, K. Fletcher, and J. Kabit-Zinn, "Three-Year Follow-up and Clinical Implications of a Mindfulness-Based Intervention in the Treatment of Anxiety Disorders," *General Hospital Psychiatry* 17 (1995): 192–200.

37. T. Hirai, *Zen Meditation and Psychotherapy* (Tokyo: Japan Publications, 1989).

CHAPTER 3

1. C. Castaneda, *Tales of Power* (New York: Touchstone, 1974).

2. A. G. Greenwald, "The Totalitarian Ego: Fabrication and Revision of Personal History," *American Psychologist* 35 (1980): 603–13; S. E. Taylor and J. D. Brown, "Illusion and Well-Being: A Social Psychological Perspective on Mental Health," *Psychological Bulletin* 103 (1988): 193–210.

3. Greenwald, "The Totalitarian Ego."

4. M. D. Alicke, M. L. Klotz, D. L. Breitenbecher, T. J. Yurak, and D. S. Vredenburg, "Personal Contact, Individuation, and the Better-than-Average Effect," *Journal of Personality and Social Psychology* 68 (1995): 804–25.

5. For a review, see V. Hoorens, "Self-Enhancement and Superiority Biases in Social Comparison," in *European Review of Social Psychology*, ed. W. Strobe and M. Hewstone, 4:113–39 (Chichester, UK: John Wiley, 1993).

6. J. M. Fields and H. Schuman, "Public Beliefs About the Beliefs of the Public," *Public Opinion Quarterly* 40 (1976): 427–48.

7. N. D. Weinstein, "Unrealistic Optimism About Future Life Events," *Journal of Personality and Social Psychology* 39 (1980): 806–20; N. D. Weinstein and E. Lachendro, "Egocentrism as a Source of Unrealistic Optimism," *Personality and Social Psychology Bulletin* 8 (1982): 195–220.

8. J. L. Sheler, "New Science Suggests a 'Grand Design' and Ways to Imagine Eternity," *U.S. News and World Report*, March 31, 1997, 65–66.

9. M. D. Alicke, F. M. LoSchiavo, J. Zerbst, and S. Zhang, "The Person Who Outperforms Me Is a Genius: Maintaining Perceived Competence in Upward Social Comparison," *Journal of Personality and Social Psychology* 72 (1997): 781–89.

10. O. P. John and R. W. Robins, "Accuracy and Bias in Self-Perception: Individual Differences in Self-Enhancement and the Role of Narcissism," *Journal of Personality and Social Psychology* 66 (1994): 206–19; Heine and Renshaw showed cultural differences in the effect—see S. J. Heine and K. Renshaw, "Interjudge Agreement, Self-Enhancement, and Liking: Cross-Cultural Divergences," *Personality and Social Psychology Bulletin* 28 (2002): 578–87.

11. B. Blaine and J. Crocker, "Self-Esteem and Self-Serving Biases in Reactions to Positive and Negative Events: An Integrative Review," in *Self-Esteem: The Puzzle of Low Self-Regard*, ed. R. F. Baumeister, 55–85 (New York: Plenum, 1993); G. W. Bradley, "Self-Serving Biases in the Attribution Process: A Reexamination of

the Fact or Fiction Question," *Journal of Personality and Social Psychology* 36 (1978): 56–71.

12. D. R. Forsyth and B. R. Schlenker, "Attributing the Causes of Group Performance: Effects of Performance Quality, Task Importance, and Future Testing," *Journal of Personality* 45 (1977): 220–36.

13. D. R. Forsyth, W. R. Pope, and J. H. McMillan, "Students' Reactions to Cheating: An Attributional Analysis," *Contemporary Educational Psychology* 10 (1985): 72–82.

14. B. R. Schlenker and R. S. Miller, "Egotism in Groups: Self-Serving Bias or Logical Information Processing," *Journal of Personality and Social Psychology* 35 (1977): 755–64.

15. M. R. Leary and D. R. Forsyth, "Attributions of Responsibility for Collective Endeavors," in *Group Processes*, ed. C. Hendrick, 167–88 (Newbury Park, CA: Sage, 1987).

16. J. K. Beggan, "On the Social Nature of Nonsocial Perception: The Mere Ownership Effect," *Journal of Personality and Social Psychology* 62 (1992): 229–37.

17. B. W. Pelham, M. C. Mirenberg, and J. T. Jones, "Why Susie Sells Seashells by the Seashore: Implicit Egoism and Major Life Decisions," *Journal of Personality and Social Psychology* 82 (2002): 469–87.

18. Ibid.

19. Ibid.

20. J. F. Fitch and R. B. Cialdini, "Another Indirect Tactic of (Self-) Image Management: Boosting," *Personality and Social Psychology Bulletin* 15 (1989): 222–32.

21. L. Ross, D. Greene, and P. House, "The False Consensus Effect: An Egocentric Bias in Social Perception and Attribution Processes," *Journal of Experimental Social Psychology* 13 (1977): 279–301; G. Marks and N. Miller, "Ten Years of Research on the False-Consensus Effect: An Empirical and Theoretical Review," *Psychological Bulletin* 102 (1987): 72–90.

22. J. Krueger and R. W. Clement, "The True False Consensus Effect: An Ineradicable and Egocentric Bias in Social Perception," *Journal of Personality and Social Psychology* 67 (1994): 596–610.

23. S. J. Sherman, C. C. Presson, and L. Chassin, "Mechanisms Underlying the False Consensus Effect: The Special Role of Threats to the Self," *Personality and Social Psychology Bulletin* 10 (1984): 127–38.

24. B. Mullen and G. R. Goethals, "Social Projection, Actual Consensus and Valence," *British Journal of Social Psychology* 29 (1990): 279–82.

25. G. Marks and N. Miller, "Target Attractiveness as a Mediator of Assumed Attitude Similarity," *Personality and Social Psychology Bulletin* 8 (1982): 728–35.

26. S. L. Murray and J. G. Holmes, "A Leap of Faith? Positive Illusions in Romantic Relationships," *Personality and Social Psychology Bulletin* 23 (1997): 586–602.

27. C. Sedikides, W. K. Campbell, G. D. Reeder, and J. J. Elliot, "The Self-Serving Bias in Relational Context," *Journal of Personality and Social Psychology* 74 (1998): 378–86.

28. M. Diehl, "The Minimal Group Paradigm: Theoretical Explanations and Empirical Findings," *European Review of Social Psychology* 1 (1990): 263–92.

29. For a review, see D. Dunning, "The Relation of Self to Social Perception," in *Handbook of Self and Identity*, ed. M. R. Leary and J. P. Tangney, 421–44 (New York: Guilford, 2003).
30. Dunning, "The Relation of Self to Social Perception," 422.
31. M. D. Alicke, M. L. Klotze, D. L. Breitenbacher, T. J. Yurak, and D. S. Vredenburg, "Personal Contact, Individuation and the Better than Average Effect," *Journal of Personality and Social Psychology* 68 (1995): 804–25.
32. E. Pronin, D. Y. Lin, and L. Ross, "The Bias Blind Spot: Perceptions of Bias in Self versus Others," *Personality and Social Psychology Bulletin* 28 (2002): 369–81.
33. Ibid.
34. J. Ehrlinger, L. Ross, and T. Gilovich, *When Do People Acknowledge and When Do They Deny Their Own Biases?* (unpublished manuscript, Cornell University, New York).
35. G. Ichheiser, "Misunderstandings in Human Relations: A Study in False Social Perception," *American Journal of Sociology* 55 (1949) suppl.: 39.
36. J. Horai, "Attributional Conflict," *Journal of Social Issues* 33 (1977): 88–100.
37. Taylor and Brown, "Illusion and Well-Being."
38. Ibid.
39. S. L. Murray, "The Quest for Conviction: Motivated Cognition in Romantic Relationships," *Psychological Inquiry* 10 (1999): 23–24; S. L. Murray, J. G. Holmes, and D. W. Griffin, "Self-Esteem and the Quest for Felt Security: How Perceived Regard Regulates Attachment Processes," *Journal of Personality and Social Psychology* 78 (2000): 478–98.
40. C. R. Colvin, J. Block, and D. C. Funder, "Overly Positive Evaluations and Personality: Negative Implications for Mental Health," *Journal of Personality and Social Psychology* 68 (1995): 1152–62.
41. C. Rogers, "A Theory of Therapy, Personality, and Interpersonal Relationships, as Developed in the Client-Centered Framework," in *Psychology: A Study of a Science*, ed. S. Koch, 3: 184–256 (New York: McGraw-Hill, 1959).
42. A. H. Maslow, *Motivation and Behavior* (New York: Harper and Row, 1954), 207.
43. S. H. Heine, D. R. Lehman, H. R. Markus, and S. Kitayama, "Is There a Universal Need for Positive Self-Regard?" *Psychological Review* 106 (1999): 766–94.
44. L. Festinger, "A Theory of Social Comparison Processes," *Human Relations* 7 (1954): 121.
45. N. Frijda, *The Emotions* (Cambridge, UK: Cambridge University Press, 1986); H. A. Simon, "Motivational and Emotional Controls of Cognition," *Psychological Review* 74 (1967): 29–39.
46. M. R. Leary and R. F. Baumeister, "The Nature and Function of Self-Esteem: Sociometer Theory," in *Advances in Experimental Social Psychology*, ed. M. P. Zanna, 32: 1–62 (San Diego: Academic Press, 2000).
47. Frijda, *The Emotions*; R. M. Neese, "What Good Is Feeling Bad?" *The Sciences* (November/December 1991): 30–37.
48. R. M. Neese, "The Smoke Detector Principle: Natural Selection and the Regulation of Defensive Responses," in *Unity of Knowledge: The Convergence of Natural and Human Science*, ed. A. R. Damasio, A. Harrington, J. Kagan, B. S. H. Moss, and R. Shaikh, 935: 75–85 (New York: New York Academy of Sciences,

2001); P. Rozin and E. B. Royzman, "Negativity Bias, Negativity Dominance, and Contagion," *Personality and Social Psychology Review* 5 (2001): 296–320.

49. C. Casteneda, *Journey to Ixtlan* (New York: Pocket, 1972).

CHAPTER 4

1. C. Darwin, *The Expression of the Emotions in Man and Animals* (New York: Oxford University Press, 1892/1998); J. M. Masson and S. McCarthy, *When Elephants Weep: The Emotional Lives of Animals* (London: Cape, 1994).

2. J. B. Watson and P. Rayner, "Conditioned Emotional Reactions," *Journal of Experimental Psychology* 3 (1920): 1–4.

3. Darwin, *The Expression of the Emotions*.

4. N. Frijda, *The Emotions* (Cambridge: Cambridge University Press, 1986); A. T. Beck and G. Emery, *Anxiety Disorders and Phobias: A Cognitive Perspective* (New York: Basic Books, 1985).

5. J. K. Norem, "Defensive Pessimism, Optimism and Pessimism," in *Optimism and Pessimism: Implications for Theory, Research and Practice,"* ed. E. C. Chang (Washington, DC: APA Press, 2000); J. K. Norem and K.S.S. Illingsworth, "Strategy Dependent Effects of Reflecting on Self and Tasks: Some Implications of Optimism and Defensive Pessimism, *Journal of Personality and Social Personality* 65 (1993): 822–35.

6. L. Martin, *Linking and the Neolithic Neuroses: Why Thinking You Can Live Happily Ever After Can Make You Unhappy* (paper presented at the meeting of the Society for Southeastern Social Psychologists, Research Triangle Park, NC, 1997).

7. Beck and Emery, *Anxiety Disorders and Phobias*.

8. G. Strawson, "The Self," in *Models of the Self*, ed. S. Gallagher and J. Shear, 1–24 (Thorverton, UK: Imprint Academic, 1999).

9. W. James, *The Principles of Psychology* (New York: Holt, 1890); R. F. Baumeister, L. Smart, and J. M. Boden, "Relation of Threatened Egotism to Violence and Aggression: The Dark Side of High Self-Esteem," *Psychological Review* 103 (1996): 5–33.

10. H. Markus and P. Nurius, "Possible Selves," *American Psychologist* 41 (1986): 954–69.

11. Ibid.

12. K. D. Markman, I. Gavanski, S. J. Sherman, and M. N. McMullen, "The Mental Simulation of Better and Worse Possible Worlds," *Journal of Experimental Social Psychology* 29 (1993): 87–109; K. D. Markman and P. E. Tetlock, "Accountability and Close-Call Counterfactuals: The Loser Who Nearly Won and the Winner Who Nearly Lost," *Personality and Social Psychology Bulletin* 26 (2000): 1213–24; N. J. Roese, "Counterfactual Thinking, " *Psychological Bulletin* 121 (1997): 133–48.

13. V. H. Medvec, S. E. Madey, and T. Gilovich, "When Less Is More: Counterfactual Thinking and Satisfaction Among Olympic Medalists," *Journal of Personality and Social Psychology* 69 (1995): 603–10.

14. James, *Principles of Psychology*.

15. D. J. Sharpsteen and L. A. Kirkpatrick, "Romantic Jealousy and Adult Romantic Attachment," *Journal of Personality and Social Psychology* 72 (1997): 627–40.

16. R. B. Cialdini, R. J. Borden, A. Thorne, M. R. Walker, S. Freeman, and L. R. Sloan, "Basking in Reflected Glory: Three (Football) Field Studies," *Journal of Personality and Social Psychology* 34 (1976): 366–75.

17. J. W. Pennebaker, *Opening Up: The Healing Power of Confiding in Others* (New York: William Morrow, 1990).

18. A. Tesser, "Toward a Self-Evaluation Maintenance Model of Social Behavior," *Advances in Experimental Social Psychology* 21 (1988): 181–227; A. Tesser, "Self-Evaluation," in *Handbook of Self and Identity*, ed. M. R. Leary and J. P. Tangney, 275–90 (New York: Guilford, 2003).

19. Tesser, "Toward A Self-Evaluation"; A. Tesser, M. Millar, and J. Moore, "Some Affective Consequences of Social Comparison and Reflective Processes: The Pain and Pleasure of Being Close," *Journal of Personality and Social Psychology* 54 (1988): 49–61.

20. S. R. Beach and A. Tesser, "Self Esteem and the Extended Self-Evaluation Maintenance Model," in *Efficacy, Agency, and Self-Esteem*, ed. M. Kernis, 145–70 (New York: Plenum, 1995); A. Tesser and J. Smith, "Some Effects of Friendship and Task Relevance on Helping: You Don't Always Help the One You Like," *Journal of Experimental Social Psychology* 16 (1980): 582–90.

21. M. Lewis and J. Brooks-Gunn, *Social Cognition and the Acquisition of Self* (New York: Plenum, 1979).

22. M. R. Leary and R. M. Kowalski, *Social Anxiety* (New York: Guilford Press, 1995).

23. B. R. Schlenker and M. R. Leary, "Social Anxiety and Self-Presentation: A Conceptualization and Model," *Psychological Bulletin* 92 (1982): 641–69.

24. R. S. Miller, *Embarrassment: Poise and Peril in Everyday Life* (New York: Guilford, 1996).

25. R. S. Miller and M. R. Leary, "Social Sources and Interactive Functions of Emotion: The Case of Embarrassment," in *Emotion and Social Behavior*, ed. M. S. Clark, 202–21 (Beverly Hills: Sage, 1992).

26. Leary and Kowalski, *Social Anxiety*.

27. S. Valins and R. E. Nisbett, "Attribution Processes in the Development and Treatment of Emotional Disorders," in *Attribution: Perceiving the Causes of* Behavior, ed. E. E. Jones, D. E. Kanouse, H. H. Kelley, R. E. Nisbett, S. Valins, and B. Weiner, 137–50 (Morristown, NJ: General Learning Press, 1972).

28. M. E. P. Seligman, L. Y. Abramson, A. Semmel, and C. von Baeyer, "Depressive Attributional Style," *Journal of Abnormal Psychology* 88 (1979): 242–47.

29. G. I. Metalsky, L. Y. Abramson, M. E. P. Seligman, A. Semmel, and C. Peterson, "Attributional Style and Life Events in the Classroom: Vulnerability and Invulnerability to Depressive Mood Reactions," *Journal of Personality and Social Psychology* 38 (1982): 704–18.

30. L. Y. Abramson, G. I. Metalsky, and L. B. Alloy, "Hopelessness Depression: A Theory-Based Subtype of Depression," *Psychological Review* 96 (1989): 358–72.

31. R. Janoff-Bulman, "Characterological versus Behavioral Self-Blame: Inquiries into Depression and Rape," *Journal of Personality and Social Psychology* 31 (1979): 1798–1809; F. W. Winkel and A. Vrij, "Crime Victims' Attributional Activities and Differential Psychological Responding to Victimizations: The Influence

of Behaviour, Character, and External Explanations," *Issues in Criminology and Legal Psychology* 20 (1993): 58–69.

32. C. B. Meyer, and S. E. Taylor, "Adjustment to Rape," *Journal of Personality and Social Psychology* 50 (1986): 1226–34.

33. J. P. Tangney, "Situational Determinants of Shame and Guilt in Young Adulthood," *Personality and Social Psychology Bulletin* 18 (1992): 199–206; J. P. Tangney, R. S. Miller, L. Flicker, and D. H. Barlow, "Are Shame, Guilt, and Embarrassment Distinct Emotions?" *Journal of Personality and Social Psychology* 70 (1996): 1256–69.

34. J. P. Tangney, P. Wagner, and R. Gramzow, "Proneness to Shame, Proneness to Guilt, and Psychopathology," *Journal of Abnormal Psychology* 101 (1992): 469–78; J. P. Tangney, P. E. Wagner, D. H. Barlow, D. E. Marschall, and R. Gramzow, "The Relation of Shame and Guilt to Constructive vs. Destructive Responses to Anger Across the Lifespan," *Journal of Personality and Social Psychology* 70 (1996): 797–809.

35. M. D. Storms and K. D. McCaul, "Attribution Processes and Emotional Exacerbation of Dysfunctonal Behavior," in *New Directions in Attribution Research*, ed. J. H. Harvey, W. J. Ickes, and R. F. Kidd, I: 143–64 (Hillsdale, NJ: Lawrence Erlbaum, 1976).

36. M. D. Storms and R. E. Nisbett, "Insomnia and the Attribution Process," *Journal of Personality and Social Psychology* 16 (1970): 319–28.

37. Storms and McCaul, "Attribution Processes."

38. Ibid.

39. R. Grigg, *The Tao of Zen* (Boston: Charles E. Tuttle, 1994).

40. N. L. Murdock, and E. M. Altmaier, "Attribution-Based Treatments," in *Handbook of Social and Clinical Psychology*, ed. C. R. Snyder and D. R. Forsyth, 563–78 (New York: Pergamon, 1991).

CHAPTER 5

1. C. Graham, *Deconstructing Ireland: Identity, Theory, Culture* (Edinburgh: Edinburgh University Press, 2001); M. Tanner, *Ireland's Holy Wars: The Struggle for a Nation's Soul, 1500–2000* (New Haven, CT: Yale University Press, 2001).

2. U. Neisser, "Five Kinds of Self-Knowledge," *Philosophical Psychology* 1 (1988): 35–59; M. Sheets-Johnstone, "Consciousness: A Natural History," *Journal of Consciousness Studies* 5 (1990): 260–94.

3. M. Lewis and J. Brooks-Gunn, *Social Cognition and the Acquisition of Self* (New York: Plenum, 1979).

4. L. A. Sass, "Schizophrenia, Self-Consciousness, and the Modern Mind," in *Models of the Self*, ed. S. Gallagher and J. Shear, 317–41 (Thorerton, UK: Imprint Academic, 1999).

5. A. Bandura, "The Self System in Reciprocal Determinism," *American Psychologist* 33 (1978): 344–58; S. Harter, *The Construction of the Self* (New York: Guilford, 1999).

6. H. Tajfel and J. C. Turner, "An Integrative Theory of Intergroup Conflict," in *The Social Psychology of Intergroup Relations*, ed. W. G. Austin and

S. Worchel, 33–47 (Monterey, CA: Brooks/Cole, 1979); H. Tajfel and J. C. Turner, "The Social Identity Theory of Intergroup Behavior," in *Psychology of Intergroup Relations*, ed. S. Worchel and W. G. Austin, 7–24 (Chicago: Nelson-Hall, 1986).

7. H. Tajfel, *Humans and Social Categories: Studies in Social Psychology* (London: Cambridge University Press, 1981); H. Tajfel and M. Billig, "Familiarity and Categorization in Intergroup Behavior," *Journal of Experimental Social Psychology* 10 (1974): 159–70.

8. M. Diehl, "The Minimal Group Paradigm: Theoretical Explanations and Empirical Findings," *European Review of Social Psychology* 1 (1990): 263–92.

9. Ibid.

10. D. Abrams and M. A. Hogg, *Social Identity and Social Cognition* (Oxford, UK: Blackwell, 1999); M. A. Hogg, "Social Identity," in *Handbook of Self and Identity*, ed. M. R. Leary and J. P. Tangney, 462–79 (New York: Guilford, 2003).

11. M. B. Brewer, "In-Group Bias in the Minimal Intergroup Situation: A Cognitive-Motivational Analysis," *Psychological Bulletin* 86 (1979): 307–24.

12. A. Hastorf and H. Cantril, "They Saw a Game: A Case Study," *Journal of Abnormal and Social Psychology* 49 (1954): 129–34.

13. R. P. Vallone, L. Ross, and M. R. Lepper, "The Hostile Media Phenomenon: Biased Perception and Perceptions of Media Bias in Coverage of the Beirut Massacre," *Journal of Personality and Social Psychology* 49 (1985): 577–85.

14. Ibid.

15. J. C. Turner and R. Onorato, "Social Identity, Personality and the Self-Concept: A Self-Categorization Perspective," in *The Psychology of the Social Self*, ed. T. R. Tyler, R. Kramer, and O. Johns, 11–46 (Hillsdale, NJ: Lawrence Erlbaum, 1999).

16. H. Tajfel, "Cognitive Aspects of Prejudice," *Journal of Social Issues* 25 (1969): 79–97; Tajfel and Turner, "An Integrative Theory."

17. M. Sherif, O. J. Harvey, B. J. White, W. E. Hood, and C. W. Sherif, *Intergroup Conflict and Cooperation: The Robber's Cave Experiment* (Norman, OK: Institute of Group Relations, 1961).

18. M. Schaller and J. Park, "Prehistoric Dangers and Contemporary Prejudices," *European Review of Social Psychology* 14 (in press).

19. Sherif, Harvey, White, Hood, and Sherif, *Intergroup Conflict*.

20. S. L. Gaertner and J. F. Dovidio, *Reducing Intergroup Bias: The Common Intergroup Identity Model* (New York: Psychology Press, 2000).

21. J. A. Nier, S. L. Gaertner, J. F. Dovidio, B. S. Banker, C. M. Ward, and M. C. Rust, "Changing Interracial Evaluations and Behavior: The Effects of a Common Group Identity," *Group Processes and Intergroup Relations* 4 (2001): 299–316; S. L. Gaertner, J. Mann, A. Murrell, and J. F. Dovidio, "Reducing Intergroup Bias: The Benefits of Recategorization," *Journal of Personality and Social Psychology* 57 (1989): 239–49.

22. W. James, *The Principles of Psychology* (New York, Holt, 1890).

23. A. Aron, "Self and Close Relationships," in *Handbook of Self and Identity*, ed. M. R. Leary and J. P. Tangney, 442–61 (New York: Guilford, 2003); A. Aron, E. N. Aron, and C. Norman, "Self-Expansion Model of Motivation and Cognition in Close Relationships and Beyond," in *Blackwell Handbook of Social Psychology:*

Interpersonal Processes, ed. G.J.O. Fletcher and M. S. Clark, 478–501 (Malden, MA: Blackwell, 2001).

24. A. Aron, E. Aron, and D. Smollan, "Inclusion of Other in the Self Scale and the Structure of Interpersonal Closeness," *Journal of Personality and Social Psychology* 83 (1992): 596–612.

25. A. Aron and B. Fraley, "Relationship Closeness as Including Other in the Self: Cognitive Underpinnings and Measures," *Social Cognition* 17 (1999): 140–60.

26. C. R. Agnew, P. A. M. Van Lange, C. E. Rusbult, and C. A. Langston, "Cognitive Interdependence: Commitment and the Mental Representation of Close Relationships," *Journal of Personality and Social Psychology* 74 (1998): 939–54.

27. Aron, Aron, and Smollan, "Inclusion of Other in the Self Scale."

28. J. Tipsord and M. R. Leary, *Correlates of the Hyperegoic and Hypoegoic Self* (unpublished manuscript, Wake Forest University, Winston-Salem, NC).

29. W. R. Cupach and B. H. Spitzberg, "Obsessional Relational Intrusion and Stalking," in *The Dark Side of Close Relationships*, ed. B. H. Spitzberg and W. R. Cupach, 233–63 (Mahwah, NJ: Lawrence Erlbaum, 1998).

30. Aron, Aron, and Norman, "Self-Expansion Model."

31. A. Tesser, "Toward a Self-Evaluation Maintenance Model of Social Behavior," *Advances in Experimental Social Psychology* 21 (1988): 181–227.

32. A. Tesser, J. Campbell, and M. Smith, "Friendship Choice and Performance: Self-Evaluation Maintenance in Children," *Journal of Personality and Social Psychology* 46 (1984): 561–74.

33. M. S. Clark and M. E. Bennett, "Research on Relationships: Implications for Mental Health," in *The Social Psychology of Mental Health: Basic Mechanisms and Applications*, ed. D. N. Ruble, P. R. Costanzo, and M. E. Oliveri, 166–98 (New York: Guilford, 1992).

34. A. Tesser and J. Smith, "Some Effects of Friendship and Task Relevance on Helping: You Don't Always Help the One You Like," *Journal of Experimental Social Psychology* 16 (1980): 582–90.

35. R. Pleban and A. Tesser, "The Effects of Relevance and Quality of Another's Performance on Interpersonal Closeness," *Social Psychology Quarterly* 44 (1981): 278–85.

36. J. Horai, "Attributional Conflict," *Journal of Social Issues* 33 (1977): 88–100.

37. M. Ross and F. Sicoly, "Egocentric Biases in Availability and Attribution," *Journal of Personality and Social Psychology* 37 (1979): 322–36.

38. B. R. Schlenker and R. S. Miller, "Egotism in Groups: Self-Serving Bias or Logical Information Processing," *Journal of Personality and Social Psychology* 35 (1977): 755–64.

39. M. R. Leary and D. R. Forsyth, "Attributions of Responsibility for Collective Endeavors," in *Group Processes*, ed. C. Hendrick, 167–88 (Newbury Park, CA: Sage, 1987).

40. M. R. Leary, R. Bednarski, D. Hammon, and T. Duncan, "Blowhards, Snobs, and Narcissists: Interpersonal Reactions to Excessive Egotism," in *Aversive Interpersonal Behaviors*, ed. R. M. Kowalski (New York: Plenum, 1997), 111–31.

41. B. R. Schlenker and M. R. Leary, "Audiences' Reactions to Self-Enhancing, Self-Denigrating, Accurate, and Modest Self-Presentation," *Journal of Experimental Social Psychology* 18 (1982): 89–104.

42. Leary, Bednarski, Hammon, and Duncan, "Blowhards, Snobs."

43. R. F. Baumeister, L. Smart, and J. M. Boden, "Relation of Threatened Egotism to Violence and Aggression: The Dark Side of High Self-Esteem," *Psychological Review* 103 (1996): 5–33.

44. Ibid.

45. R. E. Nisbett, "Violence and U.S. Regional Culture," *American Psychologist* 48 (1993): 441–49; D. Cohen, R. E. Nisbett, B. F. Bowdle, and N. Schwarz, "Insult, Aggression, and the Southern Culture of Honor: An 'Experimental Ethnography,'" *Journal of Personality and Social Psychology* 70 (1996): 945–60.

CHAPTER 6

1. T. R. Fehrenbach, *Lone Star: A History of Texas and the Texans* (New York: Collier, 1968).

2. R. E. Nisbett, "Violence and U.S. Regional Culture," *American Psychologist* 48 (1993): 441–49; D. Cohen, R. E. Nisbett, B. F. Bowdle, and N. Schwarz, "Insult, Aggression, and the Southern Culture of Honor: An 'Experimental Ethnography,'" *Journal of Personality and Social Psychology* 70 (1996): 945–60.

3. W. James, *The Principles of Psychology* (New York: Holt, 1890); C. H. Cooley, *Human Nature and the Social Order* (New York: Scribner's, 1902); G. H. Mead, *Mind, Self, and Society* (Chicago: University of Chicago Press, 1934); N. Humphrey, "Consciousness: A Just-So Story," *New Scientist* (August 19, 1982): 474–77.

4. M. R. Leary, L. R. Tchividjian, and B. E. Kraxberger, "Self-Presentation Can Be Hazardous to Your Health: Impression Management and Health Risk," *Health Psychology* 13 (1994): 461–70.

5. Centers for Disease Control and Prevention, 2000 Statistics, www.cdc.gov/nchs/fastats/acc-inj.htm.

6. K. A. Martin and M. R. Leary, "Self-Presentational Determinants of Health Risk Behavior Among College Freshmen," *Psychology and Health* 16 (2000): 17–27; K. A. Martin, M. R. Leary, and J. O'Brien, "The Role of Self-Presentation in the Health Practices of a Sample of Irish Adolescents," *Journal of Adolescent Health* 28 (2001): 259–62.

7. L. H. Chen, S. P. Baker, E. R. Braver, and G. Li, "Carrying Passengers as a Risk Factor for Crashes Fatal to 16- and 17-Year-Old Drivers," *Journal of the American Medical Association* 283 (2000): 578–82.

8. Martin and Leary, "Self-Presentational Determinants."

9. Ibid.

10. H. Nuwer, "Greek Letters Don't Justify Cult-Like Hazing of Pledges," *Chronicle of Higher Education*, November 26, 1999.

11. G. F. Linderman, *Embattled Courage* (New York: Free Press, 1987).

12. R. E. Lee, *Blackbeard the Pirate: A Reappraisal of His Life and Times* (Winston-Salem, NC: John F. Blair, 1974).

13. Information about the Darwin Awards may be found at www.darwinawards.com.

14. K. A. Martin, M. R. Leary, and W. J. Rejeski, "Self-Presentational Concerns in Older Adults: Implications for Health and Well-Being," *Basic and Applied Social Psychology* 22 (2000): 169–79.

15. M. J. Parks and M. R. Leary, *Self-Presentational Motives, Risk Taking, and Accidental Injury* (paper presented at the meeting of the Southeastern Psychological Association, Savannah, GA).

16. Martin and Leary, "Self-Presentational Determinants."

17. K. A. Martin and M. R. Leary, "Would You Drink After a Stranger? The Influence of Self-Presentational Motives on Willingness to Take a Health Risk," *Personality and Social Psychology Bulletin* 25 (1999): 1092–1100.

18. Martin and Leary, "Self-Presentational Determinants."

19. R. C. Klesges and L. M. Klesges, "Cigarette Smoking as a Dietary Strategy in a University Population," *International Journal of Eating Disorders* 7 (1988): 413–17.

20. R. C. Klesges, A. W. Meyers, L. M. Klesges, and M. E. LaVasque, "Smoking, Body Weight, and Their Effects on Smoking Behavior: A Comprehensive Review of the Literature," *Psychological Bulletin* 106 (1989): 204–30.

21. Leary, Tchividjian, and Kraxberger, "Self-Presentation Can Be Hazardous."

22. J. M. Ellwood, S. M. Whitehead, and R. P. Gallagher, "Epidemiology of Human Malignant Skin Tumors with Special Reference to Natural and Artificial Ultraviolet Radiation Exposures," in *Skin Tumors: Experimental and Clinical Aspects*, ed. C. J. Conti, T. J. Slaga, and A. J. P. Klein-Szanto, 55–84 (New York: Raven Press, 1989).

23. B. Keesling and H. S. Friedman, "Psychosocial Factors in Sunbathing and Sunscreen Use," *Health Psychology* 6 (1987): 477–93.

24. J. L. Jones and M. R. Leary, "Effects of Appearance-Based Admonitions Against Sun Exposure on Tanning Intentions in Young Adults," *Health Psychology* 13 (1994): 86–90.

25. M. R. Seary, J. L. Saltzman, and J. C. Georgeson, "Appearance Motivation, Obsessive-Compulsive Tendencies, and Excessive Suntanning in a Community Sample," *Journal of Health Psychology* 2 (1997): 493–99.

26. D. Hayes and C. E. Ross, "Concern with Appearance, Health Beliefs, and Eating Habits," *Journal of Health and Social Behavior* 28 (1987): 120–30.

27. L. Lissner, P. M. Odell, R. B. D'Agostino, J. Stokes, B. E. Kreger, A. J. Belancer, and K. D. Brownell, "Variability in Body Weight and Health Outcomes in the Framington Population," *New England Journal of Medicine* 324 (1991): 1839–44.

28. P. L. Hewitt, G. L. Flett, and E. Ediger, "Perfectionism Traits and Perfectionistic Self-Presentation in Eating Disorder Attitudes, Characteristics, and Symptoms," *International Journal of Eating Disorders* 18 (1995): 317–26; M. A. Katzman and S. A. Wolchilk, "Bulimia and Binge Eating in College Women: A Comparison of Personality and Behavioral Characteristics," *Journal of Consulting and Clinical Psychology* 52 (1984): 423–28.

29. Martin and Leary, "Self-Presentational Determinants."

30. C. J. Worringham and D. M. Messick, "Social Facilitation of Running: An Unobtrusive Study," *Journal of Social Psychology* 121 (1983): 23–29.

31. Martin and Leary, "Self-Presentational Determinants."

32. C. D. Lantz, C. J. Hardy, and B. E. Ainsworth, "Social Physique Anxiety and Perceived Exercise Behavior," *Journal of Sport Behavior* 20 (1997): 83–93; D. C.

Treasure, C. L. Lox, and B. R. Lawton, "Determinants of Physical Activity in a Sedentary, Obese Female Population," *Journal of Sport and Exercise Psychology* 20 (1998): 218–24.

33. R. F. Baumeister, *Escaping the Self* (New York: Basic Books, 1991).

34. J. G. Hull and R. D. Young, "Self-Consciousness, Self-Esteem, and Success-Failure as Determinants of Alcohol Consumption in Male Social Drinkers," *Journal of Personality and Social Psychology* 44 (1983): 1097–1109.

35. J. G. Hull, R. W. Levenson, R. D. Young, and K. J. Scher, "Self-Awareness-Reducing Effects of Alcohol Consumption," *Journal of Personality and Social Psychology* 44 (1983): 461–73.

36. J. G. Hull, R. D. Young, and E. Jouriles, "Applications of the Self-Awareness Model of Alcohol Consumption: Predicting Patterns of Use and Abuse," *Journal of Personality and Social Psychology* 51 (1986): 790–96.

37. C. M. Steele and R. A. Josephs, "Alcohol Myopia: Its Prized and Dangerous Effects," *American Psychologist* 45 (1990): 921–33.

38. R. F. Baumeister, *Masochism and the Self* (Hillsdale, NJ: Lawrence Erlbaum, 1989); Baumeister, *Escaping the Self*.

39. Baumeister, *Masochism and the Self*.

40. R. F. Baumeister, "Suicide as Escape from Self," *Psychological Review* 97 (1990): 90–113.

41. Baumeister, *Escaping the Self*, 87.

42. Ibid.

43. M. R. Leary and N. Buttermore, "The Evolution of the Human Self: Tracing the Natural History of Self-Awareness," *Journal for the Theory of Social Behavior* (2003).

44. L. Martin, *Linking and the Neolithic Neuroses: Why Thinking You Can Live Happily Ever After Can Make You Unhappy* (paper presented at the meeting of the Society for Southeastern Social Psychologists, Research Triangle Park, NC); L. Martin, "I-D Compensation Theory: Some Implications of Trying to Satisfy Immediate-Return Needs in a Delayed-Return Culture," *Psychological Inquiry* 10 (1999): 195–208.

CHAPTER 7

1. J. Boisselier, *The Wisdom of the Buddha* (New York: Abrams, 1993).

2. For one perspective, see D. Shulman and G. G. Stroumsa, *Self and Self-Transformation in the History of Religions* (New York: Oxford University Press, 2002).

3. B. Walker, *Hua Hu Ching: The Unknown Teachings of Lao Tzu* (New York: HarperCollins, 1992), no. 32.

4. K. Kavanaugh and O. Rodriguez, trans., *The Collected Works of St. John of the Cross* (Washington, DC: ICS Publications, 1979).

5. M. Gupta, *The Gospel of Sri Ramakrishna*, trans. S. Nikhilananda (New York: Ramakrishna-Viveananda Center, 1958), 226.

6. Ezekial 36: 26–27.

7. John 3:3.

8. J. E. Brown, "The Question of 'Mysticism' Within Native American Traditions," in *Understanding Mysticism*, ed. R. Woods, 203–11 (Garden City, NY: Image, 1980).

9. W. B. Swann, Jr., "The Trouble with Change: Self-Verification and Allegiance to the Self," *Psychological Science* 8 (1997): 177–80.

10. E. Fox, *The Sermon on the Mount* (San Francisco: HarperSan Francisco, 1934).

11. *Mundada Upanishads* 3:1–3.

12. S. Rinpoche, *The Tibetan Book of Living and Dying* (New York: HarperCollins, 1993), 120.

13. Genesis 5:22.

14. J. Jaynes, *The Origin of Consciousness in the Breakdown of the Bicameral Mind* (Boston: Houghton-Mifflin, 1976).

15. H. Fairlie, *The Seven Deadly Sins Today* (South Bend, IN: University of Notre Dame Press, 1983).

16. Proverbs 3:34.

17. Catechism of the Catholic Church, #2094.

18. S. Noffke, trans., *Catherine of Siena: The Dialogue* (Mahwah, NJ: Paulist Press, 1980), 35.

19. C. Hamilton, "The Enemy Within: An Interview with Archimandrite Dionysios," *What Is Enlightenment?* 17 (Spring/Summer 2000): 39–49.

20. Matthew 23:12.

21. *Tao te Ching*, #30.

22. *The Essential Rumi*, 141–42.

23. G. Robinson, *Essential Judaism: A Complete Guide to Beliefs, Customs, and Rituals* (New York: Pocket Books, 2001).

24. K. S. Leong, *The Zen Teachings of Jesus* (New York: Crossroad, 1995); N. Douglas-Klotz, *The Hidden Gospel* (Wheaton, IL: Quest, 1999).

25. Ephesians 4:22–24.

26. K. Armstrong, *Islam: A Short History* (New York: Modern Library, 2000).

27. M. Levine, *The Positive Psychology of Buddhism and Yoga* (Mahwah, NJ: Lawrence Erlbaum, 2000).

28. J. Kabat-Zinn, *Wherever You Go, There You Are* (New York: Hyperion, 1994).

29. H. Gunaratana, *Mindfulness in Plain English* (Boston: Wisdom Publications, 1991).

30. I. Shah, *The Way of the Sufi* (London: Octogon Press, 1980).

31. A. B. Pinn, *Varieties of African American Religious Experience* (Minneapolis: Fortress Press, 1998).

32. R. A. Bucko, *The Lakota Ritual of the Sweat Lodge: History and Contemporary Practice* (Lincoln: University of Nebraska Press, 1998); R. L. Hall, *An Archeology of the Soul: North American Indian Belief and Ritual* (Urbana: University of Illinois Press, 1997).

33. Douglas-Klotz, *The Hidden Gospel*; H. Waddell, *The Desert Fathers* (New York: Vintage, 1998).

34. Shah, *The Way of the Sufi*.

35. D. V. Steere and E. Vining, *Quaker Spirituality: Selected Writings* (Mahwah, NJ: Paulist Press, 1984).

36. L. Freeman, ed., *John Main: Selected Writings* (New York: Orbis, 2002).

37. A. Watts, *The Way of Zen* (New York: Vintage, 1957); C. Humphreys, *A Western Approach to Zen* (Wheaton, IL: Theosophical Publishing, 1971).

38. Watts, *The Way of Zen*.

39. Several versions of this koan exist; the classic may be found in T. Cleary and J. C. Cleary, trans., *The Blue Cliff Record* (Boston: Shambala, 1992).

40. S. Heine and D. S. Wright, eds., *The Koan* (New York: Oxford University Press, 2000).

41. J. Berendt, *The Third Ear: On Listening to the World*, trans. T. Nevill (New York: Holt, 1992).

42. D. L. Carmoody and J. T. Carmoody, *Mysticism: Holiness East and West* (New York: Oxford University Press, 1996).

43. Ibid; R. Woods, ed., *Understanding Mysticism* (Garden City, NY: Image, 1980).

44. C. Castaneda, *Tales of Power* (New York: Touchstone, 1974), 231.

45. A. Glucklich, *Sacred Pain: Hurting the Body for the Sake of the Soul* (New York: Oxford University Press, 2001).

46. W. H. Clark, "The Psychedelics and Religion," in *Psychedelics*, ed. B. Aaronson and H. Osmond (New York: Doubleday, 1970).

47. R. K. C. Forman, "Mystical Consciousness, the Innate Capacity, and the Perennial Psychology," in *The Innate Capacity: Mysticism, Psychology and Philosophy*, ed. R. K. C. Forman, 33–41 (New York: Oxford University Press, 1998).

48. A. H. Maslow, *Religions, Values, and Peak Experiences* (Columbus, OH: Ohio State University Press, 1964).

49. Forman, "Mystical Consciousness."

50. E. G. Aquili and A. B. Newberg, "The Neuropsychological Basis of Religion, or Why God Won't Go Away,"

51. J. B. Ashbrook, "Neuorotheology: The Working Brain and the Work of Theology," *Zygon: Journal of Religion and Science* 19 (1984): 331–50.

52. K. D. Noble, "Psychological Health and the Experience of Transcendence," *The Counseling Psychologist* 15 (1987): 601–14; R. Wuthnow, "Peak Experiences: Some Empirical Tests," *Journal of Humanistic Psychology* 18 (1978): 59–75.

CHAPTER 8

1. R. F. Baumeister, "The Self," in *The Handbook of Social Psychology*, ed. D. Gilbert, S. T. Fiske, and G. Lindzey (New York: Oxford University Press, 1999).

2. R. F. Baumeister, T. F. Heatherton, and D. M. Tice, *Losing Control: How and Why People Fail at Self-Regulation* (San Diego: Academic Press, 1994).

3. G. Zivin, ed., *The Development of Self-Regulation Through Private Speech* (New York: John Wiley, 1979).

4. K. C. Fuson, "The Development of Self-Regulating Aspects of Speech: A Review," in *The Development of Self-Regulation Though Private Speech*, ed. G. Zivin (New York: John Wiley, 1979).

5. For reviews, see Baumeister, Heatherton, and Tice, *Losing Control*; R. F. Baumeister and K. D. Vohs, "Self-Regulation and the Executive Function of the Self," in *Handbook of Self and Identity*, ed. M. R. Leary and J. P. Tangney, 197–217

(New York: Guilford, 2003); W. Mischel, N. Cantor, and S. Feldman, "Principles of Self-Regulation: The Nature of Willpower and Self-Control," in *Handbook of Basic Principles*, ed. E. T. Higgins and A. W. Kruglanski, 329–60 (New York: Guilford, 1996).

6. Baumeister, Heatherton, and Tice, *Losing Control.*

7. S. Duval and R. A. Wicklund, *A Theory of Objective Self-Awareness* (New York: Academic Press, 1972).

8. For a review, see C. S. Carver and M. F. Scheier, *Attention and Self-Regulation: A Control-Theory Approach to Human Behavior* (New York: Springer-Verlag, 1981).

9. C. S. Carver, "Physical Aggression as a Function of Objective Self-Awareness and Attitudes Toward Punishment," *Journal of Experimental Social Psychology* 11 (1975): 510–19.

10. E. Diener, "Deindividuation, Self-Awareness, and Disinhibition," *Journal of Personality and Social Psychology* 37 (1979): 1160–1171.

11. S. Prentice-Dunn and R. W. Rogers, "Deindividuation and Aggression," in *Aggression: Theoretical and Empirical Reviews*, ed. R. G. Geen and E. I. Donnerstein, 2: 155–72 (New York: Academic Press, 1983).

12. R. D. Johnson and L. L. Downing, "Deindividuation and Valence of Cues: Effects on Prosocial and Antisocial Behavior," *Journal of Personality and Social Psychology* 37 (1979): 1532–38.

13. E. Diener, "Deindividuation: Causes and Consequences," *Social Behavior and Personality* 5 (1977): 143–55; Diener, "Deindividuation, Self-Awareness, and Disinhibition."

14. P. G. Zimbardo, "The Human Choice: Individuation, Reason, and Order versus Deindividuation, Impulse, and Chaos," *Nebraska Symposium on Motivation* 17 (1969): 237–307; S. Prentice-Dunn and R. W. Rogers, "Deindividuation and the Self-Regulation of Behavior," in *Psychology of Group Influence*, 2nd ed., ed. Paul B. Paulhus, 87–109 (Hillsdale, NJ: Lawrence Erlbaum, 1989).

15. B. Mullen, "Atrocity as a Function of Lynch Mob Composition: A Self-Attention Perspective," *Personality and Social Psychology Bulletin* 12 (1986): 187–97.

16. Ibid.

17. R. F. Baumeister, "Choking Under Pressure: Self-Consciousness and Paradoxical Effects of Incentives on Performance," *Journal of Personality and Social Psychology* 46 (1984): 610–20.

18. Baumeister, Heather, and Tice, *Losing Control.*

19. Ibid.

20. A. R. Mele, "Is Akratic Action Unfree?" *Philosophy and Phenomenological Research* 46 (1986): 673–79.

21. Baumeister, Heatherton, and Tice, *Losing Control.*

22. M. Bjoerkman, "Decision Making, Risk Taking, and Psychological Time: Review of Empirical Findings and Psychological Theory," *Scandinavian Journal of Psychology* 25 (1984): 31–49.

23. Mischel, Cantor, and Feldman, "Principles of Self-Regulation."

24. W. Mischel and B. Moore, "The Role of Ideation in Voluntary Delay for Symbolically Presented Rewards," *Cognitive Therapy and Research* 4 (1980): 211–21.

25. J. Metcalfe and W. Mischel, "A Hot/Cool-System Analysis of Delay of Gratification: Dynamics of Willpower," *Psychological Review* 106 (1999): 3–19.

26. W. Mischel, "From Good Intentions to Willpower," in *The Psychology of Action: Linking Cognition and Motivation to Behavior*, ed. P. M. Gollwitzer and J. A. Bargh, 197–218 (New York: Guilford, 1996).

27. R. F. Baumeister and T. F. Heatherton, "Self-Regulation Failure: An Overview," *Psychological Inquiry* 7 (1996): 1–15.

28. Mischel and Moore, "The Role of Ideation."

29. Baumeister and Heatherton, "Self-Regulation Failure."

30. K. D. Vohs and T. F. Heatherton, "Self-Regulatory Failure: A Resource-Depletion Approach," *Psychological Science* 11 (2000): 249–54.

31. Baumeister, Heatherton, and Tice, *Losing Control;* R. F. Baumeister, "Ego Depletion and Self-Control Failure: An Energy Model of the Self's Executive Function," *Self and Identity* 1 (2002): 129–36.

32. R. F. Baumeister, K. L. Dale, and D. M. Tice, "Replenishing the Self: Effects of Positive Affect on Performance and Persistence Following Ego Depletion," *Social Cognition* (in press).

33. M. R. Muraven and R. F. Baumeister, "Self-Regulation and Depletion of Limited Resources; Does Self-Control Resemble a Muscle?" *Psychological Bulletin* 126 (2000): 247–59.

34. M. R. Muraven, D. M. Tice, and R. F. Baumeister, "Self-Control as a Limited Resource: Regulatory Depletion Patterns," *Journal of Personality and Social Psychology* 74 (1998): 774–89; R. F. Baumeister, E. Blatslavsky, M. Muraven, and D. M. Tice, "Ego Depletion: Is the Active Self a Limited Resource?" *Journal of Personality and Social Psychology* 74 (1998): 1252–65.

35. Muraven, Tice, and Baumeister, "Self-Control as a Limited Resource."

36. Ibid.

37. Baumeister, Bratslavsky, Muraven, and Tice, "Ego Depletion."

38. R. F. Baumeister, M. Muraven, and D. M. Tice, "Ego Depletion: A Resource Model of Volition, Self-Regulation, and Controlled Processing," *Social Cognition* 18 (2000): 130–50.

39. Muraven and Baumeister, "Self-Regulation and Depletion."

40. W. Mischel, Y. Shoda, and M. L. Rodriguez, "Delay of Gratification in Children," *Science* 244 (1989): 933–38.

41. J. P. Tangney, R. F. Baumeister, and A. L. Boone, "High Self-Control Predicts Good Adjustment, Better Grades, and Interpersonal Success," *Journal of Personality* (in press).

42. Baumeister and Heatherton, "Self-Regulation Failure."

43. D. M. Wegner, D. J. Schneider, S. Carter, and L. White, "Paradoxical Effects of Thought Suppression," *Journal of Personality and Social Psychology* 53 (1987): 5–13.

44. D. M. Wegner, R. Erber, and S. Zanakos, "Ironic Processes in the Mental Control of Mood and Mood-Related Thought," *Journal of Personality and Social Psychology* 65 (1993): 1093–1104.

45. D. M. Wegner, *White Bears and Other Unwanted Thoughts* (New York: Viking, 1989).

46. D. M. Wegner, J. W. Shortt, A. W. Blake, and M. S. Page, "The Suppression of Exciting Thoughts," *Journal of Personality and Social Psychology* 58 (1990): 409–18.

47. M. Muraven and E. Slessareva, "Mechanisms of Self-Control Failure: Motivation and Limited Resources," *Personality and Social Psychology Bulletin* 29 (2003): 894–906.

48. H. Tennen and G. Afflect, "Paradox-Based Treatments," in *Handbook of Social and Clinical Psychology*, ed. C. R. Snyder and D. R. Forsyth, 624–43 (New York: Pergamon, 1991).

Index

CPSIA information can be obtained
at www.ICGtesting.com
Printed in the USA
BVHW081457031221
623140BV00001B/3

9 780195 325447